SOLARO
STUDY GUIDE

Mathematics 10 Academic
Principles of Mathematics (MPM2D)

SOLARO Study Guide is designed to help students achieve success in school. The content in each study guide is 100% curriculum aligned and serves as an excellent source of material for review and practice. To create this book, teachers, curriculum specialists, and assessment experts have worked closely to develop the instructional pieces that explain each of the key concepts for the course. The practice questions and sample tests have detailed solutions that show problem-solving methods, highlight concepts that are likely to be tested, and point out potential sources of errors. *SOLARO Study Guide* is a complete guide to be used by students throughout the school year for reviewing and understanding course content, and to prepare for assessments.

W9-BHF-295

Rao, Gautam, 1961 –
SOLARO Study Guide: Mathematics Grade 10, Academic – Principles of Mathematics (MPM2D) Ontario
ISBN: 978-1-4876-0479-0

1. Mathematics – Juvenile Literature. I. Title

Castle Rock Research Corp.
2000 First & Jasper
10065 Jasper Avenue
Edmonton, AB T5J 3B1

Canadian Curriculum Press
is an imprint of Telegraph Road Entertainment,
Toronto, ON M1V 4Z7.

Publisher
Gautam Rao

Contributors
Betty Morris
Renee Nutt
Ted Whyte

Dedicated to the memory of Dr. V.S. Rao

With the participation of the Government of Canada | Canadä

SOLARO STUDY GUIDE

Each **SOLARO STUDY GUIDE** consists of the following sections:

Key Tips for Being Successful at School gives examples of study and review strategies. It includes information about learning styles, study schedules, and note taking for test preparation.

Class Focus includes a unit on each area of the curriculum. Units are divided into sections, each focusing on one of the specific expectations, or main ideas, that students must learn about in that unit. Examples, definitions, and visuals help to explain each main idea. Practice questions on the main ideas are also included. At the end of each unit is a test on the important ideas covered. The practice questions and unit tests help students identify areas they know and those they need to study more. They can also be used as preparation for tests and quizzes. Most questions are of average difficulty, though some are easy and some are hard—the harder questions are called *Challenger Questions*. Each unit is prefaced by a **Table of Correlations**, which correlates questions in the unit (and in the practice tests at the end of the book) to the specific curriculum expectations. Answers and solutions are found at the end of each unit.

Key Strategies for Success on Tests helps students get ready for tests. It shows students different types of questions they might see, word clues to look for when reading them, and hints for answering them.

Practice Tests includes one to three tests based on the entire course. They are very similar to the format and level of difficulty that students may encounter on final tests. In some regions, these tests may be reprinted versions of official tests, or reflect the same difficulty levels and formats as official versions. This gives students the chance to practice using real-world examples. Answers and complete solutions are provided at the end of the section.

For the complete curriculum document (including specific expectations along with examples and sample problems), visit http://www.edu.gov.on.ca/eng/curriculum/

SOLARO STUDY GUIDE *Study Guides* are available for many courses. Check www.castlerockresearch.com for a complete listing of books available for your area.

For information about any of our resources or services, please call Castle Rock Research at 1.800.840.6224 or visit our website at http://www.castlerockresearch.com.

At Castle Rock Research, we strive to produce an error-free resource. If you should find an error, please contact us so that future editions can be corrected.

CONTENTS

KEY TIPS FOR BEING SUCCESSFUL AT SCHOOL...1

CLASS FOCUS

Quadratic Relations 9

    Answers and Solutions – Quadratic Relations 56

    Unit Test 71

    Answers and Solutions – Unit Test 82

Analytic Geometry 93

    Answers and Solutions – Analytic Geometry 121

    Unit Test 132

    Answers and Solutions – Unit Test 139

Trigonometry 149

    Answers and Solutions – Trigonometry 172

    Unit Test 181

    Answers and Solutions – Unit Test 189

KEY STRATEGIES FOR SUCCESS ON TESTS... 197

PRACTICE TESTS

    Practice Test 1 206

    Practice Test 2 220

    Answers and Solutions – Practice Test 1 235

    Answers and Solutions – Practice Test 2 248

FORMULA SHEET 261

KEY Tips for being Successful at School

KEY TIPS FOR BEING SUCCESSFUL AT SCHOOL

KEY FACTORS CONTRIBUTING TO SCHOOL SUCCESS

In addition to learning the content of your courses, there are some other things that you can do to help you do your best at school. You can try some of the following strategies:

- **Keep a positive attitude:** Always reflect on what you can already do and what you already know.

- **Be prepared to learn:** Have the necessary pencils, pens, notebooks, and other required materials for participating in class ready.

- **Complete all of your assignments:** Do your best to finish all of your assignments. Even if you know the material well, practice will reinforce your knowledge. If an assignment or question is difficult for you, work through it as far as you can so that your teacher can see exactly where you are having difficulty.

- **Set small goals for yourself when you are learning new material:** For example, when learning the parts of speech, do not try to learn everything in one night. Work on only one part or section each study session. When you have memorized one particular part of speech and understand it, move on to another one. Continue this process until you have memorized and learned all the parts of speech.

- **Review your classroom work regularly at home:** Review to make sure you understand the material you learned in class.

- **Ask your teacher for help:** Your teacher will help you if you do not understand something or if you are having a difficult time completing your assignments.

- **Get plenty of rest and exercise:** Concentrating in class is hard work. It is important to be well-rested and have time to relax and socialize with your friends. This helps you keep a positive attitude about your schoolwork.

- **Eat healthy meals:** A balanced diet keeps you healthy and gives you the energy you need for studying at school and at home.

HOW TO FIND YOUR LEARNING STYLE

Every student learns differently. The manner in which you learn best is called your learning style. By knowing your learning style, you can increase your success at school. Most students use a combination of learning styles. Do you know what type of learner you are? Read the following descriptions. Which of these common learning styles do you use most often?

- **Linguistic Learner:** You may learn best by saying, hearing, and seeing words. You are probably really good at memorizing things such as dates, places, names, and facts. You may need to write down the steps in a process, a formula, or the actions that lead up to a significant event, and then say them out loud.

- **Spatial Learner:** You may learn best by looking at and working with pictures. You are probably really good at puzzles, imagining things, and reading maps and charts. You may need to use strategies like mind mapping and webbing to organize your information and study notes.

- **Kinesthetic Learner:** You may learn best by touching, moving, and figuring things out using manipulatives. You are probably really good at physical activities and learning through movement. You may need to draw your finger over a diagram to remember it, tap out the steps needed to solve a problem, or feel yourself writing or typing a formula.

SCHEDULING STUDY TIME

You should review your class notes regularly to ensure that you have a clear understanding of all the new material you learned. Reviewing your lessons on a regular basis helps you to learn and remember ideas and concepts. It also reduces the quantity of material that you need to study prior to a test. Establishing a study schedule will help you to make the best use of your time.

Regardless of the type of study schedule you use, you may want to consider the following suggestions to maximize your study time and effort:

- Organize your work so that you begin with the most challenging material first.

- Divide the subject's content into small, manageable chunks.

- Alternate regularly between your different subjects and types of study activities in order to maintain your interest and motivation.

- Make a daily list with headings like "Must Do," "Should Do," and "Could Do."

- Begin each study session by quickly reviewing what you studied the day before.

- Maintain your usual routine of eating, sleeping, and exercising to help you concentrate better for extended periods of time.

CREATING STUDY NOTES

MIND-MAPPING OR WEBBING

Use the key words, ideas, or concepts from your reading or class notes to create a mind map or web (a diagram or visual representation of the given information). A mind map or web is sometimes referred to as a knowledge map. Use the following steps to create a mind map or web:

1. Write the key word, concept, theory, or formula in the centre of your page.

2. Write down related facts, ideas, events, and information, and link them to the central concept with lines.

3. Use coloured markers, underlining, or symbols to emphasize things such as relationships, timelines, and important information.

The following examples of a Frayer Model illustrate how this technique can be used to study vocabulary.

Definition • Perimeter is the distance around the outside of a polygon.	**Notes** • Perimeter is measured in linear units (e.g., metres, centimetres, and so on).	**Definition** • A cube is a solid 3-D object with six faces.	**Notes** • A cube is different from other shapes because it has six equally-sized square faces, eight vertices, and twelve equal edges.
Perimeter		**Cube**	
Examples • The length of a fence around a yard • The distance around a circle (circumference)	**Non-Examples** • The area of grass covering a lawn • The size of a rug lying on a floor	**Examples** 	**Non-Examples**

INDEX CARDS

To use index cards while studying, follow these steps:

1. Write a key word or question on one side of an index card.

2. On the reverse side, write the definition of the word, answer to the question, or any other important information that you want to remember.

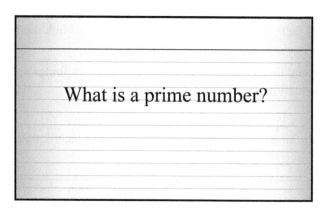

SYMBOLS AND STICKY NOTES—IDENTIFYING IMPORTANT INFORMATION

Use symbols to mark your class notes. The following are some examples:

- An exclamation mark (!) might be used to point out something that must be learned well because it is a very important idea.

- A question mark (?) may highlight something you are not certain about

- A diamond (◊) or asterisk (*) could highlight interesting information that you want to remember.

Sticky notes are useful in the following situations:

- Use sticky notes when you are not allowed to put marks in books.

- Use sticky notes to mark a page in a book that contains an important diagram, formula, explanation, or other information.

- Use sticky notes to mark important facts in research books.

MEMORIZATION TECHNIQUES

- **Association** relates new learning to something you already know. For example, to remember the spelling difference between dessert and desert, recall that the word *sand* has only one *s*. So, because there is sand in a desert, the word *desert* has only one *s*.

- **Mnemonic** devices are sentences that you create to remember a list or group of items. For example, the first letter of each word in the phrase "Every Good Boy Deserves Fudge" helps you to remember the names of the lines on the treble-clef staff (E, G, B, D, and F) in music.

- **Acronyms** are words that are formed from the first letters or parts of the words in a group. For example, RADAR is actually an acronym for Radio Detecting and Ranging, and MASH is an acronym for Mobile Army Surgical Hospital. HOMES helps you to remember the names of the five Great Lakes (Huron, Ontario, Michigan, Erie, and Superior).

- **Visualizing** requires you to use your mind's eye to "see" a chart, list, map, diagram, or sentence as it is in your textbook or notes, on the chalkboard or computer screen, or in a display.

- **Initialisms** are abbreviations that are formed from the first letters or parts of the words in a group. Unlike acronyms, an initialism cannot be pronounced as a word itself. For example, GCF is an initialism for **G**reatest **C**ommon **F**actor.

KEY STRATEGIES FOR REVIEWING

Reviewing textbook material, class notes, and handouts should be an ongoing activity. Spending time reviewing becomes more critical when you are preparing for a test. You may find some of the following review strategies useful when studying during your scheduled study time:

- Before reading a selection, preview it by noting the headings, charts, graphs, and chapter questions.

- Before reviewing a unit, note the headings, charts, graphs, and chapter questions.

- Highlight key concepts, vocabulary, definitions, and formulas.

- Skim the paragraph, and note the key words, phrases, and information.

- Carefully read over each step in a procedure.

- Draw a picture or diagram to help make the concept clearer.

KEY STRATEGIES FOR SUCCESS: A CHECKLIST

Reviewing is a huge part of doing well at school and preparing for tests. Here is a checklist for you to keep track of how many suggested strategies for success you are using. Read each question, and put a check mark (✓) in the correct column. Look at the questions where you have checked the "No" column. Think about how you might try using some of these strategies to help you do your best at school.

Key Strategies for Success	Yes	No
Do you attend school regularly?		
Do you know your personal learning style—how you learn best?		
Do you spend 15 to 30 minutes a day reviewing your notes?		
Do you study in a quiet place at home?		
Do you clearly mark the most important ideas in your study notes?		
Do you use sticky notes to mark texts and research books?		
Do you practise answering multiple-choice and written-response questions?		
Do you ask your teacher for help when you need it?		
Are you maintaining a healthy diet and sleep routine?		
Are you participating in regular physical activity?		

Quadratic Relations

QUADRATIC RELATIONS

Table of Correlations

Specific Expectation		Practice Questions	Unit Test Questions	Practice Test 1	Practice Test 2
QR1	Investigating the Basic Properties of Quadratic Relations				
QR1.1	collect data that can be represented as a quadratic relation, from experiments using appropriate equipment and technology or from secondary sources ; graph the data and draw a curve of best fit, if appropriate, with or without the use of technology	1, 2, 3	1	1	1
QR1.2	determine, through investigation with and without the use of technology, that a quadratic relation of the form $y = ax^2 + bx + c\,(a \neq 0)$ can be graphically represented as a parabola, and that the table of values yields a constant second difference	4, 5, 6	2	2	2
QR1.3	identify the key features of a graph of a parabola, and use the appropriate terminology to describe them	7, 8, 9	3, 4, 5	3	3
QR1.4	compare, through investigation using technology, the features of the graph of $y = x^2$ and the graph of $y = 2^x$, and determine the meaning of a negative exponent and of zero as an exponent	10, 11	6, 7	4	4
QR2	Relating the Graph of $y = x^2$ and Its Transformations				
QR2.1	identify, through investigation using technology, the effect on the graph of $y = x^2$ of transformations by considering separately each parameter a, h, and k	12, 13, 14	14, 15	20	21
QR2.2	explain the roles of a, h, and k in $y = a(x - h)^2 + k$, using the appropriate terminology to describe the transformations, and identify the vertex and the equation of the axis of symmetry	15, 16, 17	16, 17, 18	21	22
QR2.3	sketch, by hand, the graph of $y = a(x - h)^2 + k$ by applying transformations to the graph of $y = x^2$	18, 19, 20	19	22	23
QR2.4	determine the equation, in the form $y = a(x - h)^2 + k$, of a given graph of a parabola	21, 22, 23a, 23b, 23c	20, 21, 22a, 22b, 22c	23	24
QR3	Solving Quadratic Equations				
QR3.1	expand and simplify second-degree polynomial expressions using a variety of tools and strategies	24, 25	23, 24	24	25
QR3.2	factor polynomial expressions involving common factors, trinomials, and differences of squares using a variety of tools and strategies	26, 27, 28, 29	25, 26	25	26
QR3.3	determine, through investigation, and describe the connection between the factors of a quadratic expression and the x-intercepts of the graph of the corresponding quadratic relation, expressed in the form $y = a(x - r)(x - s)$	30, 31	27, 28	26	27
QR3.4	interpret real and non-real roots of quadratic equations, through investigation using graphing technology, and relate the roots to the x-intercepts of the corresponding relations	32, 33, 34	29, 30	27	28
QR3.5	express $y = ax^2 + bx + c$ in the form $y = a(x - h)^2 + k$ by completing the square in situations involving no fractions, using a variety of tools	35, 36, 37, 38	31, 32, 33	28	29
QR3.6	sketch or graph a quadratic relation whose equation is given in the form $y = ax^2 + bx + c$, using a variety of methods	39, 40, 41	34, 35	29	30
QR3.7	explore the algebraic development of the quadratic formula	42, 43	36, 37		

QR3.8	solve quadratic equations that have real roots, using a variety of methods	44, 45, 46, 47a, 47b, 47c	38, 39, 40a, 40b, 40c	30, 31, 32	31, 32a, 32b, 32c, 32d
QR4	Solving Problems Involving Quadratic Relations				
QR4.1	determine the zeros and the maximum or minimum value of a quadratic relation from its graph or from its defining equation	48, 49, 50	8, 9	5	5
QR4.2	solve problems arising from a realistic situation represented by a graph or an equation of a quadratic relation, with and without the use of technology.	51, 52, 53, 54a, 54b, 54c	10, 11, 12, 13a, 13b, 13c, 13d	6, 7a, 7b, 7c, 7d	6, 7, 8

QR1.1 collect data that can be represented as a quadratic relation, from experiments using appropriate equipment and technology or from secondary sources ; graph the data and draw a curve of best fit, if appropriate, with or without the use of technology

QUADRATIC RELATIONS THAT MODEL DATA

Quadratic relations can represent certain types of motion, populations, and other numerical rate problems and can therefore be used to model a specific set of **data**.

COLLECTING DATA

There are several methods in which data can be collected for mathematical analysis. These include:

- Conducting experiments in class involving motion and concrete materials.
- Conducting experiments using technology such as graphing calculators and the CBR™.
  *Note that when collecting data by conducting experiments, several trials should be done to ensure more realistic results.
- Using a secondary source such as the Internet or Statistics Canada.

GRAPHING THE DATA

After data is collected, it can be represented by a set of points on a Cartesian plane and may generate a pattern that can be represented by drawing a single curve. This curve is called the **curve of best fit** and can be drawn either by hand or by using technology.

Example

Number of Registered Apprentices in Building Construction Trades in Canada, from 1991 to 2003

Year	Year Number	Number (Thousands)
1991	1	46 925
1992	2	43 703
1993	3	40 996
1994	4	36 679
1995	5	34 786
1996	6	33 394
1997	7	32 957
1998	8	33 395
1999	9	36 496
2000	10	39 090
2001	11	42 109
2002	12	47 545
2003	13	53 606

Source: Statistics Canada, Registered Apprenticeship Information System.

Draw, by hand as well as by using technology, the curve of best fit that represents the data. Assume that the data represents a quadratic relation.

Plot the points and sketch a curve that best represents the points, as illustrated below.

Using Graph Paper:

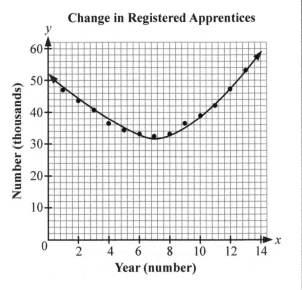

Change in Registered Apprentices

Note: the curve of best fit should be similar to the curve shown but may not be exactly the same.

Using a TI-83 Plus Graphing Calculator:

1. Enter the lists into the list editor.

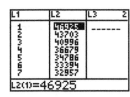

2. Perform a **quadratic regression**, and then enter the resulting equation in [$Y = $] in order to plot the curve of best fit.

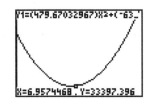

Use the following information to answer the next question.

The owner of a 300-seat theatre sells tickets for $20 each. He believes that for every dollar he increases the price of a ticket, he will lose 10 customers. He has charted his resulting revenue for each $1 increase in ticket price:

Increase in Price ($)	Revenue ($)
0	6 000
1	6 090
2	6 160
3	6 210
4	6 240
5	6 250
6	6 240

Numerical Response

1. If the owner's revenue after raising the ticket price is $5 760, then he is most likely charging $_____ per ticket.

2. Which of the following equations **best** models the given data?

    A. $y = -10x^2 + 93x + 636$

    B. $y = -10x^2 + 110x + 5990$

    C. $y = -9x^2 + 107x + 60$

    D. $y = -10x^2 + 100x + 60$

Use the following information to answer the next question.

One of the factors that determines the cost of car insurance is the age of the driver. It has been found that drivers under the age of 25 and drivers over the age of 70 are statistically more likely to have accidents compared to drivers between the ages of 25 and 70. The data in the table shows the percentage of accidents reported to a particular insurance company by their clients for various age groups.

Age Group (in years)	Group Number	Percent of Accidents
Under 20	1	20
20–30	2	16
30–40	3	12
40–50	4	10
50–60	5	11
60–70	6	14
Over 70	7	17

3. Which of the following graphs **best** shown the information in the given table?

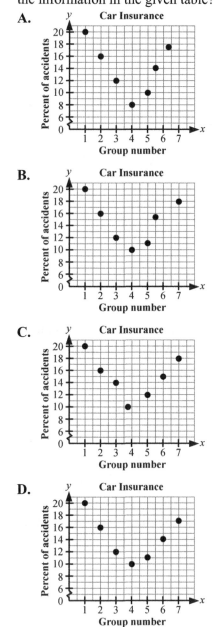

A.

B.

C.

D.

QR1.2 determine, through investigation with and without the use of technology, that a quadratic relation of the form $y = ax^2 + bx + c\,(a \neq 0)$ can be graphically represented as a parabola, and that the table of values yields a constant second difference

ANALYZING THE SECOND DIFFERENCES OF QUADRATIC RELATIONS OF THE FORM $y = ax^2 + bx + c$, $a \neq 0$

A quadratic relation of the form $y = ax^2 + bx + c$ where $a \neq 0$ will produce a graph that has the shape of a parabola (a U-shaped graph that opens upward or downward).

Consider the function $y = x^2$. The table of values and the graph of this function are shown.

x	y
-4	16
-3	9
-2	4
-1	1
0	0
1	1
2	4
3	9
4	16

When the table of values is plotted as a set of ordered pairs on a Cartesian plane, it yields the partial graph shown.

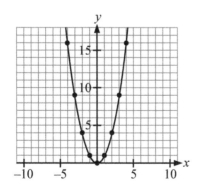

The graph of the function $y = x^2$ is U-shaped and opens upward.

When given a set of values, calculating the differences of the consecutive coordinates of the dependent variable can provide some important information about the type of relationship that exists for the data.

If the second differences from a table of values for a relation of the form $y = ax^2 + bx + c$ $(a \neq 0)$ are constant, the relation is quadratic.

To calculate the first differences of the dependent variable (y) in a table of values, the independent variable (x) has to have a constant increment. For example, this table shows a constant increment of 1.

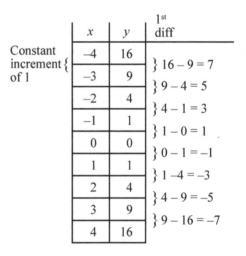

	x	y	1st diff
Constant increment of 1 {	-4	16	
	-3	9	} $16 - 9 = 7$
	-2	4	} $9 - 4 = 5$
	-1	1	} $4 - 1 = 3$
	0	0	} $1 - 0 = 1$
	1	1	} $0 - 1 = -1$
	2	4	} $1 - 4 = -3$
	3	9	} $4 - 9 = -5$
	4	16	} $9 - 16 = -7$

The second difference is calculated by taking the differences of the 1st difference as shown in this table.

	x	y	1st diff	2nd diff
Constant increment of 1	−4	16		
	−3	9	} 7	
	−2	4	} 5	} 7 − 5 = 2
	−1	1	} 3	} 5 − 3 = 2
	0	0	} 1	} 3 − 1 = 2
	1	1	} −1	} 1 − (−1) = 2
	2	4	} −3	} −1 − (−3) = 2
	3	9	} −5	} −3 − (−5) = 2
	4	16	} −7	} −5 − (−7) = 2

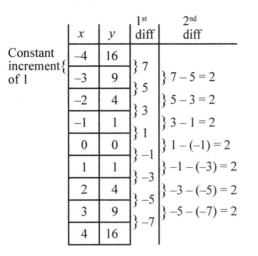

Since the 2nd difference for the function $y = x^2$ has a constant value of 2, the relation is quadratic.

Example

For the quadratic relation $y = 4x^2 - 3x - 2$, determine the constant second difference and whether the corresponding parabola opens upward or downward.

Solution

Step 1

Make a table of values to determine the constant second difference.

The table feature from a TI-83 graphing calculator can assist in setting up an appropriate table of values.

One possible table of values is shown.

x	y	1st diff	2nd diff
0	−2		
1	−1	} −1 − (−2) = 1	
2	8	} 8 − (−1) = 9	} 9 − 1 = 8
3	25	} 25 − 8 = 17	} 17 − 9 = 8
4	50	} 50 − 25 = 25	} 25 − 17 = 8
5	83	} 83 − 50 = 33	} 33 − 25 = 8
6	124	} 124 − 83 = 41	} 41 − 33 = 8

The table of values shows that the quadratic relation $y = 4x^2 - 3x - 2$ has a constant second difference of 8.

Step 2

Use a graphing calculator to graph the relation $y = 4x^2 - 3x - 2$.

The resulting graph is shown.

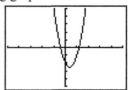

The parabola opens upward.

Example

For the quadratic relation $h = 5.5 + 6t - 3.2t^2$, determine whether the corresponding parabola opens upward or downward and then determine the constant second difference.

Solution

Step 1

Enter the equation $h = 5.5 + 6t - 3.2t^2$ into a TI-83 Plus graphing calculator.

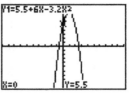

The resulting graph is shown. The graph illustrates a parabola opening downward.

Step 2

Make a table of values to determine the constant second difference.

Use the table feature from the TI-83 Plus graphing calculator to assist in setting up an appropriate table of values.

One possible table of values is shown.

	x	y	1st diff	2nd diff
	0	5.5		
			} 2.8	
	1	8.3		} −6.4
Constant			} −3.6	
increment	2	4.7		} −6.4
of 1			} −10	
	3	−5.3		} −6.4
			} −16.4	
	4	−21.7		} −6.4
			} −22.8	
	5	−44.5		} −6.4
			} −29.2	
	6	−73.7		

The table of values shows that there is a constant second difference of −6.4.

Therefore, the graph of $h = 5.5 + 6t - 3.2t^2$ is a parabola that opens downward, and the relation has a constant second difference of −6.4.

Given a quadratic relation of the form $y = ax^2 + bx + c$, where $a \neq 0$, the constant second difference is positive if $a > 0$ and negative if $a < 0$.

Example

x	−1	0	1	2	3	4
y	−1	0	1	8	27	81

By analyzing the second differences, determine if the given data represents a quadratic relation.

Solution

One possible partial table of values illustrating the second differences is shown.

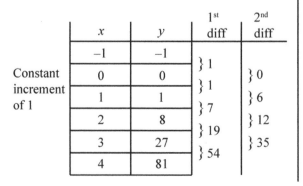

	x	y	1st diff	2nd diff
	−1	−1		
			} 1	
Constant	0	0		} 0
increment			} 1	
of 1	1	1		} 6
			} 7	
	2	8		} 12
			} 19	
	3	27		} 35
			} 54	
	4	81		

Since the second differences for this set of data are not constant, this function does not represent a quadratic relation of the form $y = ax^2 + bx + c$, $(a \neq 0)$.

---

4. Which of the following graphs **most likely** represents the graph $y = ax^2$?

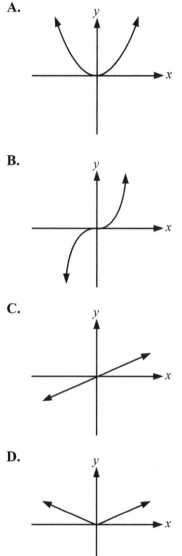

A.

B.

C.

D.

5. Which of the following partial tables of values could represent a table of values for a quadratic function?

A.

x	y	1st diff
1	8	
		} 3
2		
		} 3
3		
		} 3
4		
		} 3
5		
		} 3
6		

B.

x	y	1st diff
1	4	
		} 9
2		
		} 15
3		
		} 21
4		
		} 27
5		
		} 33
6		

C.

x	y	1st diff
1	1	
		} 2
2		
		} 5
3		
		} 9
4		
		} 14
5		
		} 20
6		

D.

x	y	1st diff
1	0	
		} 1
2		
		} 4
3		
		} 9
4		
		} 16
5		
		} 25
6		

6. Which of the following equations of quadratic functions has a corresponding parabola that opens upward and has a second difference of 5?

A. $y = -0.8x^2 - 5.5x + 23.8$

B. $y = -2.5x^2 + 6x + 5$

C. $y = 5x^2 + 4x - 3$

D. $y = 2.5x^2 - 3x - 8$

QR1.3 identify the key features of a graph of a parabola, and use the appropriate terminology to describe them

IDENTIFYING KEY FEATURES OF A PARABOLA

Recall that the graph of a quadratic function is a U-shaped curve opening either upward or downward. This U-shaped curve is called a parabola. The key features of a parabola are the maximum and minimum values, the vertex, the axis of symmetry, zeros, and the y-intercept.

MAXIMUM OR MINIMUM VALUES

A **maximum value** occurs when the parabola opens downward. The maximum value is the y-coordinate of the highest point on the curve.

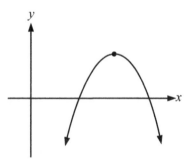

A **minimum value** occurs when the parabola opens upward. The minimum value is the y-coordinate of the lowest point on the curve.

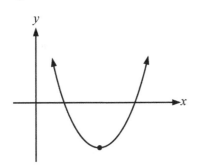

VERTEX

The **vertex** is the ordered pair where the maximum or minimum value of y occurs.

The parabola shown below has a maximum value of 1 when $x = 0$. The vertex is $(0, 1)$.

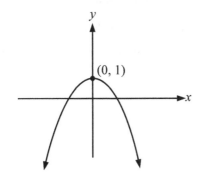

AXIS OF SYMMETRY

The **axis of symmetry** is a vertical line that passes through the vertex of the parabola and divides the parabola into two equal halves each of which is the mirror image of the other. The axis of symmetry also passes through the midpoint of any horizontal segment that connects two points on the parabola.

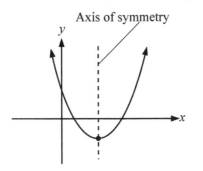

ZEROS

The **zeros** of a quadratic relation of the form $y = ax^2 + bx + c$, $(a \neq 0)$ are the value(s) of x that make the quadratic relation equal to zero. Thus, the zeros (also called the x-intercepts) are the x-coordinates of each ordered pair where the parabola touches or intersects the x-axis. For a quadratic function, there can either be 0, 1 or 2 real zeros.

y-INTERCEPT

The **y-intercept** of a quadratic relation of the form $y = ax^2 + bx + c$, $(a \neq 0)$ is the y-coordinate of the ordered pair where the parabola intersects the y-axis.

Example
Determine the following features of the parabola shown.

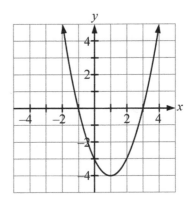

- Vertex
- Maximum or minimum value
- Zeros
- y-intercept
- Axis of symmetry

The vertex of the parabola is $(1, -4)$, the ordered pair where the minimum value of y occurs.

The minimum value is $y = -4$, (-4 is the y-coordinate of the vertex).

The zeros are $x = -1$ or $x = 3$, the x-coordinate of each ordered pair where the parabola intersects the x-axis.

The parabola passes through the y-axis at the ordered pair $(0, -3)$ so the y-intercept is -3.

The axis of symmetry is the vertical line $x = 1$ (1 is the x-coordinate of the vertex).

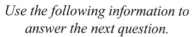

EXTRA INFORMATION

Domain – The **domain** of a relation is the permissible x-values. These are the x-values for which the relation is defined.

The domain of the quadratic relation $y = ax^2 + bx + c$, $(a \neq 0)$ will always be $x \in \mathbf{R}$.

Range – The **range** of a relation is the permissible y-values. These are the y-values for which the relation is defined. In the previous example, the range is $y \geq -4$.

Use the following information to answer the next question.

The given graph represents the quadratic function $y = f(x)$.

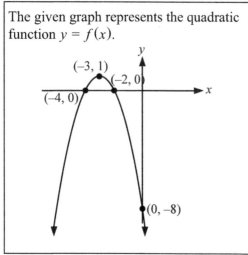

7. Which of the following statements about the graph of $y = f(x)$ is **false**?

A. The domain is $x \in R$.

B. The coordinates of the vertex are $(3, -1)$.

C. The equation of the axis of symmetry is $x + 3 = 0$.

D. The y-intercept is located at the ordered pair $(0, -8)$.

Use the following information to answer the next question.

The given graph shows a parabola.

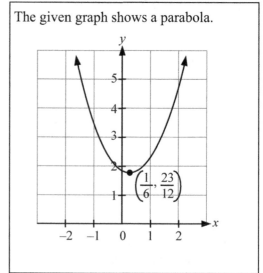

8. Which of the following statements about the given graph is **true**?

A. The minimum value is $y = \dfrac{1}{6}$, and the equation of the axis of symmetry is $x = \dfrac{23}{12}$.

B. The maximum value is $y = \dfrac{23}{12}$, and the equation of the axis of symmetry is $x = \dfrac{1}{6}$.

C. The minimum value is $y = \dfrac{23}{12}$, and the equation of the axis of symmetry is $x = \dfrac{1}{6}$.

D. The maximum value is $y = \dfrac{1}{6}$, and the equation of the axis of symmetry is $x = \dfrac{23}{12}$.

Use the following information to answer the next question.

The y-intercept of the graph of the quadratic function $y = -2(x + 3)^2 - 4$ is located at the ordered pair $(0, -K)$.

Numerical Response

9. The value of K is _____.

QR1.4 compare, through investigation using technology, the features of the graph of $y = x^2$ and the graph of $y = 2^x$, and determine the meaning of a negative exponent and of zero as an exponent

COMPARING QUADRATIC RELATIONS AND THE EXPONENTIAL RELATION $y = 2^x$

A **quadratic relation** of the form $y = ax^2 + bx + c$, $(a \neq 0)$ differs in several ways when compared to an **exponential relation** of the form $y = ab^x$.

COMPARING THE FEATURES OF THE FUNCTIONS $y = x^2$ AND $y = 2^x$

A **quadratic function** of the form $y = ax^2 + bx + c$ $(a \neq 0)$ differs in several ways when compared to an **exponential function** of the form $y = ab^x$.

To see how the two functions differ, compare the equations of each graph and the features of the graph of each function including the vertex, maximum value, minimum value, the x- and y-intercepts, and the axis of symmetry. Also, compare the second differences of each function.

When examining the equations of the two functions, notice that in an exponential function such as $y = ab^x$, the variable x is an exponent rather than part of the base as in the equation $y = ax^2 + bx + c$ $(a \neq 0)$.

Using a TI-83 Plus graphing calculator, these graphs of $y = x^2$ and $y = 2^x$ are shown.

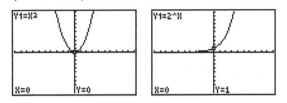

The graph of the function $y = x^2$ is a parabola opening upward. The vertex is located at $(0, 0)$. The minimum value is 0, and the equation of the axis of symmetry is $x = 0$.

The graph of the exponential function $y = 2^x$ is a continuous curve that rises from the left to the right but never intersects the x-axis. The graph is asymmetrical and does not have a maximum or a minimum value; therefore, it does not have a vertex.

The x-intercept for the graph of the function $y = x^2$ is $x = 0$.

The function $y = 2^x$ does not cross or touch the x-axis. Thus, the graph of $y = 2^x$ has no x-intercept.

The y-intercept for the graph of the function $y = x^2$ is $y = 0$.

For the function $y = 2^x$, the graph crosses the y-axis at $(0, 1)$. Therefore, the intercept is $y = 1$.

The first and second differences for the equation $y = x^2$ are shown in this table of values.

$y = x^2$		1st diff	2nd diff
x	y		
-3	9		
		$\}-5$	
-2	4		$\}2$
		$\}-3$	
-1	1		$\}2$
		$\}-1$	
0	0		$\}2$
		$\}1$	
1	1		$\}2$
		$\}3$	
2	4		$\}2$
		$\}5$	
3	9		

Since the table of values is for a quadratic function of the form $y = ax^2 + bx + c$, the second difference is a constant. In this case, the second difference is 2.

The first and second differences for the equation $y = 2^x$ are shown in this table of values.

$y = 2^x$

x	y	1st diff	2nd diff
−3	0.125		
		} 0.125	
−2	0.25		} 0.125
		} 0.25	
−1	0.5		} 0.25
		} 0.5	
0	1		} 0.5
		} 1	
1	2		} 1
		} 2	
2	4		} 2
		} 4	
3	8		

For this function, neither the first nor second difference has a constant value. Therefore, the function is not linear or quadratic.

Note: Each y-value in the table can be obtained by multiplying the previous y-value by 2.

THE NEGATIVE EXPONENT

When a number or variable has a negative exponent in the numerator, the expression can be rewritten with a positive exponent in the denominator;

$$x^{-n} = \frac{1}{x^n}.$$

Example

Using the negative exponent rule, evaluate 3^{-3}.

$$3^{-3} = \frac{1}{3^3} = \frac{1}{27}$$

SIMPLIFYING NUMERICAL EXPRESSIONS USING THE ZERO EXPONENT LAW

Any number (except 0) or variable to the exponent of zero is equal to 1. This is often referred to as the zero exponent rule and is stated as $x^0 = 1$, where $x \neq 0$.

This rule is an application of other rules of exponents.

For example, you can evaluate the expression $3^2 \times 3^{-2}$ using the negative exponent rule as well as the product rule for exponents to show that $3^0 = 1$.

Apply the negative exponent rule.

$$3^2 \times 3^{-2} = 3^2 \times \frac{1}{3^2} = 9 \times \frac{1}{9} = 1$$

Apply the product rule for exponents.

$$3^2 \times 3^{-2} = 3^{2+(-2)} = 3^0$$

Thus, $3^0 = 1$.

Example

Evaluate the expression $6(2^3 + 4^0)$.

Solution

Step 1

Evaluate 4^0.

$4^0 = 1$

Step 2

Substitute 1 for 4^0 in the given expression, and then simplify.

$$6(2^3 + 4^0) = 6(2^3 + 1)$$
$$= 6(8 + 1)$$
$$= 6(9)$$
$$= 54$$

Example

Evaluate $(2^0 - 3^0)^0$.

Solution

Step 1

Apply the zero exponent rule to the terms inside the brackets and then simplify.

Remember to follow the order of operations (BEDMAS) in the process of evaluation.

$$(2^0 - 3^0)^0 = (2^0 - (3)^0)^0$$
$$= (1 - 1)^0$$
$$= 0^0$$

Step 2

Evaluate.

Since the final expression has 0 as a base, the expression 0^0 is undefined.

Thus, the expression $(2^0 - 3^0)^0$ is undefined.

10. The graph of $y = x^0$, where $x \neq 0$, is the same as the graph of

    A. $y = 1$ **B.** $y = 2$

    C. $y = 3$ **D.** $y = 4$

11. The graphs of $y = x^2$ and $y = 2^x$ will both have

    A. the same x-intercept

    B. the same y-intercept

    C. an undefined minimum value

    D. an undefined maximum value

QR2.1 identify, through investigation using technology, the effect on the graph of $y = x^2$ of transformations by considering separately each parameter a, h, and k

ANALYZING THE EFFECTS OF $a, h,$ AND k ON QUADRATIC FUNCTIONS

When the graph of the quadratic function $f(x) = x^2$ is transformed to the graph of $f(x) = a(x - h)^2 + k$, the parameters a, h, and k have specific roles in these transformations. These parameters also affect certain features of the transformed graph.

THE EFFECT OF a IN $y = ax^2$

Regardless of the a-value, each point (x_1, y_1) on the original graph becomes (x_1, ay_1).

The a-value causes a vertical stretch by a factor of a about the x-axis when $|a| > 1$ and a vertical compression by a factor of a about the x-axis when $0 < |a| < 1$.

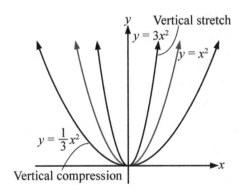

When a is negative, it causes a reflection in the x-axis, which creates a graph that is a mirror image of the original graph in the x-axis as shown.

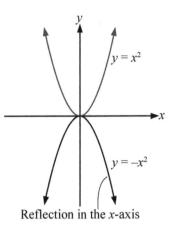

Reflection in the x-axis

The value of a also affects the following features:

- When $a > 0$, the graph opens upward, has a minimum of k, and a range of $y \geq k$.
- When $a < 0$, the graph opens downward, has a maximum of k, and a range of $y \leq k$.
- Generally, the value of a does not have an effect upon the domain, vertex, axis of symmetry, or x-intercept of the parabola.

THE EFFECT OF h IN $y = (x - h)^2$

The h-value causes a **horizontal translation**, meaning the parabola shifts left or right. When $h < 0$, the whole graph shifts left h units, and when $h > 0$, the whole graph shifts right h units.

The h-value affects the following features of the graph:

- The vertex moves from $(0, 0)$ to $(h, 0)$.

- The axis of symmetry changes from $x = 0$ to $x = h$.

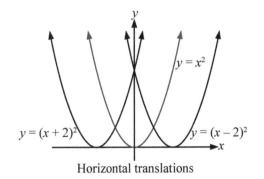

Horizontal translations

THE EFFECT OF k IN $y = x^2 + k$

The k-value causes a **vertical translation**, meaning the parabola shifts upward or downward. When $k < 0$, the whole graph shifts down k units, and when $k > 0$, the whole graph shifts up k units.

The k-value affects the following features of the graph:

- The vertex moves from $(0, 0)$ to $(0, k)$.
- The range becomes $y \geq k$.

- The minimum or maximum value becomes k.

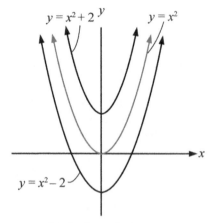

Vertical translations

Example

Two transformations were applied to the graph of $y = x^2$ to obtain the second graph of the form $y = a(x - h)^2 + k$.

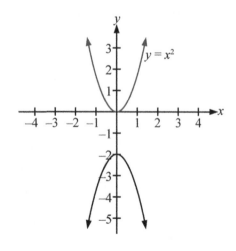

Describe the transformations in terms of the parameters a, h, and k.

Solution

Because the transformed graph has a maximum value and opens downward, there is a reflection in the x-axis. There is no vertical stretch, since the original graph and the transformed graph have the same basic shape and size. Therefore, $a = -1$.

The transformed graph has also been translated vertically downward 2 units since the vertex is at $(0, -2)$, so $k = -2$.

Since there is no horizontal change, $h = 0$.

⎯⎯⎯⎯⎯⎯⎯⎯⎯⎯

Example

For the quadratic function $f(x) = -4(x - 1)^2 - 7$, describe the transformations on the graph of $f(x) = x^2$ to produce the function, and describe its new features.

Solution

- The value of $a = -4$ means that the graph of $f(x) = x^2$ is stretched vertically by a factor of 4 and reflected in the x-axis ($a < 0$).
- The value of $h = 1$ means that the graph of $f(x) = x^2$ is translated horizontally to the right by 1 unit.
- The value of $k = -7$ means that the graph of $f(x) = x^2$ is translated vertically downward 7 units.

The new features of the graph are as follows:

Vertex (h, k)	$(1, -7)$
Axis of symmetry	$x = 1$
Maximum (k)	-7
Range ($y \leq k$)	$y \leq -7$
Direction of opening	Downward

The domain for any quadratic function is always $x \in R$.

⎯⎯⎯⎯⎯⎯⎯⎯⎯⎯

12. If the value of k increases in the equation $y = x^2 + k$, then the graph is shifted

   A. left   **B.** right

   C. upward   **D.** downward

13. Which of the following graphs could be the graph of the quadratic function $y = ax^2 + k$, where $a > 0$?

   A.

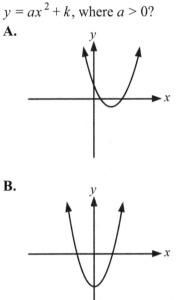

   B.

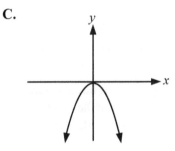

   C.

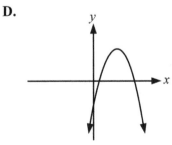

   D.

Use the following information to answer the next question.

> The graph of the function $y = x^2$ can be transformed to the graph of the function $y = 2(x + 3)^2 - 5$ by performing a vertical stretch about the x-axis by a factor of ____*i*____, a horizontal translation of ____*ii*____ units to the left, and a vertical translation downward by ____*iii*____ units.

14. This statement is completed by the information in which of the following tables?

A.

i	*ii*	*iii*
5	3	2

B.

i	*ii*	*iii*
2	5	3

C.

i	*ii*	*iii*
2	3	5

D.

i	*ii*	*iii*
5	2	3

QR2.2 explain the roles of a, h, and k in $y = a(x - h)^2 + k$, using the appropriate terminology to describe the transformations, and identify the vertex and the equation of the axis of symmetry

DESCRIBING TRANSFORMATIONS OF A PARABOLA

For the quadratic function $y = a(x - h)^2 + k$, the parameters a, h, and k as well as the vertex and equation of the axis of symmetry reveal important information about the transformations of a parabola.

THE ROLE OF *a*

- a is responsible for vertical stretches and compressions, as well as the reflection in the x-axis
- If $a > 1$, there is a vertical stretch by a factor of a.
- If $0 < a < 1$, there is a vertical compression by a factor of a.

When $a > 0$:

- The parabola opens upward.
- The function has a minimum value of k.
- The range of the function is $y \geq k$.

When $a < 0$:

- The parabola opens downward, and there is a reflection in the x-axis.
- The function has a maximum value of k.
- The range of the function is $y \leq k$.

THE ROLE OF h

- h represents a horizontal translation of h units:
  - left if $h < 0$.
  - right if $h > 0$.

THE ROLE OF k

- k represents a vertical translation of k units
  - downward if $k < 0$.
  - upward if $k > 0$.

VERTEX, AXIS OF SYMMETRY, AND DOMAIN

- The vertex is (h, k).
- The equation of the axis of symmetry is $x = h$.
- The domain of the function is the set of real numbers, which can be written as $x \in \mathbf{R}$.

Example
Write the equation of the transformed function if the graph of the quadratic function $y = x^2$ is reflected in the x-axis and then translated 7 units to the right and 9 units down.

A reflection in the x-axis will change the a-value from 1 to -1.
Translations of 7 right and 9 down give h- and k-values of 7 and -9, respectively.
The equation of the transformed graph is
$y = -1(x - (7))^2 - 9$ or $y = -(x - 7)^2 - 9$.

Example
For the quadratic function $y = 2(x + 3)^2 - 5$, determine the following:

1. The values of a, h, and k, and describe the transformations of this graph when compared to the graph of $y = x^2$.

The equation $y = 2(x + 3)^2 - 5$ can be written as $y = 2(x - (-3))^2 - 5$.
Therefore, $a = 2$, $h = -3$, and $k = -5$.
Compared with the graph of the function $y = x^2$, the graph of the function $y = 2(x + 3)^2 - 5$ has been vertically stretched by a factor of 2 ($|a| = 2$) about the x-axis and then translated 3 units to the left ($h = -3$) and 5 units downward ($k = -5$).

2. The vertex and the equation of the axis of symmetry.

Since $h = -3$ and $k = -5$, the vertex is $(-3, -5)$, and the axis of symmetry is the vertical line $x = -3$.

---

15. The graph of the quadratic function $y = -2(x - 1)^2 + 3$ is symmetric about the line
    - **A.** $x = 1$
    - **B.** $x = 3$
    - **C.** $x = -1$
    - **D.** $x = -3$

16. If a quadratic function has a minimum value of k and its graph has an axis of symmetry of $x - 5 = 0$, then the function could be
    - **A.** $y = (x - 5)^2 + k$
    - **B.** $y = (x + 5)^2 + k$
    - **C.** $y = -(x + 5)^2 + k$
    - **D.** $y = -(x - 5)^2 + k$

Use the following information to answer the next question.

The parabola $y = x^2$ is vertically stretched about the x-axis by a factor of $\frac{1}{2}$, horizontally stretched about the y-axis by a factor of 5, and translated 5 units right and 3 units down.

17. If the equation of the transformed function is in the standard form $y - k = a(x - h)^2$, then the respective values of a, h, and k are

A. 50, −5, and −3

B. $\frac{1}{50}$, 5, and −3

C. 5, $\frac{1}{50}$, and 3

D. $\frac{1}{5}$, −5, and 3

QR2.3 sketch, by hand, the graph of $y = a(x - h)^2 + k$ by applying transformations to the graph of $y = x^2$

SKETCHING THE GRAPH OF $y = x^2$

In order to sketch the graph of $y = a(x - h)^2 + k$ by hand, transformations can be applied to the graph of $y = x^2$. All points on the transformed graph must satisfy the given transformations.

For example, consider the following graphs:

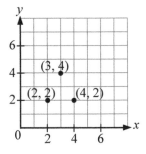

Compared to the graph of $y = x^2$, the graph of the function $y = (x - 2)^2 + 1$ has been translated 2 units right and 1 unit up and has a vertex of (2, 1) rather than (0, 0). Similarly, the point (3, 9), which is on the graph of $y = x^2$, will become the point (5, 10) on the graph of $y = (x - 2)^2 + 1$, since 5 is 2 units right of 3 and 10 is 1 unit up from 9.

SKETCHING THE GRAPH OF $y = a(x - h)^2 + k$ BY APPLYING TRANSFORMATIONS TO THE GRAPH OF $y = x^2$

In order to sketch the graph of $y = a(x - h)^2 + k$, transformations can be applied to the graph of $y = x^2$. All points on the transformed graph must satisfy the given transformations as applied to a, h, and k.

For example, consider the following graphs:

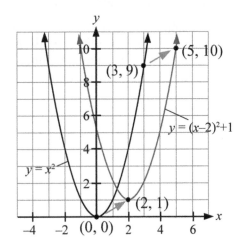

Compared to the graph of $y = x^2$, the graph of the function $y = (x - 2)^2 + 1$ has been translated 2 units right and 1 unit up, and has a vertex of (2, 1) rather than (0, 0). Similarly, the point (3, 9), which is on the graph of $y = x^2$, became the point (5, 10) on the graph of $y = (x - 2)^2 + 1$, since 5 is 2 units right of 3, and 10 is 1 unit up from 9.

Quadratic Relations

When sketching the graph of $y = a(x - h)^2 + k$ by applying transformations to the graph of $y = x^2$, the order of transformations should be as follows:

1. Vertical stretch or compression
2. Reflection in the *x*-axis
   (Steps 1 and 2 can be reversed.)
3. Vertical and/or horizontal translations (in either order)

Example

Sketch the graph of $y = -(x + 6)^2 + 5$ by applying transformations to the graph of $y = x^2$.

Solution

Step 1

Compare the equation of the graph $y = -(x + 6)^2 + 5$ with the vertex form $f(x) = a(x - h)^2 + k$ to determine the parameters *a*, *h*, and *k*, as well as the transformations that should be applied.

Since *a* is negative, the graph of $y = x^2$ will be reflected in the *x*-axis. Since $h = -6$, the graph will be translated 6 units to the left. Since $k = 5$, the graph will be translated up 5 units.

Step 2

Apply the transformations as follows:

1. Reflect the graph of $y = x^2$ in the *x*-axis. The equation of the resulting graph is $y = -x^2$.

2. Horizontally translate the graph of $y = -x^2$ six units to the left. The equation of the resulting graph is $y = -(x + 6)^2$.

3. Vertically translate the graph of $y = -(x + 6)^2$ five units up. The equation of the resulting graph is $y = -(x + 6)^2 + 5$.

This image shows the translations performed in order on the graph of $y = x^2$ that result in the graph of $y = -(x + 6)^2 + 5$.

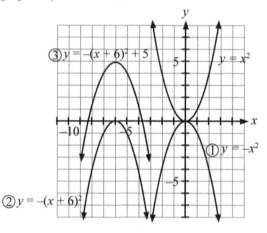

Quadratic Relations   28   Castle Rock Research

Example

Sketch the graph of $y = 3(x - 1)^2 + 4$ by applying transformations to the graph of $y = x^2$, and verify using technology.

Solution

Step 1

Sketch the graph by hand.

Compared to the graph of $y = x^2$, the graph of $y = 3(x - 1)^2 + 4$ has the following transformations applied to it:

1. It is vertically stretched by a factor of 3.
2. It is vertically translated 4 units up.
3. It is horizontally translated 1 unit right.

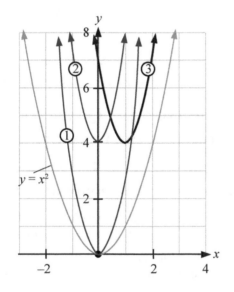

Step 2

Verify with technology.

Using a T1-83 graphing calculator, enter the equation $y = 3(x - 1)^2 + 4$ into the $\boxed{Y =}$ menu.

Press $\boxed{\text{WINDOW}}$ and set the following window settings: x:$[-10, 10, 1]$ and y:$[-10, 10, 1]$.

Press $\boxed{\text{GRAPH}}$.

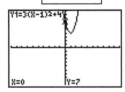

18. Which of the following graphs **best** illustrates the equation $y = -x^2 + \dfrac{7}{2}$?

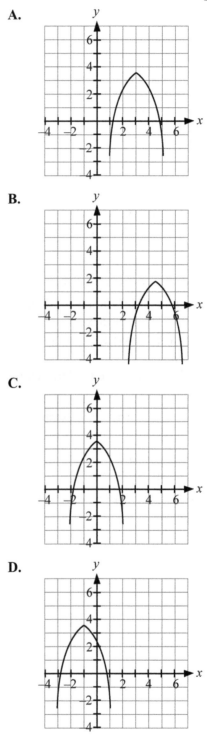

Quadratic Relations

Use the following information to answer the next question.

A student performed a series of transformations on the graph of $y = x^2$ to produce the graph shown.

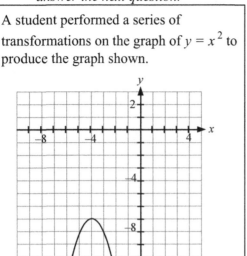

19. If the first transformation was a reflection in the *x*-axis, then the next two transformations were a horizontal translation

A. 4 units left and a vertical translation 7 units down

B. 4 units right and a vertical translation 7 units down

C. 4 units right and a vertical translation 7 units up

D. 4 units left and a vertical translation 7 units up

Use the following information to answer the next question.

The following four transformations are applied, in order, to the graph of $y = x^2$.

- a reflection about the *x*-axis
- a vertical stretch about the *x*-axis by a factor of 2
- a horizontal translation 5 units to the left
- a vertical translation 4 units upward

20. Point $(4, 16)$ on the graph of $y = x^2$ becomes point $(-1, y)$ on the transformed graph. The value of y is

A. -12 **B.** -28

C. -68 **D.** -72

QR2.4 determine the equation, in the form $y = a(x - h)^2 + k$, of a given graph of a parabola

DETERMINING THE QUADRATIC FUNCTION IN THE FORM OF $y = a(x - h)^2 + k$ USING FEATURES FROM ITS CORRESPONDING GRAPH

Follow these steps in order to determine the defining equation of the graph of a quadratic function (a parabola) in the form $y = a(x - h)^2 + k$ by making use of the coordinates of the vertex and a point on the parabola.

Note: Once a quadratic relation is expressed in the vertex form $y = a(x - h)^2 + k$ it can be expressed in the form $y = ax^2 + bx + c$ by expanding the equation.

1. Identify the coordinates of the vertex (h, k).
2. Substitute the respective values for h and k into the equation $y = a(x - h)^2 + k$.
3. Choose any point (x_1, y_1) from the graph that has coordinates that can be identified.
4. Substitute the respective values of x_1, y_1 into the equation created in step 2.

Note: Although steps 1 to 4 can be done in a single step, it is often easier to do them in separate steps.

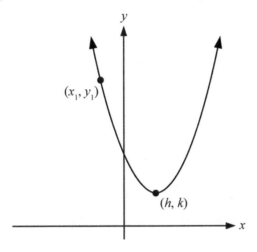

5. Solve for a.
6. Rewrite the equation $y = a(x - h)^2 + k$, substituting in the calculated values of a, h, and k.

Example
The following graph is the graph of a particular quadratic function.

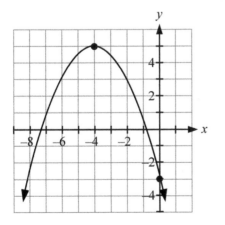

If the y-intercept of the given parabola is -3, determine the equation of the corresponding quadratic function in the form $y = a(x - h)^2 + k$.

1. The vertex is $(-4, 5)$.
2. $y = a(x + 4)^2 + 5$
3. The y-intercept is -3, so the corresponding ordered pair is $(0, -3)$.
4. Substitute and solve for a.
$$-3 = a(0 + 4)^2 + 5$$
$$-3 = a(16) + 5$$
$$-8 = 16a$$
$$-\frac{1}{2} = a$$
5. The equation of the corresponding quadratic function is $y = -\frac{1}{2}(x + 4)^2 + 5$.

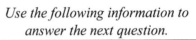

Use the following information to answer the next question.

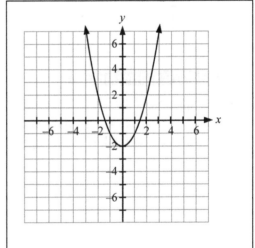

21. The parabola shown can be represented by the equation
   A. $y = (x + 2)^2$
   B. $y = 2x^2$
   C. $y = (x - 2)^2$
   D. $y = x^2 - 2$

*Use the following information to
answer the next question.*

The partial graph of a particular quadratic
relation is shown.

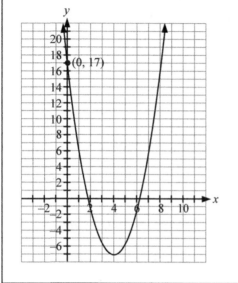

Numerical Response

22. If the equation of the parabola shown is
$y = a(x - 4)^2 - 7$, $a \in \mathbb{R}$, then the value
of a to the nearest tenth is _____.

*Use the following information to
answer the next multipart question.*

23. The graph of a quadratic function
is shown.

Open Response

a) Determine the equation of the quadratic
function of the graph shown. Write your
answer in the form of $y = a(x - h)^2 + k$.
Show your work.

b) What is the y-intercept of the graph of the
given quadratic equation?
Show your work.

c) Is the ordered pair $(-8, -12)$ on the graph of the given quadratic function? Justify your answer.

QR3.1 expand and simplify second-degree polynomial expressions using a variety of tools and strategies

EXPANDING AND SIMPLIFYING POLYNOMIALS

Before getting started, there are some key terms to review. Recall that a **monomial** is a single term expression; i.e., $5, 5x, 5xy$.

A **binomial** is the sum or difference of two monomials; i.e., $2x + 9y, 2x - 9y, 3x^2 - 5x$.

EXPANDING AND SIMPLIFYING USING ALGEBRA TILES

Algebra tiles can be used to model several types of operations relating to polynomial expressions. For these purposes, the positive x^2, x, and constants are shaded, and the negative x^2, x, and constants are white.

To represent the product of $2x(x + 3)$, make a rectangle that is two x-tiles wide and $x + 3$-tiles long, and then form the resulting rectangle.

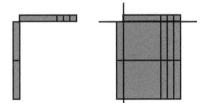

The tiles show that the product is $2x^2 + 6x$.

EXPANDING AND SIMPLIFYING USING AN ALGEBRAIC APPROACH

When expanding and simplifying polynomial expressions algebraically, these main mathematical processes are used:

- Distributive property: $a(x + y) = ax + ay$
- Product law of exponents: $x^a \cdot x^b = x^{a+b}$
- Collecting and simplifying all like terms

Example
Simplify $2xy(3x - 1)$.

$$= 2xy(3x) + 2xy(-1)$$
$$= 6x^2y - 2xy$$

MULTIPLYING TWO BINOMIALS

FOIL is a *mnemonic* device used to help remember how to multiply two binomials.
F: multiply the <u>first</u> term in each binomial together
O: multiply the two <u>outside</u> terms together
I: multiply the two <u>inside</u> terms together
L: multiply the <u>last</u> two terms together
After multiplying the terms together, gather like terms.

Example
Expand and simplify $(2x + 1)(x - 3)$.

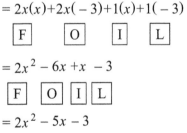

$$= 2x(x) + 2x(-3) + 1(x) + 1(-3)$$

| F | O | I | L |

$$= 2x^2 - 6x + x - 3$$

| F | O I | L |

$$= 2x^2 - 5x - 3$$

EXPANDING PERFECT SQUARE BINOMIALS

A perfect square binomial is a binomial of the form $(a + b)^2$. The following formulas can be used to expand a perfect square binomial.

$$(a + b)^2 = a^2 + 2ab + b^2$$
$$(a - b)^2 = a^2 - 2ab + b^2$$

Example

Expand and simplify $(2x + 5)^2$.

This perfect square will follow the formula

$(a + b)^2 = a^2 + 2ab + b^2$

In this case, $a = 2x$ and $b = 5$.

Substitute these values into the formula, as follows.

$(2x)^2 + 2(2x)(5) + (5)^2$

$= 4x^2 + 20x + 25$

---

24. What is the coefficient of x in the expanded form of the expression $(x - 5)(4x + 5)$?

    A. -25 **B.** -15

    C. 1 **D.** 4

25. If $(3x - 4)(4x - 1) = 12x^2 + bx + 4$, what is the value of b?

    A. -16 **B.** -19

    C. -27 **D.** -33

QR3.2 factor polynomial expressions involving common factors, trinomials, and differences of squares using a variety of tools and strategies

FACTORING POLYNOMIALS

Factoring is the process of expressing polynomials as a product of polynomials of lesser degree.

FACTORING OUT THE GREATEST COMMON FACTOR

When factoring out the greatest common factor or GCF (the largest factor common to two or more terms), look at what is common in each term of the polynomial expression. Once the greatest common factor has been identified, divide it out of each term in the polynomial.

Example

    Factor $30x^2y^3 - 12xy^2 + 24x^2y$.

Solution

    First, find the GCF of the three terms of the polynomial expression.

    Method 1: Division List

    Determine the factors of each term, and then find the GCF.

    $30x^2y^3 \rightarrow$

    1, 2, 3, 5, **6**, 10, 15, 30, $\boldsymbol{x}$, x^2, $\boldsymbol{y}$, y^2, y^3

    $12xy^2 \rightarrow$

    1, 2, 3, 4, **6**, 12, $\boldsymbol{x}$, $\boldsymbol{y}$, y^2

    $24x^2y \rightarrow$

    1, 2, 3, 4, **6**, 8, 12, 24, $\boldsymbol{x}$, x^2, $\boldsymbol{y}$

    The greatest common factor is $6xy$.

Method 2: Prime Factorization
Determine the prime factors of each term, and then select the maximum shared prime factors.

$30x^2y^3 = \mathbf{2} \times \mathbf{3} \times 5 \times \mathbf{x} \times x \times \mathbf{y} \times y \times y$
$12xy^2 = 2 \times \mathbf{2} \times \mathbf{3} \times \mathbf{x} \times \mathbf{y} \times y$
$24x^2y = 2 \times 2 \times 2 \times 3 \times \mathbf{x} \times x \times \mathbf{y}$

The greatest common factor is
$2 \times 3 \times x \times y = 6xy$.

Now, divide each term by the GCF.
$30x^2y^3 - 12xy^2 + 24x^2y$
$= 6xy(5xy^2 - 2y + 4x)$

The factored expression can be verified by multiplying the factors and then comparing the result to the original polynomial.

$6xy(5xy^2 - 2y + 4x)$
$= 6xy(5xy^2) + 6xy(-2y) + 6xy(4x)$
$= 30x^2y^3 - 12xy^2 + 24x^2y$

FACTORING BY GROUPING

Factoring by grouping involves rewriting a polynomial that has an even number of terms into smaller groups that contain a common factor.
To use this method, remove the greatest common factor (GCF) from each group, and then factor out the common binomial.

Example

Factor the expression $x^2 + 2x + x + 2$.

Solution

Step 1
Group the terms.
$x^2 + 2x + x + 2$
$= (x^2 + 2x) + (x + 2)$

Step 2
Remove the GCF from each group.
$(x^2 + 2x) + (x + 2)$
$= x(x + 2) + 1(x + 2)$

Step 3
Factor out the common binomial.
$x(x + 2) + 1(x + 2)$
$= (x + 2)(x + 1)$

FACTORING $x^2 + bx + c$ USING ALGEBRA TILES

To factor a polynomial, begin by arranging the algebra tiles into a rectangle, and then add algebra tiles to the outside of the rectangle.

The tiles representing $x^2 + 5x + 6$ can be arranged into the following rectangle:

Now, add algebra tiles to the left and upper sides of the rectangle to form the two factors.

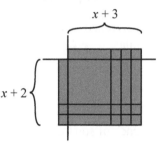

The factors are $(x + 2)(x + 3)$.

FACTORING TRINOMIALS OF THE FORM $ax^2 + bx + c$

One commonly used procedure for factoring trinomials of this form is **decomposition**. Decomposition starts by taking the middle term (bx) of the trinomial and splitting it into two separate monomials such that the resulting expression can be factored by grouping.

In order to factor $2x^2 - 5x - 3$:

1. Find two numbers that have a product of -6 ($a \times c$) and a sum of -5 (the b-value). In this case, the numbers are -6 and 1.
2. Rewrite the expression by replacing the term $-5x$ with $-6x$ and $1x$.
3. Group using brackets.
4. Remove the GCF from each group.
5. Factor out the common binomial.

$$2x^2 - 5x - 3 \qquad = 2x^2 - 6x + x - 3$$
$$= \left(2x^2 - 6x\right) + 1(x - 3)$$
$$= 2x(x - 3) + 1(x - 3)$$
$$= (x - 3)(2x + 1)$$

FACTORING A DIFFERENCE OF SQUARES

In factoring a difference of squares, use the following formula:

$$a^2 - b^2 = (a - b)(a + b)$$

Example

Factor $4x^2 - 9$.

This is a difference of squares where $a^2 = 4x^2$, so $a = 2x$, and $b^2 = 9$, so $b = 3$.

Since $a^2 - b^2 = (a - b)(a + b)$,

$4x^2 - 9 = (2x)^2 - (3)^2 = (2x - 3)(2x + 3)$.

26. What is one of the factors of the binomial $16a^2b^2 - 9c^2$?

   A. $8ab - 3c$ **B.** $8ab - 9c$

   C. $4ab + 3c$ **D.** $4ab - 9c$

27. Which of the following expressions is a factor of the trinomial $2x^2 + x - 28$?

   A. $2x + 1$ **B.** $2x - 7$

   C. $x + 7$ **D.** $x - 4$

Use the following information to answer the next question.

Rachel is asked to factor four different polynomials. The given table shows the four polynomials and the student's solutions.

	Polynomial	Student's Solution
I	$8x^3 + 4x^2$	$4x^2(2x + 1)$
II	$25a^2 - 4b^2c^2$	$(5a + 2bc)(5a - 2bc)$
III	$2x^2 - 18y^2$	$2(x + 3y)(x - 3y)$
IV	$4a^3 - a$	$a(2a - 1)^2$

28. Which polynomial did Rachel factor **incorrectly**?

   A. Polynomial I   **B.** Polynomial II

   C. Polynomial III   **D.** Polynomial IV

Use the following information to answer the next question.

The polynomial expression $x^2 - 3x - 4$ is factored as $(x - m)(x + n)$.

Numerical Response

29. The value of $m + n$ is _____.

QR3.3 determine, through investigation, and describe the connection between the factors of a quadratic expression and the x-intercepts of the graph of the corresponding quadratic relation, expressed in the form $y = a(x - r)(x - s)$

THE FACTORS AND X-INTERCEPTS OF A QUADRATIC RELATION

Recall the following:

- The x-intercepts of a graph are located at the points where the graph touches or crosses the x-axis.
- The x-intercepts of the graph of a quadratic function can be used to determine the zeros of the quadratic function.

MAKING CONNECTIONS BETWEEN THE ZEROS OF THE FACTORS OF A QUADRATIC FUNCTION AND THE x-INTERCEPTS OF ITS CORRESPONDING GRAPH

A quadratic function and its corresponding graph has these characteristics:

- The x-intercepts of a graph are located at the points where the graph touches or crosses the x-axis.
- The x-intercepts of the graph of a quadratic function can be used to determine the zeros of the quadratic function.
- In order to algebraically determine the x-intercepts of the graph from its defining function, substitute 0 for y, and then solve for x in the corresponding equation.

The graph of the function $y = (x + 3)(x - 1)$ is shown.

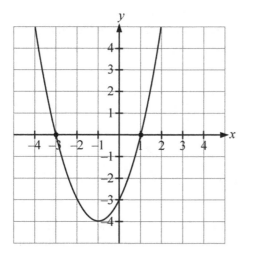

Since the graph of the function $y = (x + 3)(x - 1)$ crosses the x-axis at the points $(-3, 0)$ and $(1, 0)$, the x-intercepts are $x = -3$ and $x = 1$.

The x-intercepts of the graph of the quadratic function $y = (x + 3)(x - 1)$ can be determined algebraically by substituting 0 for y and solving for x in the corresponding quadratic equation.
$y = (x + 3)(x - 1)$
$0 = (x + 3)(x - 1)$

Apply the zero product property.

$0 = x + 3$ and $0 = x - 1$
$x = -3$ and $x = 1$

Notice the connection between the x-intercepts of the graph of the quadratic function, $x = -3$ and $x = 1$, and the zeros of the factors of the quadratic function $y = (x + 3)(x - 1)$, namely $x = -3$ and $x = 1$. They are the very same.

In general, when a quadratic function is expressed in the factored form $y = a(x - r)(x - s)$, the x-intercepts of the graph and the zeros of the quadratic function are $x = r$ and $x = s$.

Because the solutions to quadratic equations are the zeros of corresponding quadratic functions, questions that require finding these zeros involve solving quadratic equations.

Use the following information to answer the next question.

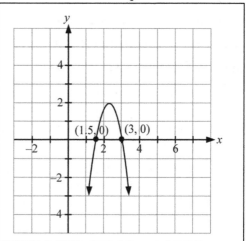
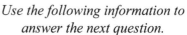

30. Which of the following equations **best** represents the graph shown?

  A. $y = 2x^2 + 9x - 9$

  B. $y = -2x^2 + 9x - 9$

  C. $y = -2x^2 + 4.5x - 4.5$

  D. $y = 2x^2 + 4.5x + 4.5$

31. The quadratic equation
$6x^2 + 13x - 28 = 0$ can be written in
factored form as $(3x - 4)(2x + 7) = 0$.
The roots of this quadratic equation are

A. $\frac{4}{3}$ and $-\frac{7}{2}$

B. $-\frac{4}{3}$ and $\frac{7}{2}$

C. $\frac{3}{4}$ and $-\frac{2}{7}$

D. $-\frac{3}{4}$ and $\frac{2}{7}$

*QR3.4 interpret real and non-real roots of
quadratic equations, through investigation using
graphing technology, and relate the roots to
the x-intercepts of the corresponding relations*

INTERPRETING THE NATURE OF THE ROOTS OF A QUADRATIC EQUATION USING A GRAPHICAL APPROACH

The **roots** of a quadratic equation are the values of
the variable that satisfy the given quadratic
equation. In other words, they are the solutions to
the equation.

The nature of the roots of a quadratic equation can
be shown graphically by determining if and where
the graph of the corresponding function intersects
the x-axis.

There are three possible scenarios:

1. Two real and distinct roots occur when the graph
   of the corresponding quadratic function
   intersects the x-axis at two distinct points.

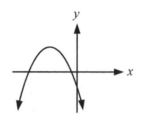

2. One real root (two equal solutions) occurs when
   the graph of the corresponding quadratic
   function touches the x-axis at one distinct point.

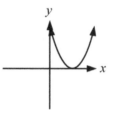

3. Non-real roots occur when the graph of the
   corresponding quadratic function does not touch
   the x-axis at any point.

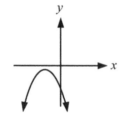

Non-real numbers, or imaginary numbers, are
numbers that cannot be placed onto a number line.
Examples of non-real roots are numbers such as
$\sqrt{-5}$, $\sqrt{-16}$, and $\frac{6}{0}$.

Example

Using technology, you can graph the function $y = -3x^2 - 2x + 10$ to determine the nature of the roots.

Graphing the function $y = -3x^2 - 2x + 10$ gives this image.

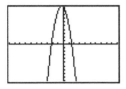

Since there are two distinct x-intercepts, this means there are two real and different roots.

Use the following information to answer the next question.

The roots of the equation $2x^2 + 9x - 5 = 0$ can be determined using technology. The first step of each of two possible procedures is shown.

Procedure A

Step 1: Graph the function $y = 2x^2 + 9x - 5$.

Procedure B

Step 1: Graph the functions $y = 2x^2$ and $y = 5 - 9x$.

32. Which of the following statements is **false**?

   A. Two distinct roots will be obtained regardless of whether procedure A or procedure B is used.

   B. With procedure A, the solution is to determine the x-intercepts on the graph of the given function.

   C. With procedure B, the solution is to determine the x-coordinate of each of the points of intersection of the graphs of the two given functions.

   D. The zeros in procedure A will be exactly the same as the y-coordinates of the points of intersection of the graphs of the two given functions in procedure B.

33. Which of the following quadratic equations has real roots?

   A. $\dfrac{1}{3}x^2 - \dfrac{4}{3}x + \dfrac{5}{3} = 0$

   B. $-\dfrac{1}{2}x^2 + 2x - 3 = 0$

   C. $3x^2 - 18x + 29 = 0$

   D. $x^2 - 5x + 6 = 0$

Use the following information to answer the next question.

Two quadratic equations are given.

I. $x^2 + x + 1 = 0$

II. $x^2 + 5x + 3 = 0$

34. Which of the following statements **best** describes the roots of the given quadratic equations?

   A. Both equations have real roots.

   B. Both equations have non-real roots.

   C. Equation I has real roots, and equation II has non-real roots.

   D. Equation I has non-real roots, and equation II has real roots.

QR3.5 express $y = ax^2 + bx + c$ in the form $y = a(x - h)^2 + k$ by completing the square in situations involving no fractions, using a variety of tools

EXPRESSING $y = ax^2 + bx + c$ IN THE FORM $y = a(x - h)^2 + k$

Completing the square is the mathematical process used to change the form of a quadratic function from the general form $y = ax^2 + bx + c$ to the standard form $y = a(x - h)^2 + k$.

COMPLETING THE SQUARE USING ALGEBRA TILES

Completing the square is the mathematical process used to change the form of a quadratic function from the general form $y = ax^2 + bx + c$ to the standard form $y = a(x - h)^2 + k$.

When using algebra tiles to complete the square, the focus needs to be on creating a figure that represents a perfect square trinomial.

Example

Using algebra tiles, create a perfect square trinomial for $x^2 + 6x + c = (x + ?)^2$.

Solution

Step 1
Create a partial square with algebra tiles to represent $x^2 + 6x$. Start with the x^2-tile, and arrange the x-tiles around x^2 to create a square.

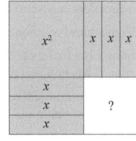

Step 2
Determine how many unit tiles are needed to complete the square.

In this case, 9 unit tiles are needed to completely fill this square.

Step 3
Determine the dimensions of the completed square.

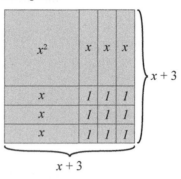

Therefore,
$$(x + 3)(x + 3) = (x + 3)^2 = x^2 + 6x + 9$$

EXPRESSING $y = ax^2 + bx + c$ IN THE FORM $y = a(x - h)^2 + k$ BY COMPLETING THE SQUARE

Completing the square is the mathematical process used to change the form of a quadratic function from the form $y = ax^2 + bx + c$ to the form $y = a(x - h)^2 + k$.

The following example shows the steps to algebraically complete the square.

Example

Complete the square for $y = -2x^2 + 8x + 3$.

Solution

Step 1
Identify and remove the common factor from the x^2- and x-terms of the expression such that the coefficient of the x^2 term is 1.

In this example, the common factor is -2.
$$y = -2(x^2 - 4x) + 3$$

Step 2
Divide the coefficient of the x-term by 2, and then square it.

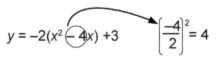

Step 3

Both add and subtract this value (4) inside the brackets in order to keep the value of the expression the same.

$y = -2(x^2 - 4x + \underline{4 - 4}) + 3$

Step 4

Move the value that will not contribute to a perfect square trinomial outside the brackets. Remember to multiply the value by the coefficient in front of the brackets.

$y = -2(x^2 - 4x + 4(-4)) + 3$

$y = -2(x^2 - 4x + 4) + 8 + 3$

Step 5

Factor the perfect square trinomial inside the brackets and collect like terms outside the brackets.

$y = -2(x - 2)^2 + 11$

Use the following information to answer the next question.

To convert the quadratic function $y = -3x^2 + 24x + 5$ into the completed square form $y = a(x - h)^2 + k$, a student performed the following steps:

1. $y = 3(x^2 + 8x) + 5$
2. $y = 3(x^2 + 8x + 12) + 5 - 36$
3. $y = 3(x^2 + 8x + 12) - 31$
4. $y = 3(x + 4)^2 - 31$

35. In which step did the student's first error occur?

   A. 1   **B.** 2

   C. 3   **D.** 4

36. The equation $y = 4x^2 + 32x + 59$ can be expressed in the form

$y = a(x - h)^2 + k$ as

   A. $y = 4(x + 4)^2 - 5$

   B. $y = 4(x + 5)^2 - 4$

   C. $y = 4(x + 4)^2 + 5$

   D. $y = 4(x + 5)^2 + 4$

37. The quadratic function $y = x^2 - 8x + 23$ can be expressed in the form

$y = a(x - h)^2 + k$ as

   A. $y = (x - 7)^2 + 4$

   B. $y = (x - 4)^2 + 7$

   C. $y = (x - 8)^2 + 23$

   D. $y = (x - 4)^2 + 23$

Numerical Response

38. If the equation $y = -2x^2 + 12x + \dfrac{1}{3}$ is written in the completed square form $y = a(x - h)^2 + k$, then the value of k, correct to the nearest tenth, is _____.

QR3.6 sketch or graph a quadratic relation whose equation is given in the form $y = ax^2 + bx + c$, using a variety of methods

Methods of Graphing a Quadratic Relation

There are three main methods of graphing a quadratic relation: by using intercepts and symmetry, completing the square, and using technology.

Graph Sketching Using Intercepts and Symmetry

To use this sketching method, begin by determining the x-intercept(s) and the y-intercept of the graph of the quadratic relation. Then, use symmetry and the vertex of the graph to complete the sketch. For example, graph the function $y = -x^2 + x + 6$, as follows:

        Quadratic Relations

Step 1: Find the x-intercepts.

$0 = -x^2 + x + 6$

$0 = -(x - 3)(x + 2)$

$x = 3$

$x = -2$

Step 2: Find the y-intercept.

$y = -(0)^2 + 0 + 6$

$y = 6$

Step 3: Find the **midpoint** of the x-intercepts in order to find the equation of the axis of symmetry.

$$M = \left(\frac{x_1 + x_2}{2}\right), \left(\frac{y_1 + y_2}{2}\right)$$

$$= \left(\frac{3 + (-2)}{2}\right), \left(\frac{0 + 0}{2}\right)$$

$$= \left(\frac{1}{2}, 0\right)$$

The equation of the axis of symmetry is $x = \dfrac{1}{2}$.

Step 4: Find the vertex (substitute $\dfrac{1}{2}$ for x).

$$y = -\left(\frac{1}{2}\right)^2 + \left(\frac{1}{2}\right) + 6$$

$$y = \frac{25}{4} \text{ or } y = 6.25$$

The vertex is at point $\left(\dfrac{1}{2}, \dfrac{25}{4}\right)$ or $(0.5, 6.25)$.

Step 5: Using the information from steps 1, 2, 3, and 4, sketch the graph of $y = -x^2 + x + 6$.

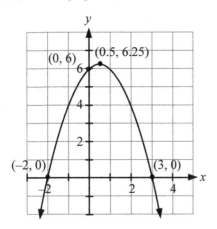

SKETCHING THE GRAPH OF $y = ax^2 + bx + c$ BY COMPLETING THE SQUARE AND APPLYING TRANSFORMATIONS TO THE GRAPH OF $y = x^2$

This method of graphing involves changing the quadratic function from the form $y = ax^2 + bx + c$ to the form $y = a(x - h)^2 + k$ by compleating the square and then applying transformations to the graph of $y = x^2$.

Consider the quadratic function $y = 4x^2 - 8x + 1$. Recall the steps for completing the square.

First, identify and remove the coefficient of the x term greatest common factor from the x^2- and x-terms of the expression. In this example, the common factor is 4.

$y = 4(x^2 - 2x) + 1$

Notice the coefficient of the x-term. Divide this value by 2, and then square it.

$y = 4(x^2 \underset{\frown}{-\,2x}) + 1 \qquad \left(\frac{-2}{2}\right)^2 = 1$

Then, both add and subtract this value (1) inside the brackets in order to maintain equality.

$y = 4(x^2 - 2x + 1 - 1) + 1$

Isolate the perfect square trinomial by moving the negative value (-1) outside the brackets. Remember to multiply this value by the coefficient in front of the brackets.

$y = 4(x^2 - 2x + 1(-1)) + 1$

$y = 4(x^2 - 2x + 1) - 4 + 1$

Factor the perfect square trinomial inside the brackets, and collect like terms outside the brackets.

$y = 4(x - 1)(x - 1) - 4 + 1$

$\quad = 4(x - 1)^2 - 3$

Thus, the function $y = 4x^2 - 8x + 1$ can be written in the form $y = 4(x - 1)^2 - 3$.

Now, sketch the graph of $y = 4(x - 1)^2 - 3$ by applying transformations to the graph of $y = x^2$. The transformations are as follows:

1. Vertical stretch by a factor of 4 about the x-axis (shown by graph 1).
2. Horizontal translation 1 unit to the right (shown by graph 2).
3. Vertical translation 3 units downward (shown by graph 3).

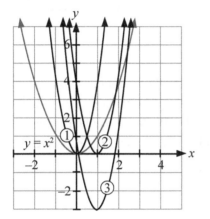

The graph of $y = 4(x - 1)^2 - 3$ is labeled graph 3, as shown.

GRAPHING VARIOUS FORMS OF THE QUADRATIC FUNCTION USING TECHNOLOGY

Using technology, such as a TI-83 Plus calculator, to graph a quadratic function requires the use of proper window settings and the appropriate selection of calculator buttons.

To graph a quadratic function on a graphing calculator, follow these steps:

1. Make sure the function is written in terms of the y-variable or unsquared variable.
2. Press the $\boxed{Y =}$ button on your graphing calculator, and type in the function.
3. Set an appropriate WINDOW setting for the graph so that the resulting parabolic graph will be adequately portrayed on the screen. For most quadratic functions, a good starting WINDOW setting can be created by pressing the $\boxed{\text{ZOOM}}$ button and selecting either the 6:ZStandard or 0:Zoom Fit feature.
4. Press the $\boxed{\text{GRAPH}}$ button if necessary to view the parabolic graph representing the quadratic function.

Example

Graph $y = 2(x - 3)^2 - 5$ on a graphing calculator.

Solution

Step 1

Press the $\boxed{Y =}$ button.

Type in the function by pressing the following sequence of buttons:

$$\boxed{2}\ \boxed{(}\ \boxed{x, T, \theta, n}\ \boxed{-}\ \boxed{3}\ \boxed{)}\ \boxed{x^2}\ \boxed{-}\ \boxed{5}$$

Step 2

Set an appropriate WINDOW setting.

Press the $\boxed{\text{ZOOM}}$ button, and select the 6:ZStandard feature. This graph should appear on the calculator screen.

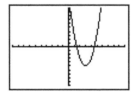

An adequate graph of the parabola representing the function is visible.

Quadratic Relations

Example

Graph $P = -25s^2 + 1\ 010s - 3\ 253$ using technology.

Solution

Step 1

Press the ☐ Y = ☐ button.

When a function like $P = -25s^2 + 1\ 010s - 3\ 253$ is not defined in terms of x- and y-variables, it can still be entered into a graphing calculator as though it was, namely as $y = -25x^2 + 1\ 010x - 3\ 253$.

Type in the function by pressing the following sequence of buttons:

(−)	2	5	x, T, θ, n	x^2	+	1	0	1	0

x, T, θ, n	−	3	2	5	3

Step 2

Set an appropriate WINDOW setting.

Press the ☐ ZOOM ☐ button, and select the 0:Zoom Fit feature. This graph should appear on the calculator screen.

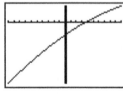

Since there is an inadequate amount of the parabola visible, the WINDOW setting needs to be adjusted manually.

Step 3

Press the ☐ WINDOW ☐ button.

To see more of the graph, the top and right side of the graph needs to be made more visible. To do so, increase the Xmax value by pressing the down arrow key so that it highlights the Xmax value.

Enter a greater value than 10, such as 50. Then, press ☐ ZOOM ☐ again, and highlight the 0:Zoom Fit feature again. A more adequate parabola will appear on the screen.

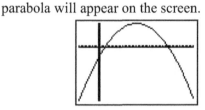

The WINDOW setting can be continually adjusted as necessary by pressing the ☐ WINDOW ☐ button and entering values for Xmin, Xmax, Xscl, Ymin, Ymac, or Yscl.

Example

Graph $y = -0.5(x - 6)(x + 5)$ using a graphing calculator.

Solution

Step 1

Press the ☐ Y = ☐ button.

Type in the function by pressing the following sequence of buttons:

(−)	0	.	5	(	x, T, θ, n	−	6	)	(

x, T, θ, n	+	5	)

Step 2

Set an appropriate WINDOW setting.

Press the ☐ ZOOM ☐ button, and select the 6:ZStandard feature. This graph should appear on the calculator screen.

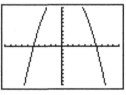

Since the top part of the parabola is not visible, the WINDOW setting needs to be adjusted manually.

Step 3

Press the | WINDOW | button.

To see more of the upper part of the graph, the Ymax value needs to be increased. Press the down arrow key so that it highlights the Ymax value. Enter a greater value than 10, such as 20. Then, press the | GRAPH | button. A more adequate graph of the parabola should appear on the screen.

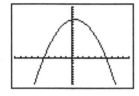

Use the following information to answer the next question.

John is attempting to sketch the graph of a particular quadratic function. He correctly determines that

the x-intercepts of the graph are $\dfrac{1}{2}$ and -4.

39. What is the equation of the axis of symmetry of this graph?

A. $x = -\dfrac{7}{2}$ **B.** $x = -\dfrac{7}{4}$

C. $x = \dfrac{7}{4}$ **D.** $x = \dfrac{7}{2}$

40. The sketch of the graph of $y = x^2 - 6x + 4$ is completed by applying transformations to the graph of $y = x^2$. The vertex of the graph of $y = x^2 - 6x + 4$ is located

    A. 3 units right and 5 units down from the vertex of the graph of $y = x^2$

    B. 3 units left and 5 units down from the vertex of the graph of $y = x^2$

    C. 6 units left and 4 units up from the vertex of the graph of $y = x^2$

    D. 6 units right and 4 units up from the vertex of the graph of $y = x^2$

Use the following information to answer the next question.

Gladys would like to graph the quadratic function $y = -4.9x^2 + 30x + 1$ using her graphing calculator. Four possible window settings are given.

	Window Setting			
	I	**II**	**III**	**IV**
x_{min}	−10	−20	−15	−10
x_{max}	10	20	15	10
x_{scl}	1	2	2	1
y_{min}	−10	−30	−10	−20
y_{max}	10	30	40	60
y_{scl}	1	3	2	4
x_{res}	1	1	1	1

41. In order to display the graph with its vertex in view, Gladys must use window setting

    A. I   **B.** II

    C. III   **D.** IV

QR3.7 explore the algebraic development of the quadratic formula

THE QUADRATIC FORMULA

Since not all quadratic equations can be factored, using technology to find the roots will only give an approximate answer. In order to obtain the exact roots of a quadratic equation, a formula (called the **quadratic formula**) can be developed by completing the square of the general form of a quadratic equation $ax^2 + bx + c = 0$.

DEVELOPING AND USING THE QUADRATIC FORMULA TO SOLVE QUADRATIC EQUATIONS

The quadratic formula is used to determine the exact roots of a quadratic equation that is not easily factorable or to determine the approximate roots to a quadratic equation that is not factorable. The formula is developed by isolating x in the equation $ax^2 + bx + c = 0$ by completing the square.

Factor out a from the x^2- and x-terms.

$$ax^2 + bx + c = 0$$

$$a\left(x^2 + \frac{b}{a}x\right) + c = 0$$

Identify the coefficient of the x-term in the brackets (denoted by $\frac{b}{a}$), divide this value by 2, and then square it.

$$\left(\frac{b}{2a}\right)^2 = \frac{b^2}{4a^2}$$

Add and subtract the resulting value, $\frac{b^2}{4a^2}$, inside the brackets to maintain equality.

$$a\left(x^2 + \frac{b}{a}x + \frac{b^2}{4a^2} - \frac{b^2}{4a^2}\right) + c = 0$$

Move the value that will not contribute to a perfect square outside the brackets, remembering to multiply the value by a to maintain equality.

Factor the trinomial inside the brackets to form a perfect square.

$$a\left(x + \frac{b}{2a}\right)^2 - \frac{b^2}{4a} + c = 0$$

Isolate the variable x.

$$a\left(x + \frac{b}{2a}\right)^2 = \left(\frac{b^2}{4a} - c\right)$$

$$\left(x + \frac{b}{2a}\right)^2 = \frac{b^2}{4a^2} - \frac{c}{a}$$

$$\left(x + \frac{b}{2a}\right)^2 = \frac{b^2}{4a^2} - \frac{4ac}{4a^2}$$

$$\left(x + \frac{b}{2a}\right)^2 = \frac{b^2 - 4ac}{4a^2}$$

$$\sqrt{\left(x + \frac{b}{2a}\right)^2} = \pm\sqrt{\frac{b^2 - 4ac}{4a^2}}$$

$$x + \frac{b}{2a} = \pm\frac{\sqrt{b^2 - 4ac}}{2a}$$

$$x = -\frac{b}{2a} \pm \frac{\sqrt{b^2 - 4ac}}{2a}$$

$$x = \frac{-b \pm \sqrt{b^2 - 4ac}}{2a}$$

The exact roots as well as the approximate roots of the quadratic equation $ax^2 + bx + c = 0$, where $a \neq 0$, can be determined using the quadratic formula:

$$x = \frac{-b \pm \sqrt{b^2 - 4ac}}{2a}$$

Example

Determine the exact roots to the equation $x^2 - 8x + 5 = 0$ by applying the quadratic formula.

Solution

Step 1
Identify the values of a, b, and c.
$a = 1 \quad b = -8 \quad c = 5$

Step 2

Substitute the values for a, b and c into the quadratic formula, and solve for x.

$$x = \frac{-b \pm \sqrt{b^2 - 4ac}}{2a}$$

$$= \frac{-(-8) \pm \sqrt{(-8)^2 - 4(1)(5)}}{2(1)}$$

$$= \frac{8 \pm \sqrt{64 - 20}}{2}$$

$$= \frac{8 \pm \sqrt{44}}{2}$$

$$= \frac{8 \pm \sqrt{4 \times 11}}{2}$$

$$= \frac{8 \pm 2\sqrt{11}}{2}$$

$$= \frac{2(4 \pm \sqrt{11})}{2}$$

$$= 4 \pm \sqrt{11}$$

The roots of the given equation are $4 + \sqrt{11}$ and $4 - \sqrt{11}$.

Use the following information to answer the next question.

Marianne used the quadratic formula to solve the equation $2x^2 - 3x - 1 = 0$. She followed these steps to arrive at a solution:

1. $x = \dfrac{-3 \pm \sqrt{(-3)^2 - 4(2)(-1)}}{2(2)}$

2. $x = \dfrac{-3 \pm \sqrt{9 + 8}}{4}$

3. $x = \dfrac{-3 \pm \sqrt{17}}{4}$

4. $x = -1.78, \; x = 0.28$

42. There is an error in one of the steps Marianne followed. In which step did the error occur?

  A. Step 1   **B.** Step 2

  C. Step 3   **D.** Step 4

Use the following information to answer the next question.

The first three steps in the algebraic development of the quadratic formula $ax^2 + bx + c = 0$ are given as follows:

1. $a\left(x^2 + \dfrac{b}{a}x\right) + c = 0$

2. $a\left(x^2 + \dfrac{b}{a}x + \dfrac{b^2}{4a^2} - \dfrac{b^2}{4a^2}\right) + c = 0$

3. $a(x + K)^2 - \dfrac{b^2}{4a} + c = 0$

43. Which expression is represented by the variable K?

  A. $\dfrac{b^2}{4a^2}$ **B.** $\dfrac{b^2}{2a^2}$

  C. $\dfrac{b}{4a}$ **D.** $\dfrac{b}{2a}$

QR3.8 solve quadratic equations that have real roots, using a variety of methods

Solving Quadratic Equations

Quadratic equations can be solved using factoring, the quadratic formula, and graphing.

The following tips can help you solve a quadratic equation of the form $ax^2 + bx + c = 0$:

1. Attempt to solve the equation by factoring.
2. If the equation cannot be solved by factoring or is difficult to factor, use the quadratic formula.
3. Use a graphical procedure to solve the equation or verify your solution.
4. Simplify the roots (solution values), if necessary, and clearly state the solution(s) using "$x =$".

                           Quadratic Relations

Example

Solve the equation $0 = x^2 + 4x - 21$.

Solution

Method 1: Factoring

$0 = x^2 + 4x - 21$
$0 = (x - 3)(x + 7)$
$0 = (x - 3)$ or $0 = (x + 7)$
$x = 3$ or $x = -7$

Method 2: Using the quadratic formula
Substitute the values $a = 1$, $b = 4$, and $c = -21$, and then solve for x.

$$x = \frac{-b \pm \sqrt{b^2 - 4ac}}{2a}$$

$$x = \frac{-(4) \pm \sqrt{(4)^2 - 4(1)(-21)}}{2(1)}$$

$$x = \frac{-4 \pm \sqrt{16 + 84}}{2}$$

$$x = \frac{-4 \pm \sqrt{100}}{2}$$

$$x = \frac{-4 \pm 10}{2}$$

$$x = \frac{-4 + 10}{2} \text{ or } x = \frac{-4 - 10}{2}$$

$$x = \frac{6}{2} \text{ or } x = \frac{-14}{2}$$

$$x = 3 \text{ or } x = -7$$

Method 3: Graphing
Enter the equation into the calculator by pressing the $\boxed{Y =}$ button. Then, access the CALCULATE menu by pressing $\boxed{2nd}$ $\boxed{Trace}$, and choose 2:Zero to determine the x-intercepts of the graph.

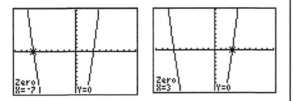

From the ZERO feature, the x-intercepts or zeros are $x = 3$ and $x = -7$.

Thus, the solution to the equation
$0 = x^2 + 4x - 21$ is $x = 3$ or $x = -7$.

Use the following information to answer the next question.

A math teacher asks her class to solve the quadratic equation $8x^2 - 2x = 3$. The partial solution of two students is given.

Tanya's Solution

$$8x^2 - 2x = 3$$
$$8x^2 - 2x - 3 = 0$$
$$8x^2 - 6x + 4x - 3 = 0$$
$$2x(4x - 3) + 1(4x - 3) = 0$$
$$(4x - 3)(2x + 1) = 0$$

Hilary's Solution

$$8x^2 - 2x = 3$$
$$8x^2 - 2x - 3 = 0$$
$$x = \frac{-(-2) \pm \sqrt{(-2)^2 - 4(8)(-3)}}{2(8)}$$
$$x = \frac{2 \pm \sqrt{4 + 96}}{16}$$
$$x = \frac{2 \pm \sqrt{100}}{16}$$

44. Which of the following statements is **true**?

   A. Tanya's work and Hilary's work will each lead to a correct solution.

   B. Tanya's work and Hilary's work will each lead to an incorrect solution.

   C. Tanya's work will lead to an incorrect solution, and Hilary's work will lead to a correct solution.

   D. Tanya's work will lead to a correct solution, and Hilary's work will lead to an incorrect solution.

45. The solutions to the quadratic equation $7x^2 + 2x - 5 = 11x^2 - 6x - 4$ are

   A. $x = \dfrac{2 \pm \sqrt{3}}{2}$ **B.** $x = 1 \pm 4\sqrt{3}$

   C. $x = \dfrac{2 \pm \sqrt{5}}{2}$ **D.** $x = 1 \pm 4\sqrt{5}$

46. What are the solutions to the quadratic equation $10x + 3 = 7x^2$?

A. $x = \dfrac{3 + \sqrt{46}}{7}$ or $x = \dfrac{3 - \sqrt{46}}{7}$

B. $x = \dfrac{4 + \sqrt{46}}{7}$ or $x = \dfrac{4 - \sqrt{46}}{7}$

C. $x = \dfrac{5 + \sqrt{46}}{7}$ or $x = \dfrac{5 - \sqrt{46}}{7}$

D. $x = \dfrac{7 + \sqrt{46}}{7}$ or $x = \dfrac{7 - \sqrt{46}}{7}$

Use the following information to answer the next multipart question.

47. The graph of the quadratic function $y = 2x^2 - x - 15$ is shown.

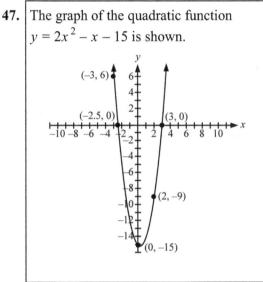

Open Response

a) What are the roots of the quadratic equation $2x^2 - x - 15 = 0$?

b) Algebraically, solve the quadratic equation $2x^2 - x - 15 = 30$.

c) If a student were to solve the equation $2x^2 - x - 15 = 0$ by using the quadratic formula, would the value of $b^2 - 4ac$ be a number that is a perfect square? Justify your answer.

QR4.1 determine the zeros and the maximum or minimum value of a quadratic relation from its graph or from its defining equation

DETERMINING THE ZEROS AND THE MAXIMUM OR MINIMUM VALUE OF A PARABOLA

DETERMINING THE FEATURES OF A QUADRATIC FUNCTION USING TECHNOLOGY

Technology such as a TI-83 graphing calculator can be used to determine the features of the graph of a quadratic function.

Enter a quadratic function into a graphing calculator by first pressing $\boxed{Y=}$ and then entering the given equation. Next, press the $\boxed{\text{GRAPH}}$ button, and use an appropriate window setting to properly view the parabola.

Follow these steps to determine the features of the graph of a function using a TI-83 graphing calculator:

- The direction of opening can be observed upon inspection of the graph.
- The vertex of the graph corresponds to the coordinates of the maximum or minimum point. The coordinates of the maximum or minimum point can be determined by pressing 2nd TRACE and choosing 3:Minimum if the graph opens upward or 4:Maximum if the graph opens downward and then following the calculator prompts.
- The maximum or minimum value is the y-coordinate of the vertex.
- The x-coordinate of the vertex is used to determine the equation of the axis of symmetry.
- To determine the x-intercept(s) of the graph (the zeros of a function), press 2nd TRACE, choose **2:Zero**, and then follow the calculator prompts.
- The y-intercept is found by pressing TRACE and then entering 0 so that $X = 0$ appears on the bottom of the screen. The corresponding value, on the screen, for y is the y-intercept.
- The range will depend on the y-value of the vertex and how the graph opens

Remember that the domain for all quadratic functions is $x \in \mathbb{R}$.

Example
Using a graphing calculator, determine all the features of the graph of the function $y = x^2 + 6x - 11$.

Press Y = and enter $x^2 + 6x - 11$.

An appropriate window setting is x:[-10, 4, 1] y: [-25, 5, 2]. Press GRAPH to display the resulting graph.

Since this graph opens upward, use the MINIMUM feature on the graphing calculator to determine the coordinates of the vertex of the graph.

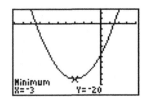

The following features of the graph of the function $y = x^2 + 6x - 11$ can now be stated:

- The vertex is (-3, -20).
- The minimum value is -20.
- The equation of the axis of symmetry is $x = -3$.
- The range of the function is $y \geq -20$.
- The domain is $x \in \mathbb{R}$.

To the nearest hundredth, the zeros of the function $y = x^2 + 6x - 11$ are $x = 1.47$ and $x = -7.47$.

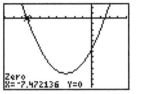 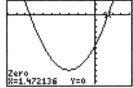

The y-intercept is -11.

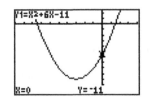

USING AN ALGEBRAIC APPROACH

Recall that when using an algebraic approach:

- The zero(s) of a function can be determined by substituting 0 for y into the equation $y = ax^2 + bx + c$, $a \neq 0$ and then solving for x.
- The maximum or minimum value can be determined when the function is written in the form $y = a(x - h)^2 + k$.
- The maximum value is k when $a < 0$.
- The minimum value is k when $a > 0$.

Example

Determine the zero(s) and the maximum or minimum value for the function

$y = -2(x + 6)^2 + 5.$

To determine the zero(s) of the function, substitute 0 for y, and solve for x.

$0 = -2(x + 6)^2 + 5$

$-5 = -2(x + 6)^2$

$\dfrac{5}{2} = (x + 6)^2$

$\pm\sqrt{\dfrac{5}{2}} = \sqrt{(x + 6)^2}$

$\pm\sqrt{\dfrac{5}{2}} = x + 6$

$\pm\sqrt{\dfrac{5}{2}} - 6 = x$

Thus, either $x = -6 + \sqrt{\dfrac{5}{2}}$ or $x = -6 - \sqrt{\dfrac{5}{2}}$

$x = -4.4$ and $x = -7.6$

To the nearest tenth, the zeros for the function $y = -2(x + 6)^2 + 5$ are $x = -4.4$ or $x = -7.6$.

The function $y = -2(x + 6)^2 + 5$ is written in the form $y = a(x - h)^2 + k$. Since $a < 0$, the graph of the function opens downward. Therefore, a maximum value occurs at k. For the function $y = -2(x + 6)^2 + 5$, the maximum value is 5.

---

48. The minimum value of the function $y = ax^2 + bx + c$ is -1. If the zeros of the function are 1 and 2, then the value of c is

A. 5   B. 6

C. 8   D. 9

Use the following information to answer the next question.

> Megan was given a math problem that required her to design a pigpen with maximum area given a fixed amount of fencing. She was able to generate a quadratic function expressed in standard form, $y = a(x - h)^2 + k$, to help her determine the maximum area of the pigpen. Megan wants to confirm that the pigpen has a maximum area rather than a minimum area.

49. To determine whether the function has a minimum or maximum, Megan should look at

A. the *a*-variable only

B. the *k*-variable only

C. both the *k*- and *h*-variables

D. both the *a*- and *k*-variables

Numerical Response

50. To the nearest whole number, what is the minimum value of the function $y = 40 - 12x + x^2$? _____

QR4.2 solve problems arising from a realistic situation represented by a graph or an equation of a quadratic relation, with and without the use of technology.

SOLVING REAL-WORLD PROBLEMS INVOLVING GRAPHS OF QUADRATIC FUNCTIONS

Quadratic functions can be used to model real-world situations and solve problems that require an analysis of the graph of the given quadratic function. It is also possible to solve problems, with or without the use of technology, that require the analysis of a quadratic function.

Most real-world problems involving quadratic functions can be solved by analyzing the graph of the corresponding parabola and identifying the y-intercept, the x-intercept, the coordinates of the vertex, or another particular point on the parabola.

Example

The trajectory of a baseball is represented by the given graph.

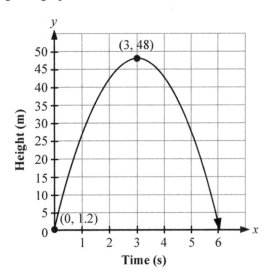

What is the maximum height of the baseball's trajectory?

Solution

The given parabola opens downward and has a vertex at (3, 48).

The maximum value (since the parabola opens downwards) of the quadratic function represented by the given parabola is equal to the *y*-coordinate of the vertex of the parabola.

Therefore, the maximum height of the baseball is 48 m.

What was the initial height of the baseball when it was hit?

Solution

At 0 s, the baseball was at its initial height. This corresponds to the ordered pair (0, 1.2) on the parabola.

Thus, the baseball was hit from an initial height of 1.2 m.

How long does the baseball remain in the air?

Solution

The ball remains in the air until it hits the ground. This occurs at the point where the parabola intersects the *x*-axis after reaching its maximum value.

Since the graph intersects the *x*-axis at 6, the ball remains in the air for 6 s.

Technology, such as a graphing calculator, can be a useful tool in solving real world problems that can be modelled by using quadratic functions.

Example

A city's population can fluctuate from year to year. The population of a small Ontario city with a declining population is expected to begin increasing in the near future because of the introduction of several industrial development initiatives.

The city planners predict that the city's population can be modelled by the function $P = 150t^2 - 1\ 200t + 14\ 900$, $t \geq 0$, where t is the time in years since January 1, 2007 and P is the population.

In which year will the city's population be at its lowest point?

Solution

Graph the function
$y = 150x^2 - 1\ 200x + 14\ 900$.

Use the MINIMUM feature of a TI-83 Plus graphing calculator and a window setting such as $x:[-5, 20, 2]\ y:[7\ 500, 30\ 000, 2\ 500]$.

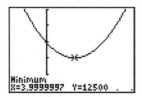

Since the graphing calculator's cursor is at $x = 4$, which corresponds to $t = 4$, the city's minimum population 4 years after January 1, 2007.

$2\ 007 + 4 = 2\ 011$

Therefore, the city's population will be at its lowest point at the beginning of 2011.

What is the first year that the city's population will be more than 24 000?

Solution

Use a TI-83 Plus graphing calculator to graph the line $y = 24\ 000$, and use the INTERSECTION feature to determine the x-coordinates, where $x > 0$, of the point of intersection of the graph of $y = 24\ 000$ and the graph of $y = 150x^2 - 1\ 200x + 14\ 900$.

This x-coordinate is $x = 12.76$, as shown.

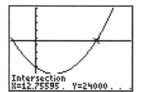

Since $t = 12.76$ it follows that
$2\ 007 + 12.76 = 2\ 019.76$.

The first entire year that the city's population will be more than 24 000 is at the end of 2020.

51. Ben observed that an arrow shot from a bow followed a parabolic path for which the height is approximated by the quadratic function

$h = -4.9(t - 1.5)^2 + 12, t \geq 0$, where h is the height in metres and t is the time in seconds. Which of the following graphs **best** represents this quadratic function?

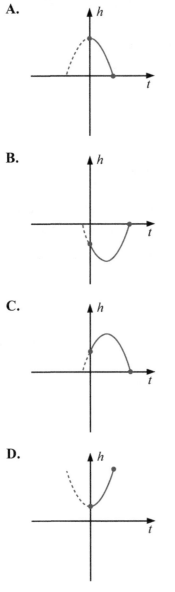

A.

B.

C.

D.

Use the following information to answer the next question.

A rectangular lot is bordered on one side by a river and on the other three sides by a total of 60 m of fencing, as shown in the diagram. If x represents the width of the lot and y represents the length of the lot, the equation $2x + y = 60$ represents the total amount of fencing, expressed in terms of x and y. The area, A, of the lot in terms of x is given by the equation $A = -2x^2 + 60x$.

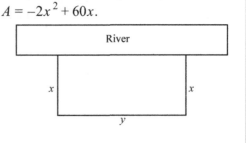

52. What is the length of the lot with maximum area?

    A. 15 m   **B.** 25 m

    C. 30 m   **D.** 40 m

Use the following information to answer the next question.

For the first section of the ride, the path of a roller coaster car can be modelled by the function $h = -7t^2 + 61t + 98$, where $1 \leq t \leq 10$. For this function, h is the height, in feet, of the car above the ground and t is the time, in seconds, elapsed since the beginning of the ride.

53. To the nearest tenth, the maximum height reached by the roller coaster car in the interval $1 \leq t \leq 10$ is

    A. 61.0 ft   **B.** 98.0 ft

    C. 115.5 ft   **D.** 230.9 ft

Use the following information to answer the next multipart question.

54. The daily profit, P, in dollars of a hot dog vendor in Toronto is described by the equation $P = -40x^2 + 240x - 75$, where x dollars is the selling price per hot dog.

Open Response

a) Describe the financial impact if the hot dog vendor does not sell any hot dogs.

b) What should the selling price per hot dog be in order for the vendor to maximize his daily profit? Justify your answer algebraically.

c) What is the maximum daily profit for the hot dog vendor?

Quadratic Relations

Copyright Protected

ANSWERS AND SOLUTIONS
QUADRATIC RELATIONS

1. 32	13. B	c) OR	35. A	47. a) OR
2. D	14. C	24. B	36. A	b) OR
3. D	15. A	25. B	37. B	c) OR
4. A	16. A	26. C	38. 18.3	48. C
5. B	17. B	27. B	39. B	49. A
6. D	18. C	28. D	40. A	50. 4
7. B	19. A	29. 5	41. D	51. C
8. C	20. B	30. B	42. A	52. C
9. 22	21. D	31. A	43. D	53. D
10. A	22. 1.5	32. D	44. A	54. a) OR
11. D	23. a) OR	33. D	45. A	b) OR
12. C	b) OR	34. D	46. C	c) OR

1. 32

Graph the function obtained from the quadratic regression, $y = -10x^2 + 100x + 6\ 000$, in the calculator, and graph the line $y = 5\ 760$. Find the point of intersection between the two graphs. The x-coordinate of the point of intersection is the value of the increases in price that corresponds to a revenue of $5 760.

The owner must have increased his price by $12 to generate a revenue of $5 760. This corresponds to a ticket price of $32. ($20 + $12).

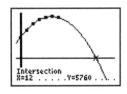

2. D

Enter the data into a graphing calculator and perform a quadratic regression, as shown.

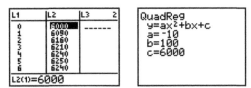

The following quadratic regression equation will result: $y = -10x^2 + 100x + 60$

3. D

Sketch the specified ordered pairs by hand to get the following graph:

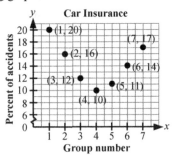

Therefore, graph D is the best display of information given in the table.

4. A

The graph of any quadratic $y = ax^2$ is a parabola. Graph B is the shape of a third degree or cubic function of the form, $y = ax^3$. Graph C is the graph of a linear function of the form, $y = ax$, and graph D is the V-shaped graph of an absolute value function of the form, $y = a\,|\,x\,|$. Therefore, the graph that most likely represents the relation $y = ax^2$ is graph A.

5. B

In order for a relation to be quadratic, the second differences from a table of values must be constant and must not be equal to zero.

Answers and Solutions   56   Castle Rock Research

Calculate the second differences for each of the given tables of values.

x	y	1st diff	2nd diff
1	8		
		} 3	
2			} 0
		} 3	
3			} 0
		} 3	
4			} 0
		} 3	
5			} 0
		} 3	
6			

x	y	1st diff	2nd diff
1	4		
		} 9	
2			} 6
		} 15	
3			} 6
		} 21	
4			} 6
		} 27	
5			} 6
		} 33	
6			

x	y	1st diff	2nd diff
1	1		
		} 2	
2			} 3
		} 5	
3			} 4
		} 9	
4			} 5
		} 14	
5			} 6
		} 20	
6			

x	y	1st diff	2nd diff
1	0		
		} 1	
2			} 3
		} 4	
3			} 5
		} 9	
4			} 7
		} 16	
5			} 9
		} 25	
6			

The table of values with a constant second difference of 6, represents a table of values for a quadratic function.

6. D

If the corresponding parabola opens upward, $a > 0$ in the equation $y = ax^2 + bx + c$. Therefore, of the given equations, $y = 5x^2 + 4x - 3$ and $y = 2.5x^2 - 3x - 8$ are possible.

Use an appropriate table of values to determine the constant second difference for each of these two equations.

$y = 5x^2 + 4x - 3$

x	y	1st diff	2nd diff
1	6		
		} 19	
2	25		} 10
		} 29	
3	54		} 10
		} 39	
4	93		} 10
		} 49	
5	142		} 10
		} 59	
6	201		

$y = 2.5x^2 - 3x - 8$

x	y	1st diff	2nd diff
1	−8.5		
		} 4.5	
2	−4		} 5
		} 9.5	
3	5.5		} 5
		} 14.5	
4	20		} 5
		} 19.5	
5	39.5		} 5
		} 24.5	
6	64		

The equation of a quadratic function that opens upward and has a second difference of 5 is $y = 2.5x^2 - 3x - 8$.

7. B

The vertex of the parabola is $(-3, 1)$, the ordered pair where the maximum value of y occurs, not $(3, -1)$. The parabola passes through the y-axis at the ordered pair $(0, -8)$, so the y-intercept is -8. The axis of symmetry is the vertical line $x = -3$ (-3 is the x-coordinate of the vertex). The domain of the quadratic function is $x \in \mathbb{R}$.

8. C

The graph shows a parabola that opens upward; therefore, a minimum value occurs at the vertex $\left(\dfrac{1}{6}, \dfrac{23}{12} \right)$.

Solutions – Quadratic Relations

The minimum value is $y = \dfrac{23}{12}$ ($\dfrac{23}{12}$ is the y-coordinate of the vertex).

The axis of symmetry is the vertical line $x = \dfrac{1}{6}$ ($\dfrac{1}{6}$ is the x-coordinate of the vertex).

9. 22

The y-intercept of the quadratic function $y = -2(x + 3)^2 - 4$ can be found by substituting 0 for x into the equation and solving for y.

$y = -2(0 + 3)^2 - 4$
$y = -2(9) - 4$
$y = -18 - 4$
$y = -22$

Therefore, the value of K in the ordered pair $(0, -K)$ is 22.

10. A

Recall that any number (except 0) or variable with an exponent of zero is equal to 1: $x^0 = 1$.

The graphs of $y = x^0$ and $y = 1$ are shown below.

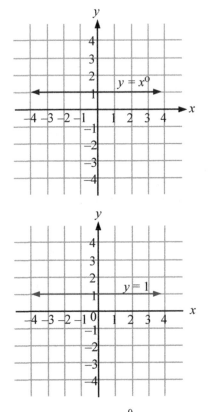

Therefore, the graph of $y = x^0$, where $x \neq 0$, is the same as the graph of $y = 1$.

11. D

Step 1
Determine the x-intercepts of both graphs.

The x-intercept of $y = x^2$ is $x = 0$. The relation $y = 2^x$ does not cross or touch the x-axis; thus, the graph of $y = 2^x$ has no x-intercept. Therefore, the graphs of $y = x^2$ and $y = 2^x$ do not have the same x-intercept.

Step 2
Determine the y-intercepts of both graphs.

The y-intercept of $y = x^2$ is $y = 0$. For the relation $y = 2^x$, the graph crosses the y-axis at $(0, 1)$; thus, the y-intercept is $y = 1$. Therefore, the graphs of $y = x^2$ and $y = 2^x$ do not have the same y-intercept.

Step 3
Determine the minimum and maximum values of both graphs.

The minimum value of $y = x^2$ is 0, and it has an undefined maximum value. The graph of the exponential relation $y = 2^x$ has an undefined maximum value and an undefined minimum value. Although their minimum values differ, the graphs of $y = x^2$ and $y = 2^x$ each have an undefined maximum value.

12. C

The k-value causes a vertical translation (shifting the parabola upward or downward). When $k > 0$, the whole graph shifts up k units. Therefore, if the value of k increases in the equation $y = x^2 + k$, the graph is shifted upward.

13. B

Since $a > 0$, the graph of the quadratic function $y = ax^2 + k$ must open upward. The k-value causes a vertical translation (shifting the parabola upward or downward). Since the only parameters are a and k, there is no horizontal translation. Therefore, the following graph best models the quadratic function $y = ax^2 + k$.

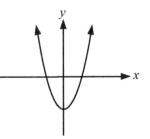

14. C

Given the function $y = 2(x + 3)^2 - 5$, it follows that $a = 2$, $h = -3$, and $k = -5$ when compared to the general quadratic function $y = a(x - h)^2 + k$.

- Since $a = 2$, there is a vertical stretch about the x-axis by a factor of 2.
- Since $h = -3$, there is a horizontal translation of 3 units to the left.
- Since $k = -5$, there is a vertical translation downward by 5 units.

15. A

The quadratic function $y = -2(x - 1)^2 + 3$ is of the form $y = a(x - h)^2 + k$. The axis of symmetry of a quadratic function of the form $y = a(x - h)^2 + k$ is at $x = h$.

The graph of $y = -2(x - 1)^2 + 3$ is symmetric about the line $x = 1$.

16. A

Since the equation of the axis of symmetry for a quadratic function is $x = h$ and for this quadratic function, the axis of symmetry is $x - 5 = 0$ or $x = 5$, it follows that $h = 5$.

Also, since the quadratic function has a minimum value, the graph opens upward, which means that $a > 0$.

Substitute 5 for h into the equation $y = a(x - h)^2 + k$, where $a > 0$ to get $y = (x - 5)^2 + k$.

17. B

Step 1

Apply the vertical and horizontal stretch transformations.

Replace y with $2y$ to produce a vertical stretch by a factor of $\frac{1}{2}$ and replace x with $\frac{1}{5}x$ to produce a horizontal stretch by a factor of 5.

$$y = x^2$$
$$2y = \left(\frac{1}{5}x\right)^2$$

Simplify.

$$2y = \frac{1}{25}x^2$$

Divide both sides of the equation by 2.

$$y = \frac{1}{2}\left(\frac{1}{25}x^2\right)$$
$$y = \frac{1}{50}x^2$$

Step 2

Apply the vertical and horizontal translations.

The parabola is defined by the equation $y = \frac{1}{50}x^2$.

To translate the graph of the parabola 5 units right, replace x with $x - 5$. Similarly, to translate the graph of the parabola 3 units down, replace y with $y + 3$.

$$y + 3 = \frac{1}{50}(x - 5)^2$$

In standard form, the equation of the transformed parabola is $y + 3 = \frac{1}{50}(x - 5)^2$. The values of a, h, and k are $a = \frac{1}{50}$, $h = 5$, and $k = -3$.

18. C

The equation is $y = -x^2 + \frac{7}{2} = -x^2 + 3.5$.

Comparing this with the equation $y = a(x - h)^2 + k$, $a = -1$, $h = 0$, and $y = 3.5$.

Since $a = -1$ and $-1 < 0$, the parabola will open downward.

The graph of $y = -x^2 + \frac{7}{2}$ can be obtained by reflecting the graph of $y = x^2$ in the x-axis and then translating the graph 3.5 units upward.

Therefore, the graph is as shown:

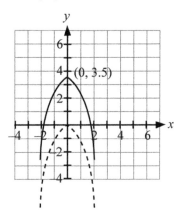

19. A

Begin with the graph of $y = x^2$.

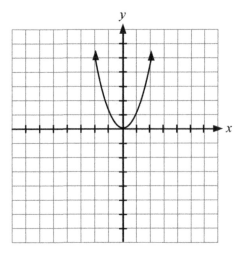

Perform a reflection in the x-axis.

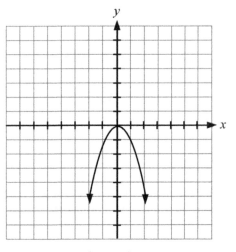

The vertex is at $(-4, -7)$ in the original graph, so after the reflection, the graph was translated left 4 units and down 7 units.

20. B

All points on the transformed graph must satisfy the given transformations.

A reflection about the x-axis will change $(4, 16)$ to $(4, -16)$

A vertical stretch about the x-axis by a factor of 2 will change $(4, -16)$ to $(4, -32)$.

A horizontal translation 5 units to the left changes $(4, -32)$ to $(-1, -32)$.

A vertical translation 4 units upward changes $(-1, -32)$ to $(-1, -28)$.

The value of y is -28.

21. D

The parabola shown has an equation of the form $y = a(x - h)^2 + k$, where (h, k) is the vertex. Since the vertex is at $(0, -2)$, $h = 0$ and $k = -2$.

Substitute 0 for h and -2 for k into the equation $y = a(x - h)^2 + k$ to get $y = ax^2 - 2$.

Locate a point on the parabola. Perhaps $(2, 2)$.

Substitute 2 for x and 2 for y in the equation $y = ax^2 - 2$ and then solve for a.

$2 = a(2)^2 - 2$
$2 = 4a - 2$
$4 = 4a$
$1 = a$

Substitute 1 for a into the equation $y = ax^2 - 2$ to get $y = x^2 - 2$.

Thus, the equation for this parabola is $y = x^2 - 2$.

22. 1.5

Step 1

Substitute a known point into the equation.

The y-intercept of the graph is $(0, 17)$. Substitute 0 for x and 17 for y in the equation $y = a(x - 4)^2 - 7$.

$17 = a(0 - 4)^2 - 7$

Step 2

Solve for a.

$17 = a(16) - 7$
$24 = 16a$
$\dfrac{3}{2} = a$
$1.5 = a$

The value of a to the nearest tenth is 1.5.

23. a) OR

Begin by locating the vertex of the parabola shown. This ordered pair is $(-2, 6)$.

Now, make use of equation $y = a(x - h)^2 + k$. Substitute -2 for h and 6 for k.

$y = a(x - (-2))^2 + 6$

$y = a(x + 2)^2 + 6$

Since the parabola passes through the ordered pair $(4, -12)$, solve for a as follows:

$y = a(x + 2)^2 + 6$

Substitute 4 for x and -12 for y.

$-12 = a(4 + 2)^2 + 6$

$-12 = a(6)^2 + 6$

$-12 = 36a + 6$

$-18 = 36a$

$\dfrac{-18}{36} = a$

$-\dfrac{1}{2} = a$

Thus, the equation of the quadratic function of the graph shown is $y = -\dfrac{1}{2}(x + 2)^2 + 6$.

b) OR

In order to determine the y-intercept of the given parabola, substitute 0 for x in the equation $y = -\dfrac{1}{2}(x + 2)^2 + 6$, and solve for y as shown:

$y = -\dfrac{1}{2}(0 + 2)^2 + 6$ Substitute 0 for x.

$y = -\dfrac{1}{2}(2)^2 + 6$

$y = -\dfrac{1}{2}\left(4\right) + 6$

$y = -2 + 6$

$y = 4$

The y-intercept of the parabola shown is 4.

c) OR

If the ordered pair $(-8, -12)$ is on the graph of the quadratic function, then the ordered pair $(-8, -12)$ must satisfy the equation $y = -\dfrac{1}{2}(x + 2)^2 + 6$.

Determine this as follows:
Substitute -8 for x and -12 for y.

$-12 = -\dfrac{1}{2}(-8 + 2)^2 + 6$

$-12 = -\dfrac{1}{2}(-6)^2 + 6$

$-12 = -\dfrac{1}{2}\left(36\right) + 6$

$-12 = -18 + 6$

$-12 = -12$

Since $-12 = -12$, the ordered pair $(-8, -12)$ is on the graph of the given quadratic function.

24. B

$(x - 5)(4x + 5)$
Use the FOIL strategy to multiply each term within the first set of brackets by each term within the second set of brackets.
$x(4x) + x(5) - 5(4x) - 5(5)$
$4x^2 + 5x - 20x - 25$
Collect like terms.
$4x^2 - 15x - 25$
Thus, the coefficient of x is -15.

25. B

Use the FOIL strategy, and multiply each term within the first set of brackets by each term within the second set of brackets.
$3x(4x) + 3x(-1) - 4(4x) - 4(-1)$
$= 12x^2 - 3x - 16x + 4$

Collect like terms.
$12x^2 - 3x - 16x + 4$
$= 12x^2 - 19x + 4$

Compare the expression $12x^2 - 19x + 4$ to the expression $12x^2 + bx + 4$. In order for the expressions to be equal, b must equal -19.

26. C

Step 1
Since this expression is a differences of squares, set up a product of two binomials, one with an addition operation and one with a subtraction operation.

The order of the binomials does not matter.
$(\ + \ )(\ - \ )$

Step 2

Determine the square root of the first term in the difference-of-squares expression, and use the root as the first term in each of the bracketed binomials.

$$16a^2b^2 = \sqrt{16a^2b^2}$$
$$= 4ab$$

Therefore, $(4ab + \ )(4ab - \ )$.

Step 3

Calculate the square root of the second term in the difference-of-squares expression, and use the root as the second term in each of the bracketed binomials.

$$9c^2 = \sqrt{9c^2}$$
$$= 3c$$

Therefore, $(4ab + 3c)(4ab - 3c)$.
One factor is $4ab + 3c$.

27. **B**

Step 1

Since this is a trinomial of the form $ax^2 + bx + c$, find two numbers that have a product of $(a \times c)$ and a sum of b.

$$(a \times c) = (2 \times -28)$$
$$= -56$$

The factors of -56 are $\pm(1)(56)$, $\pm(2)(28)$, $\pm(4)(14)$, and $\pm(7)(8)$. The required factors must have a sum of b, or 1.

The required factors are $(-7)(8)$, since $-7 + 8 = 1$.
Let $h = 8$ and $k = -7$.

Step 2

Rewrite the expression by replacing the middle term with the terms (hx) and (kx).

$$2x^2 + x - 28 = 2x^2 + 8x - 7x - 28$$

Step 3

Group using brackets.

$$2x^2 + 8x - 7x - 28$$
$$= (2x^2 + 8x) + (-7x - 28)$$

Step 4

Remove the GCF from each group.

$$(2x^2 + 8x) + (-7x - 28)$$
$$= 2x(x + 4) - 7(x + 4)$$

Step 5

Factor out the common binomial.

$$2x(x + 4) - 7(x + 4)$$
$$= (x + 4)(2x - 7)$$

The expression $2x - 7$ is a factor of the trinomial $2x^2 + x - 28$.

28. **D**

Step 1

Factor polynomial I by removing the greatest common factor of $4x^2$ from each term.

$$8x^3 + 4x^2 = 4x^2(2x + 1)$$

Polynomial I was factored correctly by Rachel.

Step 2

Factor polynomial II as a difference of squares: $a^2 - b^2 = (a + b)(a - b)$.

$$25a^2 - 4b^2c^2$$
$$= \left(\begin{array}{c} (\sqrt{25a^2}) + (\sqrt{4b^2c^2}) \\ \times \ (\sqrt{25a^2}) - (\sqrt{4b^2c^2}) \end{array} \right)$$
$$= (5a + 2bc)(5a - 2bc)$$

Polynomial II was factored correctly by Rachel.

Step 3

Factor polynomial III by removing the greatest common factor of 2 from each term and factoring the result as a difference of squares.

$$2x^2 - 18y^2$$
$$= 2(x^2 - 9y^2)$$
$$= 2(\sqrt{x^2} + \sqrt{9y^2}) \times (\sqrt{x^2} - \sqrt{9y^2})$$
$$= 2(x + 3y)(x - 3y)$$

Polynomial III was factored correctly by Rachel.

Step 4

Factor polynomial IV by removing the greatest common factor of a and factoring the result as a difference of squares.

$$4a^3 - a$$
$$= a(4a^2 - 1)$$
$$= a(\sqrt{4a^2} + \sqrt{1}) \times (\sqrt{4a^2} - \sqrt{1})$$
$$= a(2a + 1)(2a - 1)$$

Polynomial IV was not factored correctly by Rachel.

29. **5**

Step 1

Factor $x^2 - 3x - 4$.

In order to factor $x^2 - 3x - 4$, find two numbers that have a product of -4 (c-value) and a sum of -3 (b-value). In this case, the two numbers are -4 and 1.

The factored form of $x^2 - 3x - 4$ is $(x - 4)(x + 1)$.

Step 2

Determine the value of $m + n$.
$m = 4$ and $n = 1$
$$m + n = 4 + 1$$
$$= 5$$

30. B

The x-intercepts of the graph shown are 1.5 and 3. Therefore, substitute 1.5 for r and 3 for s in the equation $y = a(x - r)(x - s)$ as follows:

$y = a(x - 1.5)(x - 3)$

$y = a(x^2 - 4.5x + 4.5)$

Since the graph of the parabola shown opens downward, $a < 0$.

$y = -a(x^2 - 4.5x + 4.5)$

$y = -ax^2 + 4.5ax - 4.5a$

Therefore, the equation that best models the parabola is $y = -2x^2 + 9x - 9$ since it can be arrived at by substituting 2 for a into the equation

$y = -ax^2 + 4.5ax - 4.5a$.

$y = -(2)x^2 + 4.5(2)x - 4.5(2)$

$y = -2x^2 + 9x - 9$

31. A

When a quadratic function is expressed in the factored form $y = a(x - r)(x - s)$, the x-intercepts (roots) of the graph of the quadratic function are $x = r$ and $x = s$.

Apply the zero property of multiplication.

Set $3x - 4$ equal to zero, and solve for x.

$3x - 4 = 0$

$3x = 4$

$x = \dfrac{4}{3}$

Set $2x + 7$ equal to zero, and solve for x.

$2x + 7 = 0$

$2x = -7$

$x = -\dfrac{7}{2}$

The roots of $6x^2 + 13x - 28 = 0$ are $\dfrac{4}{3}$ and $-\dfrac{7}{2}$.

32. D

Procedure A

Step 2: Using the CALCULATE feature and the "zero" option, determine the x-intercepts of the graph.

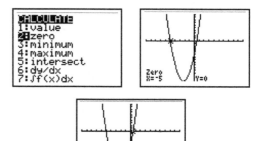

The zeros are displayed as the x-value, when $y = 0$.
$x = -5, 0.5$

Procedure B

Step 2: Using the CALCULATE feature and the "intersect" option, determine the x-coordinate of each of the points of intersection of the graphs.

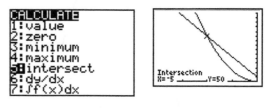

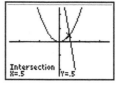

$x = -5, 0.5$

The zeros in procedure A will be exactly the same as the x-coordinates (not the y-coordinates) of the points of intersection of the graphs of the two given functions in procedure B.

33. D

To determine the nature of the roots of each quadratic equation, graph each equation, and determine if there are any x-intercepts.

If the roots of a quadratic equation

$ax^2 + bx + c = 0$ are non-real, its graph does not intersect the x-axis.

Graph of equation in alternative A:

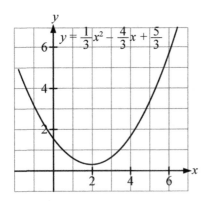

Graph of equation in alternative B:

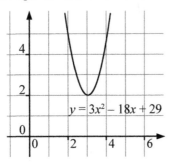

\Graph of equation in alternative C:

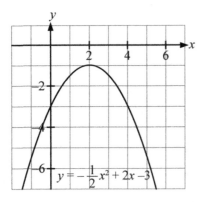

Graph of equation in alternative D:

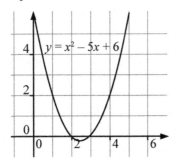

Only the equation $y = x^2 - 5x + 6$, found in alternative D, has real roots since it has x-intercepts at $(2, 0)$ and $(3, 0)$.

34. D

Determine the nature of the roots of each equation by graphing the equation and checking if there are any x-intercepts.

Step 1
Graph equation I.

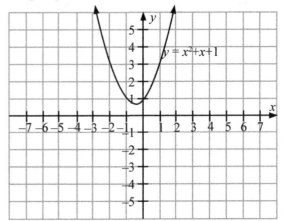

The graph has no x-intercepts, meaning equation I has non-real roots.

Step 2
Graph equation II.

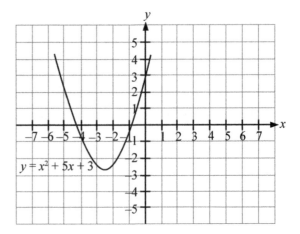

The graph has two distinct x-intercepts, meaning equation II has real roots.

Therefore, equation I has non-real roots, and equation II has real roots.

35. A

Identify and remove the common factor from the x^2 and x term of the expression. In this case, the common factor is -3.

The student's first error occurred in step 1.
The student incorrectly removed the common factor of 3; the student should have removed the common factor of -3. Step 1 should be as follows:
$$y = -3(x^2 - 8x) + 5$$

36. A

Step 1
Identify and remove the common factor from the x^2- and x-terms of the function. In this case, the common factor is 4.
$$y = 4(x^2 + 8x) + 59$$

Step 2
Notice the resulting coefficient for the x-term. Divide this value by 2, and then square it.
$$y = 4(x^2 + \underline{8x}) + 59$$
$$\left(\frac{8}{2}\right)^2 = 16$$

Step 3
Both add and subtract 16 inside the brackets.
$$y = 4(x^2 + 8x + \underline{16 - 16}) + 59$$

Step 4
Move the value that will not contribute to a perfect square outside the brackets.
Note: With the distributive property, -64 and $+64$ have been added to the function, since $4(16) = 64$ and $4(-16) = -64$. To move -16 outside the brackets, it becomes -64.
$$y = 4(x^2 + 8x + 16 \underline{- 16}) + 59$$
$$y = 4(x^2 + 8x + 16) \underline{- 64} + 59$$

Step 5
Factor the perfect square trinomial inside the brackets, and collect like terms outside the brackets.
$$y = 4(x + 4)^2 - 5$$

The function can be expressed as $y = 4(x + 4)^2 - 5$.

37. B

Step 1
Identify and remove the common factor from the x^2- and x-terms in the equation.
In this case, the common factor is 1.
$$y = 1(x^2 - 8x) + 23$$

Step 2
Identify the resulting coefficient for the x-term. Divide this value by 2, and then square it.
$$y = (x^2 \underline{- 8x}) + 23$$
The coefficient of the x-term is -8.
$$\left(\frac{-8}{2}\right)^2 = 16$$

Step 3
Add and subtract this value inside the brackets.
$$y = (x^2 - 8x + \underline{16 - 16}) + 23$$

Step 4
Move the value that will not contribute to a perfect square outside the brackets.
$$y = (x^2 - 8x + 16 \underline{- 16}) + 23$$
$$y = (x^2 - 8x + 16) \underline{- 16} + 23$$

Step 5
Factor the trinomial inside the brackets to form a perfect square, and collect like terms outside the brackets.
$$y = (x - 4)^2 + 7$$

The equation can be expressed as $y = (x - 4)^2 + 7$.

38. 18.3

$y = -2(x^2 - 6x) + \frac{1}{3}$	Identify and remove the common factor from the x^2 and x term of the expression. In this case, the common factor is -2.
$y = -2(x^2 - \underline{6x}) + \frac{1}{3}$ $\left(\frac{-6}{2}\right)^2 = 9$	Notice the resulting coefficient for the x-term. Divide this value by 2, and then square it.
$y = -2(x^2 - 6x + \underline{9 - 9}) + \frac{1}{3}$	Both add and subtract this value inside the brackets.
$y = \underline{-2}(x^2 - 6x + 9 \underline{- 9}) + \frac{1}{3}$ $y = -2(x^2 - 6x + 9) \underline{+18} + \frac{1}{3}$	Move the value that will not contribute to a perfect square outside the brackets. [**Note**: With the distributive property, -18 and $+18$ have been added to the function, since $-2(9) = -18$ and $-2(-9) = 18$. To move -9 outside the brackets, it becomes $+18$.]
$y = -2(x - 3)^2 + \frac{55}{3}$	Factor the trinomial inside the brackets to form a perfect square, and collect like terms outside the bracket.

When the equation $y = -2x^2 + 12x + \dfrac{1}{3}$ is written in the completed square form $y = a(x-h)^2 + k$, it becomes $y = -2(x-3)^2 + \dfrac{55}{3}$. The k value is $\dfrac{55}{3}$ and when written as a decimal value, to the nearest tenth, is 18.3.

39. B

Determine the midpoint of the x-intercepts.

$$M = \left(\dfrac{x_1 + x_2}{2}, \dfrac{y_1 + y_2}{2}\right)$$

$$M = \left(\dfrac{\dfrac{1}{2} + (-4)}{2}, \dfrac{0+0}{2}\right)$$

$$M = \left(\dfrac{\dfrac{1}{2} + \dfrac{-8}{2}}{2}, 0\right)$$

$$M = \left(\dfrac{-\dfrac{7}{2}}{2}, 0\right)$$

$$M = \left(-\dfrac{7}{4}, 0\right)$$

Since the x-coordinate of the axis of symmetry is $-\dfrac{7}{4}$, the equation of the axis of symmetry is

$$x = -\dfrac{7}{4}.$$

40. A

To determine the vertex of the graph of $y = x^2 - 6x + 4$, complete the square.

$y = \left(x^2 - 6x\right) + 4$

$y = \left(x^2 - \underline{6x}\right) + 4$

$\left(\dfrac{-6}{2}\right)^2 = 9$

$y = \left(x^2 - 6x + \underline{9 - 9}\right) + 4$

$y = \left(x^2 - 6x + 9\right) \underline{- 9} + 4$

$y = (x - 3)^2 - 5$

When written in this form, you can see that the vertex is at the point $(3, -5)$. Therefore, the vertex of the graph of $y = x^2 - 6x + 4$ is located 3 units right and 5 units down from the vertex of the graph of $y = x^2$.

41. D

The graph of the quadratic function $y = -4.9x^2 + 30x + 1$ is displayed with each of the given window settings.

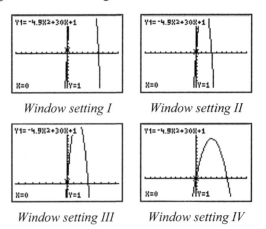

Window setting I   *Window setting II*

Window setting III   *Window setting IV*

Window setting IV will display the graph with its vertex in view.

42. A

Step 1

Apply the quadratic formula, $x = \dfrac{-b \pm \sqrt{b^2 - 4ac}}{2a}$.

Substitute 2 for a, -3 for b, and -1 for c into the quadratic formula.

$$= \dfrac{-(-3) \pm \sqrt{(-3)^2 - 4(2)(-1)}}{2(2)}$$

Step 2
Simplify

$$= \dfrac{3 \pm \sqrt{9 + 8}}{4}$$

$$= \dfrac{3 \pm \sqrt{17}}{4}$$

Step 3
The roots of the given equation are $x = 1.78$ and $x = -0.28$.

The error occurred in step 1, as Marianne did not correctly substitute -3 for b.

43. D

In step 3, the value that does not contribute to a perfect square is moved outside the brackets.

Applying the distributive property, multiply $\dfrac{b^2}{4a^2}$ by the a in front of the brackets so the value outside the brackets becomes $\dfrac{b^2}{4a}$ which agrees with what is shown.

Now, factor the remaining perfect square trinomial inside the brackets.

Divide the term $\dfrac{b}{a}$ by 2 to give $\dfrac{b}{2a}$ which can be used to express the perfect square trinomial in factored form as the following shows.

$$a\left(x + \dfrac{b}{2a}\right)^2 - \dfrac{b^2}{4a} + c = 0.$$

The variable K represents the expression $\dfrac{b}{2a}$.

44. A

Step 1

To solve by factoring (Tanya's procedure), begin by rearranging the equation $8x^2 - 2x = 3$ to $8x^2 - 2x - 3 = 0$.

Factor by decomposition by finding two numbers that have a product of -24 ($a \times c = 8 \times -3$) and a sum of -2 (b-value). In this case, these numbers are 4 and -6.

$$8x^2 - 2x - 3 = 0$$
$$8x^2 + 4x - 6x - 3 = 0$$
$$4x(2x + 1) - 3(2x + 1) = 0$$
$$(4x - 3)(2x + 1) = 0$$
$$x = \dfrac{3}{4} \text{ or } x = -\dfrac{1}{2}$$

Step 2

To solve using the quadratic formula (Hilary's solution), begin by rearranging the equation $8x^2 - 2x = 3$ to $8x^2 - 2x - 3 = 0$.

$$x = \dfrac{-b \pm \sqrt{b^2 - 4ac}}{2a}$$

Substitute 8 for a, -2 for b, and -3 for c into the quadratic formula.

$$x = \dfrac{-(-2) \pm \sqrt{(-2)^2 - 4(8)(-3)}}{2(8)}$$

$$x = \dfrac{2 \pm \sqrt{4 + 96}}{16}$$

$$x = \dfrac{2 \pm \sqrt{100}}{16}$$

$$x = \dfrac{2 \pm 10}{16}$$

$$x = \dfrac{2 + 10}{16} \qquad x = \dfrac{2 - 10}{16}$$

$$= \dfrac{12}{16} \qquad \text{or} \qquad = \dfrac{-8}{16}$$

$$= \dfrac{3}{4} \qquad\qquad = -\dfrac{1}{2}$$

Step 3

Compare the two partial solutions.

Both Tanya's work and Hilary's work will lead to a correct solution.

45. A

Step 1

Rearrange the equation to form a quadratic equation equal to 0.

$$7x^2 + 2x - 5 = 11x^2 - 6x - 4$$
$$0 = 4x^2 - 8x + 1$$

Step 2

Since the resulting equation cannot be factored, solve for x using the quadratic formula.

$$x = \dfrac{-b \pm \sqrt{b^2 - 4ac}}{2a}$$

Substitute 4 for a, -8 for b, and 1 for c into the quadratic formula.

$$x = \dfrac{-(-8) \pm \sqrt{(-8)^2 - 4(4)(1)}}{2(4)}$$

$$x = \dfrac{8 \pm \sqrt{64 - 16}}{8}$$

$$x = \dfrac{8 \pm \sqrt{48}}{8}$$

$$x = \dfrac{8 \pm \sqrt{16 \times 3}}{8}$$

$$x = \dfrac{8 \pm 4\sqrt{3}}{8}$$

$$x = \dfrac{4(2 \pm \sqrt{3})}{8}$$

$$x = \dfrac{2 \pm \sqrt{3}}{2}$$

The solutions to the given quadratic equation are $x = \dfrac{2 \pm \sqrt{3}}{2}$.

46. C

To solve using the quadratic formula, begin by rearranging the equation.

$$10x + 3 = 7x^2$$
$$0 = 7x^2 - 10x - 3.$$

Apply the quadratic formula.

$$x = \frac{-b \pm \sqrt{b^2 - 4ac}}{2a}$$

Substitute 7 for a, -10 for b, and -3 for c, and solve.

$$x = \frac{-(-10) \pm \sqrt{(-10)^2 - 4(7)(-3)}}{2(7)}$$
$$x = \frac{10 \pm \sqrt{100 + 84}}{14}$$
$$x = \frac{10 \pm \sqrt{184}}{14}$$
$$x = \frac{10 \pm \sqrt{4 \times 46}}{14}$$
$$x = \frac{10 \pm 2\sqrt{46}}{14}$$
$$x = \frac{2(5 \pm \sqrt{46})}{14}$$
$$x = \frac{5 \pm \sqrt{46}}{7}$$

47. a) OR

The roots of the quadratic equation $2x^2 - x - 15 = 0$ can be determined by locating the x-intercepts of the graph of $y = 2x^2 - x - 15$. Since the x-intercepts of the graph of $y = 2x^2 - x - 15$ are located at the ordered pairs $(-2.5, 0)$ and $(3,0)$, the roots of the quadratic equation $2x^2 - x - 15 = 0$ are $x = -2.5$ or $x = 3$.

b) OR

In order to solve the quadratic equation $2x^2 - x - 15 = 30$, set the equation equal to 0, and if possible, solve by factoring. If the equation is not factorable, solve by applying the quadratic formula.

$$2x^2 - x - 15 = 30$$
$$2x^2 - x - 45 = 0$$

The two numbers that have a product of $-90[2 \times (-45)]$ and a sum of -1 (the coefficient of x) are -10 and 9.

$$2x^2 - 10x + 9x - 45 = 0$$

Remove a common factor of $2x$ from $2x^2 - 10x$ and 5 from $9x - 45$.

$$2x(x - 5) + 9(x - 5) = 0$$
$$(x - 5)(2x + 9) = 0$$

$x - 5 = 0$	or	$2x + 9 = 0$
$x = 5$		$2x = -9$
		$x = \dfrac{-9}{2}$

c) OR

If $2x^2 - x - 15$ is factorable, then the roots of the equation $2x^2 - x - 15 = 0$ can be expressed as exact values. In order for an equation to have exact roots, the value of $b^2 - 4ac$ in the quadratic formula $x = \frac{-b \pm \sqrt{b^2 - 4ac}}{2a}$ must be a number that is a perfect square. Otherwise, the equation will only have approximate roots. Now, check to see if $2x^2 - x - 15$ is factorable.

The two numbers that have a product of $-30 [2 \times (-15)]$ and a sum of -1(the coefficient of x) are -6 and 5.

$$2x^2 - x - 15 = 2x^2 - 6x + 5x - 15$$

Remove a common factor of $2x$ from $2x^2 - 6x$ and 5 from $5x - 15$.

$$= 2x(x - 3) + 5(x - 3)$$
$$= (x - 3)(2x + 5)$$

Since $2x^2 - x - 15$ is factorable, the value of $b^2 - 4ac$ in the quadratic formula $x = \frac{-b \pm \sqrt{b^2 - 4ac}}{2a}$ must be a number that is a perfect square.

48. C

The zeros of the function $ax^2 + bx + c$ are 1 and 2. Thus,

$y = a(x - 1)(x - 2)$

$y = a(x^2 - 3x + 2)$

$y = ax^2 - 3ax + 2a$

The x-coordinate of the vertex can be determined by calculating the midpoint of the two zeros of the given function. Thus, $x = \dfrac{1 + 2}{2} = 1.5$.

Substitute 1.5 for x and -1 (the minimum value) for y in the equation $y = ax^2 - 3ax + 2a$.

$-1 = a(1.5)^2 - 3a(1.5) + 2(1.5)$

$-1 = 2.25a - 4.5a + 2a$

$-1 = -0.25a$

$4 = a$

Finally, compare the equation $y = ax^2 - 3ax + 2a$ to the equation $y = ax^2 + bx + c$. Observe $c = 2a$. Thus, $c = 2(4) = 8$.

49. A

The a-value can be used to determine if the function has a minimum or maximum.

- The maximum value is k when $a < 0$.
- The minimum value is k when $a > 0$.

Therefore, Megan only needs to examine the a-variable.

50. 4

Step 1

Change the form of the function by completing the square.

Since the coefficient of x^2 is positive, the minimum value of the given function is equal to the y-coordinate of the vertex of the graph of the function.

To find the coordinate of the vertex, rewrite the given function in completed square form.

$y = x^2 - 12x + 40$

$y = x^2 - 12x + 36 - 36 + 40$

$y = (x^2 - 12x + 36) + 4$

$y = (x - 6)^2 + 4$

Step 2

Determine the minimum value of the function.

The vertex of this parabola, is (6, 4).

Therefore, the minimum value of the given function is 4.

51. C

Since the quadratic function

$h = -4.9(t - 1.5)^2 + 12$, $t \geq 0$ is given in the form $y = a(x - h)^2 + k$, it follows that $a = -4.9$, $h = 1.5$, and $k = 12$.

Since $a = -4.9$ and $-4.9 < 0$, the graph of the function opens downward. Since $h = 1.5$ and $k = 12$, the graph of the function has been shifted right 1.5 units and 12 units upward, when compared to the graph of $y = x^2$. The graph shown best illustrates the graph of $h = -4.9(t - 1.5)^2 + 12$.

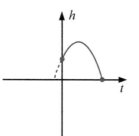

52. C

The graph of the given area function is a parabola opening downwards. The maximum value of the area function occurs at the vertex of the parabola.

Write the equation $A = -2x^2 + 60x$ in completed square form.

$A = -2x^2 + 60x$

$A = -2(x^2 - \underline{30x})$

$\left(\dfrac{-30}{2}\right)^2 = 225$

$A = -2(x^2 - 30x + \underline{225 - 225})$

$A = -2(x^2 - 30x + 225 \underline{- 225})$

$A = -2(x^2 - 30x + 225) \underline{+450}$

$A = -2(x - 15)^2 + 450$

In this form, the area function models a parabola with a vertex at (15, 450).

Thus, when $x = 15$, the area of the lot is a maximum of 450 m^2.

Substitute 15 for x into the equation $2x + y = 60$.

$2(15) + y = 60$

$30 + y = 60$

$y = 30$

The length of the lot is 30 m.

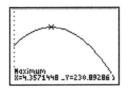

53. D

Using a TI-83 Plus graphing calculator, graph the equation $y = -7t^2 + 61t + 98$. Then, use the MAXIMUM feature and a window setting such as $x: [1, 10, 1]$ $y: [0, 300, 20]$.

Maximum
X=4.3571448 _Y=230.89286)

The function's maximum value occurs when $x = 4.35$.

The maximum height reached by the roller coaster car in the interval $1 \leq t \leq 10$, to the nearest tenth, is 230.9 ft.

54. a) OR

If the vendor does not sell any hot dogs, the value of x in the equation

$P = -40x^2 + 240x - 75$ is zero. If 0 is substituted for x, then $P = -40(0)^2 + 240(0) - 75 = -75$.
Thus, if the vendor does not sell any hot dogs, he will lose $75.

b) OR

In order to determine the selling price per hot dog to maximize the vendor's daily profit, complete the square of the equation $P = -40x^2 + 240x - 75$ as follows:

$P = -40x^2 + 240x - 75$
$P = -40(x^2 - 6x) - 75$
$P = -40(x^2 - 6x + 9 - 9) - 75$
$\rightarrow \dfrac{-6}{2} = -3, (-3)^2 = 9$
$P = -40(x^2 - 6x + 9) + 360 - 75$
$P = -40(x - 3)^2 + 285$
The maximum value of P is 285 when $x = 3$.
A selling price of $3 per hot dog will maximize the vendor's daily profit.

c) OR

The maximum daily profit for the hot dog vendor is $285.

UNIT TEST — QUADRATIC RELATIONS

*Use the following information to
answer the next question.*

The owner of a 300-seat theatre sells
tickets for $20 each. He believes that for
every dollar he increases the price of a
ticket, he will lose 10 customers.
He charts his research in the given table.

Increase in Price ($)	Revenue ($)
0	6 000
1	6 090
2	6 160
3	6 210
4	6 240
5	6 250
6	6 240

1. In order to have a total revenue of $6 120,
the most he can increase the price of the
tickets is
   A. $1.29
   B. $6.81
   C. $8.61
   D. $9.55

*Use the following information to
answer the next question.*

A partial table of values for a particular
relation is shown below

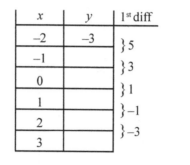

x	y	1st diff
−2	−3	} 5
−1		} 3
0		} 1
1		} −1
2		} −3
3		

2. The equation of the relation is
   A. $y = x^2 - 2x - 5$
   B. $y = x^2 - 2x - 11$
   C. $y = -2x + 5$
   D. $y = -2x - 3$

3. The graph of a particular quadratic
function passes through the ordered pairs
(−2, 6) and (8, 6). The equation of the
axis of symmetry of this graph is
   A. $x = 3$
   B. $x = 4$
   C. $x = 5$
   D. $x = 6$

The graph of a particular parabola is shown.

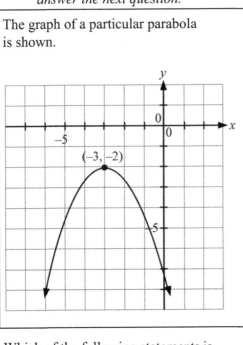

4. Which of the following statements is **true** with respect to the graph of the parabola shown?

   A. The minimum value is −2.

   B. The parabola does not have any zeros.

   C. The equation of the axis of symmetry is $x - 3 = 0$.

   D. The y-intercept of the parabola could be located at the ordered pair $(-8, 0)$.

The graph of a parabola with a vertex of $(0, 5)$ is shown.

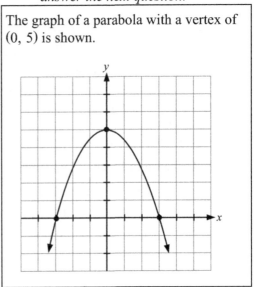

Numerical Response

5. The y-intercept of the graph of this parabola is _____.

6. The expression 2^{-x} is equivalent to the expression

   A. -2^x

   B. $(-2)^x$

   C. $\dfrac{-1}{2^x}$

   D. $\dfrac{1}{2^x}$

7. The y-intercept of $y = 2^x$ is

   A. equal to the y-intercept of $y = x^2$

   B. one less than the y-intercept of $y = x^2$

   C. two more than the y-intercept of $y = x^2$

   D. one more than the y-intercept of $y = x^2$

8. The maximum value of the graph of the quadratic relation $f(x) = -2x^2 + 8x - 19$ is at the ordered pair

   A. $(-11, -2)$

   B. $(-2, -11)$

   C. $(2, -11)$

   D. $(11, -2)$

9. What are the *x*-intercepts of the function
$y = x^2 + 3x - 18$?

   A. −9 and 2   B. −6 and 3

   C. 6 and −3   D. 9 and −2

Use the following information to answer the next question.

A soccer ball is kicked upward. The height, *x*, of the ball in metres is given by the function $x = -5t^2 + 30t$, where *t* is the time in seconds.

10. At what time does the ball reach its maximum height?

   A. 2 s   B. 3 s

   C. 4 s   D. 5 s

Use the following information to answer the next question.

The parabolic shape obtained from a quadratic function can be used to design arches. A construction company used the quadratic function $y = a(x - h)^2 + k$ and the resulting graph, as shown, to plan a bridge support for a road.

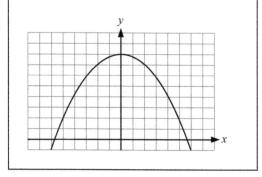

11. Which variable represents the maximum height of the bridge support?

   A. *h*   B. *a*

   C. *x*   D. *k*

Use the following information to answer the next question.

A rocket is launched from a platform. Its height, *h*, in metres above the ground, is given as a function of time, *t*, in seconds after launch by the equation
$h = -4.9t^2 + 98t + 5$.

Numerical Response

12. What is the maximum height, to the nearest tenth, that the rocket can reach? _____

Use the following information to answer the next multipart question.

13. A rectangular area is to be enclosed by a fence in order to create a playground for kindergarten students. A part of the wall of the school will be used as one side of the rectangular enclosure, as shown.

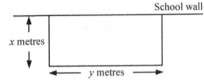

If 300 m of fencing material is to be used, then the table shown illustrates the area, A, in square metres for various values of x.

x (m)	A (m^2)
10	2 800
20	5 200
50	10 000
75	11 250
90	10 800
100	10 000
125	6 250
140	2 800

Open Response

a) On the grid, draw a graph that illustrates the data given in the table.

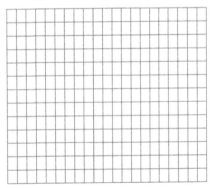

b) What is the maximum possible area of the rectangular enclosure?

c) The area, A, in square metres of the playground can be defined by the equation $A = -2x^2 + 300x$, where x is the width of the rectangular enclosure in metres. Using this equation, verify algebraically that your answer in part B is correct.

d) What will be the dimensions of the playground that produce a maximum area?

14. A change in the value of a could affect which of the following aspects of the graph of $y = ax^2$?

A. The direction in which the parabola opens

B. The vertical stretch that the parabola experiences

C. Both the direction in which the parabola opens and the vertical stretch that it experiences

D. The x-intercepts, the direction in which the parabola opens, and the vertical stretch that it experiences

The partial graph of the quadratic function $y = a(x - 2)^2 + K$ is shown.

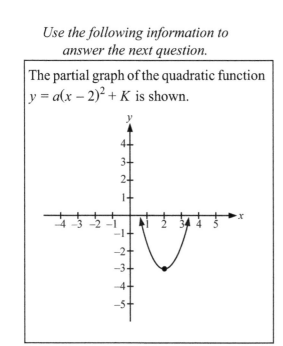

15. The values of a and K in the function
$y = a(x - 2)^2 + K$ must be such that
   A. $a < 0$ and $K < 0$
   B. $a < 0$ and $K > 0$
   C. $a > 0$ and $K > 0$
   D. $a > 0$ and $K < 0$

16. The graph of the function $y = x^2$ is
vertically stretched by a factor of 4 about
the x-axis and then translated such that the
vertex of the transformed graph is at
$(-2, 51)$. The equation of the transformed
function is
   A. $y = 4(x - 2)^2 - 51$
   B. $y = 4(x - 51)^2 - 2$
   C. $y = 4(x + 2)^2 + 51$
   D. $y = -4(x + 2)^2 - 51$

The graph of a quadratic function of the form $y = a(x - h)^2 + k$ is shown.

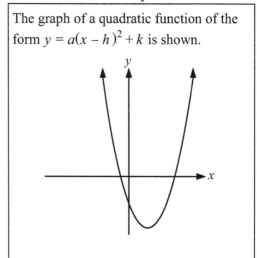

17. Which of the following conditions with
respect to the variables, a, h, and k is
correct?
   A. $a > 0$, $h > 0$, and $k < 0$
   B. $a \geq 0$, $h > 0$, and $k > 0$
   C. $a < 0$, $h > 0$, and $k > 0$
   D. $a \geq 0$, $h < 0$, and $k < 0$

The graph of the quadratic function
$y = -3(x + 2)^2 - 5$ is symmetric about the
line $x + B = 0$.

Numerical Response

18. What is the value of B? _____

19. Which of the following partial graphs **best** illustrates the graph of the equation $y = (x + 3)^2 + 2.5$?

    A.

    B.

    C.

    D.

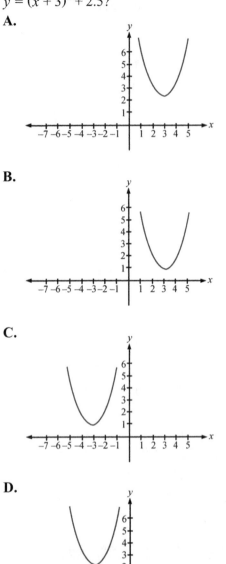

Use the following information to answer the next question.

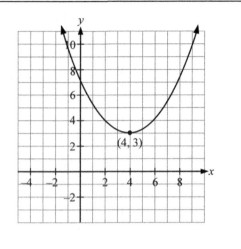

The given diagram shows a partial graph of a quadratic relation.

20. What is the equation of this partial graph?

    A. $y = (x - 4)^2 + 3$

    B. $y = (x - 4)^2 - 3$

    C. $y = \dfrac{1}{4}(x + 4)^2 - 3$

    D. $y = \dfrac{1}{4}(x - 4)^2 + 3$

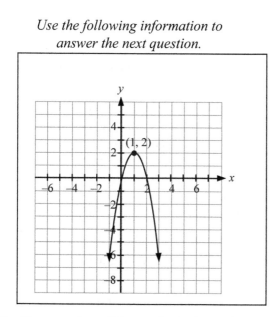

21. The equation of the parabola shown is

   A. $y = 2(x + 1)^2 + 2$

   B. $y = 2(x - 1)^2 + 2$

   C. $y = -2(x + 1)^2 + 2$

   D. $y = -2(x - 1)^2 + 2$

22. The graph of a particular quadratic function is shown.

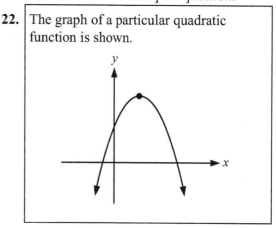

Open Response

a) If the equation of the axis of symmetry of the graph of this quadratic function is $x = 2$ and an x-intercept is defined by the ordered pair $(-1, 0)$, then what are the coordinates of the other x-intercept? Show your work.

b) Write the equation of this quadratic function in the form $y = a(x - r)(x - s)$ given that the y-intercept of the graph is 10. Show your work.

c) Write the equation of this quadratic function in the form $y = a(x - h)^2 + k$. Show your work.

Use the following information to answer the next question.

$$(4x - 3)(3x - 2) - 2(3x - 2)^2$$

23. Which of the following expressions is a simplified form of the given expression?

   A. $-6x^2 - 5x - 2$

   B. $-6x^2 - 5x + 14$

   C. $-6x^2 + 7x - 2$

   D. $-6x^2 - 7x - 14$

24. If $(3x + 2)(2x + 3) = 6x^2 + bx + c$, where b and c are real numbers, what is the value of $b + c$?

   A. 6   **B.** 13

   C. 19   **D.** 25

25. If $5x + k$ is a factor of $10x^2 + 19x + 6$, then what is the value of k?

   A. 1   **B.** 2

   C. 3   **D.** 6

26. The polynomial $2xy - 3ay + 2xz - 3az$ can be written in factored form as

   A. $(2x + 3a)(y - z)$

   B. $(2x + 3a)(y + z)$

   C. $(2x - 3a)(y - z)$

   D. $(2x - 3a)(y + z)$

Use the following information to answer the next question.

Olivia was asked to factor the quadratic function $y = x^2 - 2x - 15$. She let $y = 0$ and then wrote the equation $0 = x^2 - 2x - 15$. She then factored this equation to obtain $0 = (x + 3)(x - 5)$.

27. Olivia can use this factored form to determine the

   A. y-intercepts of the graph of $y = x^2 - 2x - 15$

   B. x-intercepts of the graph of $y = x^2 - 2x - 15$

   C. minimum y-value of the graph of $y = x^2 - 2x - 15$

   D. coordinates of the vertex of the graph of $y = x^2 - 2x - 15$

28. The x-intercepts of the graph of $y = a(x - r)(x - s)$ are $(3, 0)$ and $(2, 0)$. If $r > s$, what are the values of r and s, respectively?

   A. 3 and 2   **B.** 2 and 3

   C. 6 and 1   **D.** 1 and 6

29. Which of the following graphs represents a quadratic equation that has two real and distinct roots?

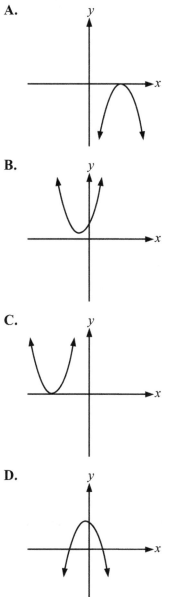

A.

B.

C.

D.

Use the following information to answer the next question.

Two equations are given.

I. $2x^2 + 2.5x - 5 = 0$

II. $x^2 + 0.5x - 0.5 = 0$

30. Which of the following statements about these equations is **true**?

A. Both equations have real roots.

B. Both equations have non-real roots.

C. Equation I has real roots, and equation II has non-real roots.

D. Equation I has non-real roots, and equation II has real roots.

31. If the equation $y = 3x^2 - 24x + \frac{1}{2}$ is written in the completed square form $y = a(x - h)^2 + k$, then the value of k is

A. 97

B. $\frac{97}{2}$

C. -95

D. $\frac{-95}{2}$

32. Which of the following functions represents the quadratic function $y = 2x^2 + 16x + 26$ when it is changed to its completed square form of $y = a(x - h)^2 + k$?

A. $y = 2(x + 4)^2 - 3$

B. $y = 2(x + 4)^2 - 6$

C. $y = 2(x + 8)^2 + 10$

D. $y = 2(x + 8)^2 - 19$

Numerical Response

33. When the equation $y = -2x^2 + 16x - 27$ is expressed in the form $y = a(x - h)^2 + k$, the value of h is

_____.

34. What are the x-intercepts of the quadratic function $y = x^2 - 10x - 24$?

A. 6 and -4

B. -6 and 4

C. 12 and -2

D. -12 and 2

35. What is the vertex of the graph of the quadratic function

$y = kx^2 - 4kx - 2(1 - 2k)$, $k \neq 0$, $k \in \mathbb{R}$?

A. $(2, -2)$

B. $(-2, -2)$

C. $(2, 4k - 2)$

D. $(2, -2k + 1)$

Use the following information to answer the next question.

Samuel decided to use the quadratic formula to solve a particular quadratic equation. Step one of Samuel's solution was the equation

$x = \dfrac{4 \pm \sqrt{(-4)^2 - 4(7)(-2)}}{2(7)}$.

36. The quadratic equation Samuel was attempting to solve was

A. $-2x^2 + 4x + 7 = 0$

B. $-2x^2 - 4x - 7 = 0$

C. $7x^2 + 4x - 2 = 0$

D. $7x^2 - 4x - 2 = 0$

Use the following information to answer the next question.

A student's attempt at developing the quadratic formula is partially shown.

$ax^2 + bx + c = 0$

1. $x^2 + \dfrac{b}{a}x + \dfrac{c}{a} = 0$

2. $x^2 + \dfrac{b}{a}x = -\dfrac{c}{a}$

3. $x^2 + \dfrac{b}{a}x + \dfrac{b^2}{4a^2} - \dfrac{b^2}{4a^2} = -\dfrac{c}{a}$

4. $x^2 + \dfrac{b}{a}x + \dfrac{b^2}{4a^2} = \dfrac{b^2}{4a^2} - \dfrac{c}{a}$

5. $\left(x + \dfrac{b}{2a}\right)^2 = \dfrac{b^2}{4a^2} - \dfrac{c}{a}$

37. If steps 1 to 5 are correct, what is the next correct step?

A. $x + \dfrac{b}{2a} = \dfrac{b}{2a} - \dfrac{c}{a}$

B. $x + \dfrac{b}{2a} = \dfrac{b}{2a} - \sqrt{\dfrac{c}{a}}$

C. $\left(x + \dfrac{b}{2a}\right)^2 = \dfrac{b^2 - 4ac}{4a^2}$

D. $\left(x + \dfrac{b}{2a}\right)^2 = \dfrac{b^2 - 4ac}{2a}$

38. What are the solutions to the quadratic equation $2z^2 + 5z - 3 = 0$?

A. $z = \dfrac{1}{2}$ or 3

B. $z = \dfrac{1}{2}$ or -3

C. $z = 2$ or -1

D. $z = 1$ or -1

39. One of the roots of the quadratic equation $10x^2 - 19x + 14 = 8$ is $x = 1.5$. Rounded to the nearest tenth, the value of the other root is

A. -1.5 B. -0.4

C. 0.4 D. 2.2

Use the following information to answer the next multipart question.

40. A diver in Acapulco, Mexico dives from a cliff into the sea below. His height y metres above the sea x seconds after diving from the cliff is given by the equation $y = -4.9x^2 + 2x + 40$, where $x \geq 0$.

Open Response

a) What is the height of the cliff? Justify your answer.

b) Algebraically, determine the number of seconds, to the nearest tenth, that it takes the diver to reach the water. Show your work.

c) Explain how a graphical procedure could be used to determine the number of seconds that have elapsed when the diver is 15 m above the water.

Quadratic Relations

ANSWERS AND SOLUTIONS — UNIT TEST

1.	C	11.	D	18.	2	26.	D	36.	D
2.	B	12.	495.0	19.	D	27.	B	37.	C
3.	A	13.	a) OR	20.	D	28.	A	38.	B
4.	B		b) OR	21.	D	29.	D	39.	C
5.	5		c) OR	22.	a) OR	30.	A	40.	a) OR
6.	D		d) OR		b) OR	31.	D		b) OR
7.	D	14.	C		c) OR	32.	B		c) OR
8.	C	15.	D	23.	C	33.	4		
9.	B	16.	C	24.	D	34.	C		
10.	B	17.	A	25.	B	35.	A		

1. C

Step 1

Find the quadratic regression equation.

Enter the given data into a graphing calculator, and perform a quadratic regression, as shown.

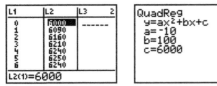

The resulting quadratic regression equation is

$y = -10x^2 + 100x + 60$.

Step 2

Enter the function obtained from the quadratic regression $y = -10x^2 + 100x + 6\,000$ into the calculator, and graph the line $y = 6\,120$.

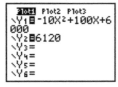

Step 3

Determine the point of intersection between the two graphs.

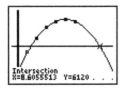

The x-coordinate of the point of intersection is the number of dollar increases in price that correspond to a revenue of $6 120.

In order to have a total revenue of $6 120, the most he can increase the price of the tickets is $8.61.

2. B

Calculate the second differences in order to classify the relation.

Since the table of values shows a constant second difference, this relation represents a quadratic relation of the form $y = ax^2 + bx + c$, $(a \neq 0)$. Therefore, alternatives C and D are incorrect (linear relations are given).

x	y	1st diff	2nd diff
−2	−3		
		} 5	
−1			} 2
		} 3	
0			} 2
		} 1	
1			} 2
		} −1	
2			} 2
		} −3	
3			

To determine whether alternative A or B is correct, substitute −2 for x into each of the given equations, $y = x^2 - 2x - 5$ and $y = x^2 - 2x - 11$, in order to determine which of the equations has a corresponding y-value of −3.

$y = x^2 - 2x - 5$
$y = (-2)^2 - 2(-2) - 5$
$y = 4 + 4 - 5$
$y = 3$

$y = x^2 - 2x - 11$
$y = (-2)^2 - 2(-2) - 11$
$y = 4 + 4 - 11$
$y = -3$

Therefore, the equation of the relation is
$y = x^2 - 2x - 11$.

3. A

Recall that the axis of symmetry also passes through the midpoint of any horizontal segment that connects two points on the parabola.

Now, find the midpoint of the ordered pairs $(-2, 6)$ and $(8, 6)$ in order to find the equation of the axis of symmetry.

$$M = \left(\frac{x_1 + x_2}{2}\right), \left(\frac{y_1 + y_2}{2}\right)$$
$$= \left(\frac{(-2) + 8}{2}\right), \left(\frac{6 + 6}{2}\right)$$
$$= (3, 6)$$

The equation of the axis of symmetry is $x = 3$.

4. B

The parabola has no zeros since the parabola does not intersect the x-axis.
The vertex of the parabola is $(-3, -2)$.
The axis of symmetry is the vertical line $x = -3$ or $x + 3 = 0$ (-3 is the x-coordinate of the vertex).
Since the parabola opens downward, the maximum value is $y = -2$ (-2 is the y-coordinate of the vertex).
The parabola passes through the y-axis approximately at the ordered pair $(0, -7)$, so the y-intercept is -7.

5. 5

The y-intercept of a quadratic relation of the form $y = ax^2 + bx + c$, $(a \neq 0)$ is the y-coordinate of the ordered pair where the parabola intersects the y-axis. In the graph shown this occurs at the y-value of the vertex, which is 5.

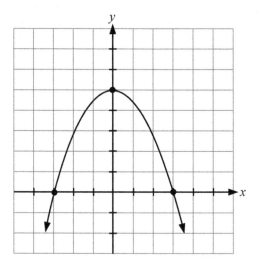

6. D

When a number or variable has a negative exponent in the numerator, the expression can be rewritten with a positive exponent in the denominator. $x^{-n} = \dfrac{1}{x^n}$

Therefore, the expression 2^{-x} is equivalent to the expression $\dfrac{1}{2^x}$.

7. D

For the function $y = 2^x$, the graph crosses the y-axis at $(0, 1)$. This means that the y-intercept is $y = 1$.

The y-intercept of $y = x^2$ is $y = 0$. Therefore, the y-intercept of $y = 2^x$ is one more than the y-intercept of $y = x^2$.

8. C

Step 1

Change the form of the function by completing the square.

$$f(x) = -2x^2 + 8x - 19$$
$$= -2(x^2 - 4x) - 19$$
$$= -2\left(x^2 - 4x + \left(\frac{-4}{2}\right)^2 - \left(\frac{-4}{2}\right)^2\right) - 19$$
$$= -2(x^2 - 4x + 4 - 4) - 19$$
$$= -2(x^2 - 4x + 4) + 8 - 19$$
$$= -2(x - 2)^2 - 11$$

This function is in the form $f(x) = a(x - h)^2 + k$, where $a = -2$, $h = 2$, and $k = -11$.

Step 2

Determine the maximum value of the function.
The vertex of the parabola is at $(2, -11)$, and the parabola opens downward because $a < 0$. Therefore, the maximum value of the graph of the given quadratic function is located at its vertex.
The maximum value is at the ordered pair $(2, -11)$.

9. B

There are two methods you can use to find the x-intercepts of the function.

Method 1

Factor and solve the equation $0 = x^2 + 3x - 18$.

$0 = x^2 + 3x - 18$
$0 = (x - 3)(x + 6)$
$0 = x - 3$
$x = 3$
$0 = x + 6$
$x = -6$

The x-intercepts are 3 and -6.

Method 2

Apply the quadratic formula.

$x = \dfrac{-b \pm \sqrt{b^2 - 4ac}}{2a}$

$x = \dfrac{-(3) \pm \sqrt{(3)^2 - 4(1)(-18)}}{2(1)}$

$x = \dfrac{-3 \pm \sqrt{9 - (-72)}}{2}$

$x = \dfrac{-3 \pm \sqrt{81}}{2}$

$x = \dfrac{-3 \pm 9}{2}$

$x = \dfrac{-3 + 9}{2}$ or $x = \dfrac{-3 - 9}{2}$

$x = \dfrac{6}{2}$ or $x = \dfrac{-12}{2}$

$x = 3$ or $x = -6$

Both methods provide the same answer, so the x-intercepts of the function $y = x^2 + 3x - 18$ are 3 and -6.

10. B

The graph of the given height function is a parabola opening downward. The maximum height reached by the ball occurs at the vertex of the parabola.

Write the equation $x = -5t^2 + 30t$ in completed square form.

$x = -5t^2 + 30t$
$x = -5(t^2 - 6t)$
$\left(\dfrac{-6}{2}\right)^2 = 9$

$x = -5(t^2 - 6t + 9 - \underline{9})$
$x = -5(t^2 - 6t + 9 - \underline{9})$
$x = -5(t^2 - 6t + 9) + \underline{45}$
$ = -5(t - 3)^2 + 45$

The soccer ball follows a parabolic path with $(3, 45)$ as its vertex; i.e., $t = 3$ and $x = 45$ at the vertex.

Therefore, the ball reaches its maximum height of 45 m in 3 s.

11. D

The maximum or minimum value can be determined when the function is written in the form $y = a(x - h)^2 + k$. The maximum value is k when $a < 0$.

12. 495.0

Using a TI-83 Plus graphing calculator, graph the equation $y = -4.9t^2 + 98t + 5$. Then, use the MAXIMUM feature and a window setting such as $x: [0, 20, 1]$ $y: [-10, 600, 50]$.

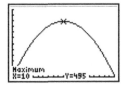

The function's maximum value occurs when $x = 10$. Therefore, the maximum height, to the nearest tenth, that the rocket can reach is 495.0 m.

13. a) OR

Playground Enclosure

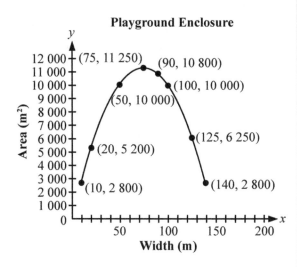

b) OR

The maximum area of the rectangular enclosure can be determined by evaluating the y-coordinate of the vertex of the parabola. The vertex (the highest point on the parabola) is (75, 11 250). Therefore, the maximum area of the rectangular enclosure is 11 250 m^2.

c) OR

The maximum area of the rectangular enclosure can be determined by completing the square of the equation as follows:

$A = -2x^2 + 300x$

$A = -2x^2 + 300x$

$A = -2(x^2 - 150x)$

$A = -2(x^2 - 150x + 5625 - 5625)$

$\rightarrow \left(-\dfrac{150}{2}\right)^2 = 5\ 625$

$A = -2(x^2 - 150x + 5\ 625) + 11\ 250$

$A = -2(x - 75)^2 + 11\ 250$

The maximum value of A is 11 250 m^2 when $x = 75$ m. The value 11 250 m^2 is exactly the same as the value for the maximum area obtained in part B.

d) OR

Recall $A = LW$ or $A \div W = L$. Since $x = 75$ m, the value of y is 150 m(11 250 ÷ 75). Therefore, the dimensions of the playground that produce a maximum area will have a width (the value of x) of 75 m and a length (the value of y) of 150 m.

14. C

Changing the value of a would affect the graph of $y = ax^2$ in the following ways:

- The direction in which the parabola opens could change since the value of a determines the direction of opening.
- The graph would be be vertically stretched by a factor of a.

Changing the value of a in the equation $y = ax^2$ would not have an effect on the domain, vertex, axis of symmetry, or x-intercepts of the parabola.

15. D

Since the partial graph of $y = a(x - 2)^2 + K$ has a minimum value and opens upward, it follows that $a > 0$.

The vertex of the graph is located in quadrant IV. When compared to the graph of $y = x^2$, the graph of $y = a(x - 2)^2 + K$ has been translated 2 units to the left and vertically downward K units. Therefore, $K < 0$.

16. C

When the graph of $y = x^2$ is vertically stretched by factor of 4 about the x-axis, the equation of the transformed function is $y = 4x^2$.
In order for the graph of the transformed function to have a vertex of (−2, 51), the graph of $y = 4x^2$ must be translated 2 units left and 51 units up, therefore, $h = -2$ and $k = 51$.
Now, substitute 4 for a, −2 for h, and 51 for k into $y = a(x - h)^2 + k$.
$y = 4(x + 2)^2 + 51$.
Thus, the equation of the transformed function is $y = 4(x + 2)^2 + 51$.

17. A

Since the graph opens upward, $a > 0$.
When compared to the graph of $y = x^2$:

- the graph shown has been translated right; therefore, $h > 0$.
- the graph shown has been translated down; therefore, $k < 0$.

18. 2

The axis of symmetry of a quadratic function of the form $y = a(x - h)^2 + k$ is at $x = h$.

Step 1

Determine the axis of symmetry of the quadratic function $y = -3(x + 2)^2 - 5$.

The function $y = -3(x + 2)^2 - 5$ is of the form $y = a(x - h)^2 + k$.

The quadratic function is symmetric about the line $x = -2$.

Step 2

Find the value of B.

Rearrange the equation of the axis of symmetry, $x = -2$, to be in the form $x + B = 0$.

$$x = -2$$
$$x + 2 = 0$$

The value of B is 2.

19. **D**

Step 1

Determine the values of a, h, and k in the equation.

Comparing the equation $y = (x + 3)^2 + 2.5$ to the $y = a(x - h)^2 + k$, gives the values $a = 1$, $h = -3$, and $k = 2.5$.

Step 2

Determine the effect of parameter h on the transformed graph.

Since $h = -3$, the graph the graph of $y = x^2$ is translated 3 units to the left to form the graph of $y = (x + 3)^2$.

This means that the x-coordinate of the vertex is located at $x = -3$,

Step 3

Determine the effect of the parameter k on the transformed graph.

Since $k = 2.5$, the graph of $y = (x + 3)^2$ is translated 2.5 units up to form the graph of $y = (x + 3)^2 + 2.5$. This means that the y-coordinate of the vertex is located at $y = 2.5$

Therefore, the graph of $y = (x + 3)^2 + 2.5$ can be obtained by translating the graph of $y = x^2$ left 3 units and upward 2.5 units.

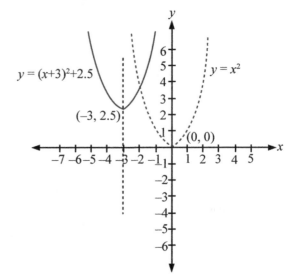

20. **D**

The parabola shown in the given diagram can have an equation of the form $y = a(x - h)^2 + k$, where (h, k) is the vertex. Since the vertex is at (4, 3), $h = 4$ and $k = 3$.

Substitute 4 for h and 3 for k into the equation $y = a(x - h)^2 + k$ to get $y = a(x - 4)^2 + 3$.

Since the equation passes through the point (0, 7), $x = 0$ and $y = 7$. Substitute 0 for x and 7 for y into the equation $y = a(x - 4)^2 + 3$. Solve for a.

$$7 = a(0 - 4)^2 + 3$$
$$7 = a(16) + 3$$
$$4 = 16a$$
$$\frac{1}{4} = a$$

Substitute $\frac{1}{4}$ for a in the equation $y = a(x - 4)^2 + 3$ to get $y = \frac{1}{4}(x - 4)^2 + 3$.

The equation for this parabola is $y = \frac{1}{4}(x - 4)^2 + 3$.

21. D

The parabola shown can have an equation of the form $y = a(x - h)^2 + k$, where (h, k) is the vertex. Since the vertex is at $(1, 2)$, $h = 1$ and $k = 2$.

Substitute 1 for h and 2 for k into $y = a(x - h)^2 + k$ to get $y = a(x - 1)^2 + 2$.

Since the equation passes through the point $(0, 0)$, $x = 0$ and $y = 0$.

Substitute 0 for x and 0 for y in the equation $y = a(x - 1)^2 + 2$ and then solve for a.

$0 = a(0 - 1)^2 + 2$
$0 = a + 2$
$a = -2$

Substitute -2 for a in the equation $y = a(x - 1)^2 + 2$ to get $y = -2(x - 1)^2 + 2$.
Thus, the equation of the graph is $y = -2(x - 1)^2 + 2$.

22. a) OR

Since the equation of the axis of symmetry of the parabola is $x = 2$, the ordered pair $(2, 0)$ must be the midpoint of the two x-intercepts. One x-intercept is given as $(-1, 0)$. This ordered pair is 3 units left of the ordered pair $(2, 0)$. Therefore, the other x-intercept must be 3 units right of the ordered pair $(2, 0)$. Thus, the coordinates of the other x-intercept are $(5, 0)$.

b) OR

The two x-intercepts of the parabola are $(-1, 0)$ and $(5, 0)$. Use the formula $y = a(x - r)(x - s)$.

Substitute -1 for r and 5 for s.
$y = a(x - (-1))(x - 5)$
$y = a(x + 1))(x - 5)$

Since the y-intercept of the parabola is 10, solve for a as follows:
$y = a(x + 1))(x - 5)$
Substitute 0 for x and 10 for y.
$10 = a(0 + 1))(0 - 5)$
$10 = a(1)(-5)$
$10 = -5a$
$\dfrac{10}{-5} = \dfrac{-5}{5}a$
$-2 = a$

The equation of the quadratic function in the form $y = a(x - r)(x - s)$ is $y = -2(x + 1)(x - 5)$.

c) OR

In order to write the equation of the quadratic function in the form $y = a(x - h)^2 + k$, expand $y = -2(x + 1)(x - 5)$ and then complete the square of the resulting equation as illustrated:

$y = -2(x + 1)(x - 5)$
$y = -2(x^2 - 5x + x - 5)$
$y = -2(x^2 - 4x - 5)$
$y = -2x^2 + 8x + 10$
$y = -2(x^2 - 4x) + 10$
$y = -2(x^2 - 4x + 4 - 4) + 10$
$y = -2(x^2 - 4x + 4) + 8 + 10$
$y = -2(x - 2)^2 + 18$

The equation of the quadratic function in the form $y = a(x - h)^2 + k$ is $y = -2(x - 2)^2 + 18$.

23. C

$(4x - 3)(3x - 2) - 2(3x - 2)^2$

Expand and simplify using **FOIL** for each group.
$= 12x^2 - 8x - 9x + 6 - 2(3x^2 - 2)(3x^2 - 2)$
$= 12x^2 - 17x + 6 - 2(9x^2 - 12x + 4)$

Collect like terms and simplify.
$= 12x^2 - 17x + 6 - 18x^2 + 24x - 8$
$= -6x^2 + 7x - 2$

24. D

$(3x + 2)(2x + 3)$
Use the FOIL procedure to multiply each term within the first set of brackets by each term within the second set of brackets.
$3x(2x) + 3x(3) + 2(2x) + 2(3)$
$6x^2 + 9x + 4x + 6$
Collect like terms.
$6x^2 + 13x + 6$
Compare the expression $6x^2 + 13x + 6$ to the expression $6x^2 + bx + c$. In order for the expressions to be equal, $b = 13$ and $c = 6$.

The value of $b + c = 13 + 6 = 19$.

25. B

Step 1

In order to factor $10x^2 + 19x + 6$, find two numbers with a product of $60(a \times c)$ and a sum of 19 (the value of b).
In this case, the numbers are 15 and 4.

Step 2

Rewrite the expression by replacing the term $19x$ with $15x + 4x$.

$10x^2 + 19x + 6$
$= 10x^2 + 15x + 4x + 6$

Step 3

Group using brackets.

$10x^2 + 15x + 4x + 6$
$= \left(10x^2 + 15x\right) + (4x + 6)$

Step 4

Remove the GCF from each group.

$\left(10x^2 + 15x\right) + (4x + 6)$
$= 5x(2x + 3) + 2(2x + 3)$

Step 5

Factor out the common binomial.

$5x(2x + 3) + 2(2x + 3)$
$= (5x + 2)(2x + 3)$

Since $5x + 2$ is one factor, $k = 2$.

26. D

The polynomial $2xy - 3ay + 2xz - 3az$ can be factored by rearranging and grouping the terms in pairs.

Step 1

Group terms and factor out a greatest common factor.

Group the terms with the coefficients 2 together (the first and third terms) and the terms with the coefficients 3 together (the second and fourth terms).

$2xy - 3ay + 2xz - 3az$
$= 2xy + 2xz - 3ay - 3az$

Once rearranged, a greatest common factor can be removed from each group, which is the greatest term that the coefficients can be divided by.

$2xy + 2xz - 3ay - 3az$
$= 2x(y + z) - 3a(y + z)$

Step 2

Remove the common binomial factor $y + z$.

$2x(y + z) - 3a(y + z)$
$= (y + z)(2x - 3a)$

The factored form of the polynomial $2xy - 3ay + 2xz - 3az$ is $(y + z)(2x - 3a)$, which is equivalent to $(2x - 3a)(y + z)$.

27. B

The solution values to $0 = ax^2 + bx + c$ are the x-intercepts of the graph of the function $y = ax^2 + bx + c$ because the x-intercepts occur when $y = 0$.

Factoring $0 = ax^2 + bx + c$ to the form $0 = a(x - r)(x - s)$ identifies the x-intercepts as r and s. Therefore, Olivia can use the factored form of the equation $0 = (x + 3)(x - 5)$ to determine the x-intercepts of the graph of the equation. The x-intercepts are -3 and 5.

28. A

In the equation $y = a(x - r)(x - s)$, $x = r$ and $x = s$ are the x-intercepts.

Hence, when $x = r$, $y = 0$, and when $x = s$, $y = 0$. In the given question $r > s$ therefore, $r = 3$ and $s = 2$.

The values of r and s are 3 and 2, respectively.

29. D

A quadratic equation with two real and distinct roots has a corresponding graph with two distinct x-intercepts.

Only this graph intersects the x-axis at two distinct points.

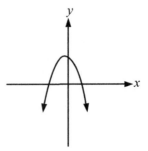

30. A

To determine the nature of the roots of each quadratic equation, graph each equation, and determine if there are any x-intercepts.

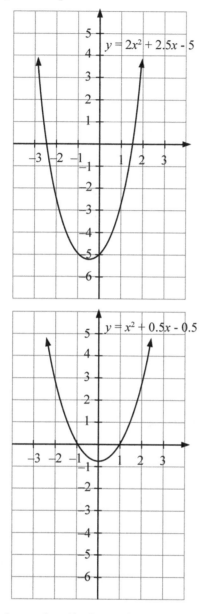

Since the graphs of both equations intersect the x-axis, both equations have real roots.

31. D

Step 1

Identify and remove the common factor from the x^2- and x-terms of the expression. In this case, the common factor is 3.

$$y = 3(x^2 - 8x) + \frac{1}{2}$$

Step 2

Notice the resulting coefficient for the x-term. Divide this value by 2, and then square it.

$$y = 3(x^2 - \underline{8x}) + \frac{1}{2}$$

$$\left(\frac{-8}{2}\right)^2 = 16$$

Step 3

Add and subtract this value inside the brackets.

$$y = 3(x^2 - 8x + \underline{16 - 16}) + \frac{1}{2}$$

Step 4

Move the value that will not contribute to a perfect square outside the brackets.

$$y = 3(x^2 - 8x + 16 \underline{- 16}) + \frac{1}{2}$$

$$y = 3(x^2 - 8x + 16) \underline{- 48} + \frac{1}{2}$$

[**Note:** To move -16 outside the brackets, use the distributive property. Since $3(16) = 48$ and $3(-16) = -48$, $+48$ and -48 have been added to the function.]

Step 5

Factor the trinomial inside the brackets to form a perfect square, and collect like terms outside the brackets.

$$y = 3(x - 4)^2 - \frac{95}{2}$$

When the equation $y = 3x^2 - 24x + \frac{1}{2}$ is written in the completed square form $y = a(x - h)^2 + k$, it becomes $y = 3(x - 4)^2 - \frac{95}{2}$. The value of k is $\frac{-95}{2}$.

32. B

Step 1

Identify and remove the common factor from the x^2- and x-terms of the expression. In this case, the common factor is 2.

$$y = 2(x^2 + 8x) + 26$$

Step 2

Notice the resulting coefficient for the x-term. Divide this value by 2, and then square it.

$$y = 2(x^2 + \underline{8x}) + 26$$

$$\left(\frac{8}{2}\right)^2 = 16$$

Step 3

Both add and subtract this value inside the brackets.

$$y = 2(x^2 + 8x + \underline{16 - 16}) + 26$$

Solutions – Quadratic Relations

Step 4

Move the value that will not contribute to a perfect square outside the brackets.

$y = 2(x^2 + 8x + 16 \underline{- 16}) + 26$

$y = 2(x^2 + 8x + 16) \underline{- 32} + 26$

[Note: With the distributive property, -32 and $+32$ have been added to the function since $2(-16) = -32$ and $2(16) = 32$. To move -16 outside the brackets, it becomes -32.]

Step 5

Factor the perfect square trinomial inside the brackets and collect like terms outside the brackets.

$y = 2(x + 4)^2 - 6$

The function can be expressed as $y = 2(x + 4)^2 - 6$.

33. **4**

Step 1

Identify and remove the common factor from the x^2- and x-terms of the equation.

In this case, the common factor is -2.

$y = -2(x^2 - 8x) - 27$

Step 2

Divide the resulting coefficient for the x-term by 2, and then square it.

$y = -2(x^2 - \underline{8x}) - 27$

$\left(\dfrac{-8}{2}\right)^2 = 16$

Both add and subtract this value inside the brackets.

$y = -2(x^2 - 8x + \underline{16 - 16}) - 27$

Step 3

Move the value that will not contribute to a perfect square trinomial outside the brackets.

The value that does not contribute to a perfect square trinomial is -16. When -16 is moved outside the brackets, it becomes $-2(-16) = 32$ because of the distributive property.

$y = \underline{-2}(x^2 - 8x + 16 \underline{- 16}) - 27$

$y = -2(x^2 - 8x + 16) \underline{+ 32} - 27$

Step 4

Factor the trinomial inside the brackets to form a perfect square, and collect like terms outside the brackets.

$y = -2(x - 4)^2 + 5$

When the equation $y = -2x^2 + 16x - 27$ is written in completed square form $y = a(x - h)^2 + k$, it becomes $y = -2(x - 4)^2 + 5$. The h-value is 4.

34. **C**

Method 1

Factor and solve the given equation.

$0 = x^2 - 10x - 24$

$0 = (x + 2)(x - 12)$

$0 = x + 2$

$x = -2$

$0 = x - 12$

$x = 12$

The x-intercepts are 12 and -2.

Method 2

Apply the quadratic formula.

$x = \dfrac{-b \pm \sqrt{b^2 - 4ac}}{2a}$

$x = \dfrac{-(-10) \pm \sqrt{(-10)^2 - 4(1)(-24)}}{2(1)}$

$x = \dfrac{10 \pm \sqrt{100 - (-96)}}{2}$

$x = \dfrac{10 \pm \sqrt{196}}{2}$

$x = \dfrac{10 \pm 14}{2}$

$x = \dfrac{10 + 14}{2}$ or $x = \dfrac{10 - 14}{2}$

$x = \dfrac{24}{2}$ or $x = \dfrac{-4}{2}$

$x = 12$ or $x = -2$

Both methods provide the same answer, so the x-intercepts of the function $y = x^2 - 10x - 24$ are $x = 12$ and $x = -2$.

35. **A**

The coordinates of the vertex of any quadratic function in the form $y = ax^2 + bx + c$ are $\left(-\dfrac{b}{2a}, -\dfrac{b^2}{4a} + c\right)$. The vertex of the function $y = kx^2 - 4kx - 2(1 - 2k)$ can be found by substituting the appropriate values into the variables $\left(-\dfrac{b}{2a}, -\dfrac{b^2}{4a} + c\right)$, where $a = k$, $b = -4k$, and $c = -2(1 - 2k)$.

$\left(-\dfrac{b}{2a}, -\dfrac{b^2}{4a} + c\right)$

$= \left(-\dfrac{-4k}{2(k)}, -\dfrac{(-4k)^2}{4(k)} + (-2(1 - 2k))\right)$

$= \left(\dfrac{4k}{2k}, -\dfrac{16k^2}{4k} - 2 + 4k\right)$

$= (2, -4k + 4k - 2)$

$= (2, -2)$

The vertex of the function $y = kx^2 - 4kx - 2(1 - 2k)$ is $(2, -2)$.

36. D

Samuel substituted 7 for a, -4 for b, and -2 for c into the quadratic formula $x = \dfrac{-b \pm \sqrt{b^2 - 4ac}}{2a}$ to obtain $x = \dfrac{4 \pm \sqrt{(-4)^2 - 4(7)(-2)}}{2(7)}$.

Therefore, $a = 7$, $b = -4$, and $c = -2$.

Next, substitute 7 for a, -4 for b, and -2 for c into the general quadratic equation $ax^2 + bx + c = 0$.

$$(7)x^2 + (-4)x + (-2) = 0$$
$$7x^2 - 4x - 2 = 0$$

The quadratic equation Samuel was attempting to solve was $7x^2 - 4x - 2 = 0$.

37. C

Step 5 is as follows:

$$\left(x + \frac{b}{2a}\right)^2 = \frac{b^2}{4a^2} - \frac{c}{a}$$

The next correct step involves placing the two terms on the right side of the equation over a common denominator.

$$\left(x + \frac{b}{2a}\right)^2 = \frac{b^2 - 4ac}{4a^2}$$

38. B

Solve $2z^2 + 5z - 3 = 0$ by using the decomposition procedure.
Begin by finding two numbers that have a product of -6 $(a \times c = 2 \times -3)$ and a sum of 5 (b-value) In this case,
these numbers are -1 and 6. Write $5z$ as $-z + 6z$.

$$2z^2 + 5z - 3 = 0$$
$$2z^2 - z + 6z - 3 = 0$$
$$z(2z - 1) + 3(2z - 1) = 0$$
$$(z + 3)(2z - 1) = 0$$
$$z = -3 \text{ or } z = \frac{1}{2}$$

39. C

Rearrange the equation so it equals 0.
$$10x^2 - 19x + 6 = 0$$

Solve the equation using the quadratic formula.
$$x = \frac{-b \pm \sqrt{b^2 - 4ac}}{2a}$$

For the formula $10x^2 - 19x + 6 = 0$, $a = 10$, $b = -19$, and $c = 6$.

Substitute these values into the quadratic formula.

$$x = \frac{-(-19) \pm \sqrt{(-19)^2 - 4(10)(6)}}{2(10)}$$
$$x = \frac{19 \pm \sqrt{361 - 240}}{20}$$
$$x = \frac{19 \pm \sqrt{121}}{20}$$
$$x = \frac{19 \pm 11}{20}$$
$$x = \frac{19 + 11}{20} = \frac{30}{20} = 1.5 \text{ and}$$
$$x = \frac{19 - 11}{20} = \frac{8}{20} = 0.4.$$

The equation $10x^2 - 19x + 6 = 0$ could also be solved using the decomposition factoring procedure.

Find two factors that have a product of 60 $(a \times c)$ and a sum of -19 (the b-value). In this case, those numbers are -15 and -4. Solve for x.

$$10x^2 - 19x + 6 = 0$$
$$10x^2 - 15x - 4x + 6 = 0$$
$$5x(2x - 3) - 2(2x - 3) = 0$$
$$(2x - 3)(5x - 2) = 0$$
$$x = \frac{3}{2} = 1.5 \text{ and } x = \frac{2}{5} = 0.4.$$

The roots of the quadratic equation $10x^2 - 19x + 14 = 8$ are 1.5 and 0.4.

40. a) OR

The height of the cliff, y metres, can be determined by substituting 0 for x in the equation $y = -4.9x^2 + 2x + 40$ since at time 0 s, the diver is standing at the top of the cliff. Thus, the height of the cliff is 40 m$\left(-4.9(0)^2 + 2(0) + 40\right)$.

b) OR

When the diver reaches the water, his height above the water will be 0 m. Therefore, to determine the number of seconds it takes the diver to reach the water, substitute 0 for y in the equation $y = -4.9x^2 + 2x + 40$, and solve for x as shown:

$$0 = -4.9x^2 + 2x + 40$$

Since $-4.9x^2 + 2x + 40$ is not factorable, solve the equation $-4.9x^2 + 2x + 40 = 0$ by applying the quadratic formula.

$$x = \frac{-b \pm \sqrt{b^2 - 4ac}}{2a}$$

Substitute -4.9 for a, 2 for b, and 40 for c.

$$x = \frac{-2 \pm \sqrt{2^2 - 4(-4.9)(40)}}{2(-4.9)}$$

$$x = \frac{-2 \pm \sqrt{4 + 784}}{-9.8}$$

$$x = \frac{-2 \pm \sqrt{788}}{-9.8}$$

$$x = \frac{-2 + \sqrt{788}}{-9.8} \qquad \text{or} \qquad x = \frac{-2 - \sqrt{788}}{-9.8}$$

$$x \approx -2.66 \qquad\qquad\qquad x \approx 3.07$$

Since time cannot be negative, it takes the diver 3.1 s to reach the water.

c) OR

In order to determine the number of seconds that have elapsed when the diver is 15 m above the water by using a graphical approach, the first step is to choose an appropriate window setting. Next, graph $y_1 = -4.9x^2 + 2x + 40$ and $y_2 = 15$. Finally, determine the x-coordinate of the point of intersection of the two graphs.

Analytic Geometry

ANALYTIC GEOMETRY

	Table of Correlations				
Specific Expectation		**Practice Questions**	**Unit Test Questions**	**Practice Test 1**	**Practice Test 2**
AG1	Using Linear Systems to Solve Problems				
AG1.1	solve systems of two linear equations involving two variables, using the algebraic method of substitution or elimination	1, 2, 3, 4, 5, 6	1, 2, 3, 4, 5	8, 9	9, 10
AG1.2	solve problems that arise from realistic situations described in words or represented by linear systems of two equations involving two variables, by choosing an appropriate algebraic or graphical method	7, 8, 9, 10, 11a, 11b	6, 7, 8, 9a, 9b	10, 11	11, 12
AG2	Solving Problems Involving Properties of Line Segments				
AG2.1	develop the formula for the midpoint of a line segment, and use this formula to solve problems	12, 13, 14	10, 11	12	13
AG2.2	develop the formula for the length of a line segment, and use this formula to solve problems	15, 16, 17, 18	12, 13, 14	13	14
AG2.3	develop the equation for a circle with centre (0, 0) and radius r, by applying the formula for the length of a line segment;	19, 20	15	14	15
AG2.4	determine the radius of a circle with centre (0, 0), given its equation; write the equation of a circle with centre (0, 0), given the radius; and sketch the circle, given the equation in the form $x^2 + y^2 = r^2$	21, 22, 23	16, 17, 18	15	16
AG2.5	solve problems involving the slope, length, and midpoint of a line segment.	24, 25, 26, 27a, 27b, 27c	19, 20, 21, 22	16, 17	17, 18
AG3	Using Analytic Geometry to Verify Geometric Properties				
AG3.1	determine, through investigation some characteristics and properties of geometric figures	28, 29	23		
AG3.2	verify, using algebraic techniques and analytic geometry, some characteristics of geometric figures	30, 31, 32	24, 25, 26	18	19
AG3.3	plan and implement a multi-step strategy that uses analytic geometry and algebraic techniques to verify a geometric property	33, 34, 35, 36a, 36b, 36c	27, 28, 29a, 29b, 29c	19	20a, 20b, 20c, 20d

AG1.1 solve systems of two linear equations involving two variables, using the algebraic method of substitution or elimination

SOLVING SYSTEMS OF TWO LINEAR EQUATIONS

A collection of linear equations involving the same set of variables is called a
system of linear equations. The solution to a system of linear equations can be found graphically or algebraically and with or without the use of technology.

THE ALGEBRAIC METHOD OF ELIMINATION

This method involves eliminating one of the variables. Some suggested steps for using the method of elimination are outlined in the following example.

Example
Solve the following:
$3x - 4y = 20$
$x + 3y = -2$

Step 1: Label the equations.

(1) $3x - 4y = 20$

(2) $x + 3y = -2$

Step 2: Multiply both sides of equation (2) by 3.

(1) $3x - 4y = 20$

(2) $3x + 9y = -6$

Step 3: Subtract the two equations. Solve for y.

$3x - 4y = 20$
$3x + 9y = -6$
$0 - 13y = 26$
$-13y = 26$
$y = -2$

Step 4: Substitute 2 for y in one of the original equations. (In this case, equation 2).

Solve for x.

$x + 3(-2) = -2$

$x - 6 = -2$

$x = 4$

Step 5: The solution is $x = 4$ and $y = -2$.

THE ALGEBRAIC METHOD OF SUBSTITUTION

The steps for solving a system of two linear equations using the method of substitution are outlined in the following example.

Example
Solve the following:
$y - 4x + 1 = 0$
$4x - 5y + 3 = 0$

Step 1: Label each equation.

(1) $y - 4x + 1 = 0$

(2) $4x - 5y + 3 = 0$

Step 2: Isolate variable y in the first equation since the coefficient of y is 1.

Thus, equation (1) becomes $y = 4x - 1$.

Step 3: Substitute $4x - 1$ for y into the second equation.

(2) $4x - 5y + 3 = 0$

$4x - 5(4x - 1) + 3 = 0$

Step 4: Solve for the variable x.

$4x - 5(4x - 1) + 3 = 0$
$4x - 20x + 5 + 3 = 0$
$-16x + 8 = 0$
$8 = 16x$

$\dfrac{8}{16} = x$ or $x = \dfrac{1}{2}$

Step 5: Substitute $\dfrac{1}{2}$ for x in either the first or second equation or in the equation $y = 4x - 1$ to determine the value for y.

$y = 4x - 1$

$y = 4\left(\dfrac{1}{2}\right) - 1$

$y = 2 - 1$

$y = 1$

Step 6: The solution is $x = \dfrac{1}{2}$ and $y = 1$.

1. If the points $(2, -5)$ and $(-5, -2)$ both satisfy the equation $Ax + By = 29$, then the value of A is

   A. -7 B. -3

   C. 3 D. 7

2. Which of the following statements about the possible solutions to various linear systems of equations is **false**?

   A. A system of parallel lines has no solution.

   B. A system of intersecting lines has exactly one solution.

   C. A system of coincident lines has infinitely many solutions.

   D. A system of intersecting lines where one line is vertical has an undefined solution.

Use the following information to answer the next question.

A student is asked to solve the following system of linear equations by using a graphical method.

$-9x + 6y = 10$

$Ax - 8y = 15$

After graphing each linear equation, the student observed that the two lines were parallel and concluded that there was no solution to the given system of linear equations.

3. Given that the student's solution is correct, the value of A is

   A. 36 B. 12

   C. -12 D. -36

Use the following information to answer the next question.

The ordered pair (x, y) is the solution to the system of linear equations $8x + 3y = -41$ and $6x - 5y = -9$.

4. What is the value of x?

   A. 4 B. $\dfrac{-89}{29}$

   C. -4 D. $\dfrac{-159}{29}$

Use the following information to answer the next question.

Rebecca is given a system of linear equations.

$x + y = 365$

$3x + 2y = 925$

5. In verifying the solution to this system of linear equations, Rebecca must replace x with

   A. 170 and y with 195 in both equations

   B. 195 and y with 170 in both equations

   C. 170 in the first equation and y with 195 in the second equation

   D. 195 in the first equation and y with 170 in the second equation

Numerical Response

6. For the system of linear equations $12x + Ky = -9$ and $-16x - 20y = 12$ to have an infinite number of solutions, what is the value of K? _____

AG1.2 solve problems that arise from realistic situations described in words or represented by linear systems of two equations involving two variables, by choosing an appropriate algebraic or graphical method

PROBLEM SOLVING USING SYSTEMS OF LINEAR EQUATIONS

When solving problems that arise from realistic situations represented by a linear system of two equations, use some of these general hints.

- Assign a different variable to each of the unknown quantities.
- Set up a system of two linear equations, and solve the system using either an algebraic or graphical method.
- Clearly state the solution to the given problem.

Example

Four cabbages and five heads of lettuce cost $8.40, whereas six cabbages and two heads of lettuce cost $8.20. Determine the price of one cabbage and one head of lettuce.

Let the price in dollars of one cabbage = x.

Let the price in dollars of one head of lettuce = y.

Using the information given in the problem, the following system of equations can be formed:

$(1) 4x + 5y = 8.40$

$(2) 6x + 2y = 8.20$

Multiply equation (1) by 2 and equation (2) by 5 to obtain a common coefficient for y.

$(3)\quad 8x + 10y = 16.80\ [2 \times (1)]$
$(4)\ \underline{30x + 10y = 41.00}\ [5 \times (2)]$

Subtract equation (4) from equation (3).

$-22x + 0y = -24.20$
$x = \dfrac{-24.20}{-22}$
$x = 1.10$

Substitute 1.10 for x into equation (1).

$4(1.10) + 5y = 8.40$
$\quad 4.40 + 5y = 8.40$
$\qquad\qquad 5y = 4.00$
$\qquad\qquad\ y = 0.80$

The price of a cabbage is $1.10, and the price of a head of lettuce is $0.80.

Example

A car rental company offers two plans to rent compact cars at a weekly rate.

Plan A: $50 plus $0.05 / km

Plan B: $80 plus $0.03 / km

a. For each rental plan, write an equation to represent the total weekly cost in dollars, C, to rent a compact car for x kilometres driven.
   Since x = the number of kilometres driven and C = the weekly cost, it follows that
   for Plan A: $C = 50 + 0.05x$
   for Plan B: $C = 80 + 0.03x$

b. Determine which plan is more economical if the car is driven 800 km in one week.
   To determine which weekly plan is more economical if the car is driven 800 km, substitute 800 for x into each equation.
   For Plan A, the cost is
   $C = 50 + 0.05(800) = \$90$.
   For Plan B, the cost is
   $C = 80 + 0.03(800) = \$104$.
   Therefore, since Plan A costs $14 ($104 − $90) less than Plan B, Plan A is more economical.

c. Determine the distance that must be driven for Plan B to be more economical than Plan A.
   Plan B will be more economical than Plan A after the plans have an equal weekly cost. Recall that graphically, the solution to the system of equations is the intersection point of the two lines.
   The graphs displayed with the window setting $x: [0, 2\ 000, 250]$, $y: [0: 200, 50]$ are shown below.

   Using the INTERSECTION feature, the intersection point is the ordered pair (1 500, 125).
   Therefore, Plan B is more economical if the car is driven more than 1 500 km in one week.

Use the following information to answer the next question.

> The perimeter of a road marker is in the shape of an isosceles triangle is 71 inches. The base measures 1 inch less than double the length of each of the other two sides.

7. Which of the following systems of linear equations would allow a person to find the dimensions of the road marker?

A. $x + y = 71$
$2x + y = 1$

B. $x + y = 71$
$2x - y = 1$

C. $2x + y = 71$
$2x + y = 1$

D. $2x + y = 71$
$2x - y = 1$

Use the following information to answer the next question.

> At a particular theatre, adult tickets cost $7 each and student tickets cost $5 each. For a certain show, three times as many student tickets as adult tickets were sold. The total sales for the show were $880.

8. If *a* represents the number of adult tickets sold and *b* represents the number of student tickets sold, then the system of linear equations that could be solved in order to determine the number of adult and student tickets sold is

A. $7a + 5b = 880$ and $3b = a$

B. $7a + 5b = 880$ and $b = 3a$

C. $a + b = 880$ and $3(5b) = 7a$

D. $a + b = 880$ and $5b = 3(7a)$

Use the following information to answer the next question.

> Steve and Noel belong to different fitness gyms. They were comparing the cost of using each gym and were unable to decide who was getting the better deal.
> To help them compare, they graphed the cost of using each facility, as shown.

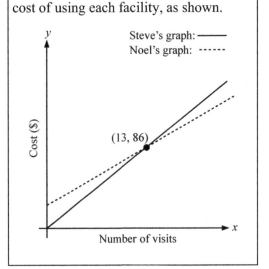

9. Which of the following statements about the information given in the graph is **false**?

A. The point of intersection (13, 86) represents the fact that 13 visits costs $86 at each facility.

B. Noel's gym has an initial membership fee that must be paid even if he never goes to the gym.

C. For a person planning to go to the gym only 8 times, Steve's gym would be the most cost-effective.

D. For a person planning to go to the gym every day for a year, Steve's gym would be the most cost-effective.

10. Sally purchased 2 pens and 8 pencils for a total cost of $5.20. If she had purchased 3 pens and 4 pencils, the total cost would have been $5.80. The cost of one pen is

A. $1.20   B. $1.40

C. $1.50   D. $1.60

Use the following information to answer the next multipart question.

11. Ken earned $6 000 working during July and August. He wants to invest these earnings, and decides to investigate some different investments to determine how much interest he might earn from these investments.

Open Response

a) Ken is thinking of investing $2 500 in an account that pays 4.2 % simple interest per year. How much interest will Ken earn at the end of the first year of his investment?

b) Ken decided to invest part of the $6 000 in an account that pays 4 % simple interest per year and the remainder of the money in a government bond that pays 3.5 % simple interest per year. After one year, the 4 % investment earned $30 more interest than the 3.5 % investment. How much interest did Ken earn at each rate?

Set up a system of two linear equations showing two variables, and then use this system to solve the problem. Show your work.

AG2.1 develop the formula for the midpoint of a line segment, and use this formula to solve problems

MIDPOINT OF A LINE SEGMENT

The **midpoint** of a line segment is a point on the line segment that is the same distance from either endpoint of the line segment. As shown below, the midpoint of a line segment is often referred to as the middle point of the line segment.

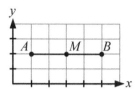

In general, the midpoint of the line segment with endpoints $A(x_1, y_1)$ and $B(x_2, y_2)$ is given by the formula $M_{AB} = \left(\dfrac{x_1 + x_2}{2}, \dfrac{y_1 + y_2}{2} \right)$.

Example
Determine the midpoint of each side of the triangle shown below.

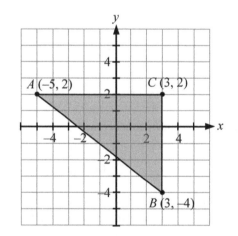

Analytic Geometry

Use the midpoint formula $M = \left(\dfrac{x_1 + x_2}{2}, \dfrac{y_1 + y_2}{2} \right)$.

For line segment AB:

$M_{AB} = \left(\dfrac{-5 + 3}{2}, \dfrac{2 + (-4)}{2} \right) = \left(\dfrac{-2}{2}, \dfrac{-2}{2} \right)$

$M_{AB} = (-1, -1)$

For line segment BC:

$M_{BC} = \left(\dfrac{3 + 3}{2}, \dfrac{-4 + 2}{2} \right) = \left(\dfrac{6}{2}, \dfrac{-2}{2} \right)$

$M_{BC} = (3, -1)$

For line segment AC:

$M_{AC} = \left(\dfrac{-5 + 3}{2}, \dfrac{2 + 2}{2} \right) = \left(\dfrac{-2}{2}, \dfrac{4}{2} \right)$

$M_{AC} = (-1, 2)$

Use the following information to answer the next question.

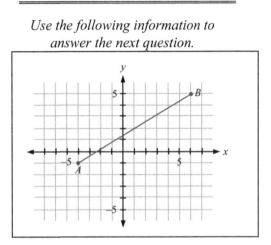

12. The midpoint of line segment AB is

   A. (1, 2)   **B.** (2, 1)

   C. (2, 4)   **D.** (4, 2)

13. One endpoint of a line segment is located at point (6, 5). The midpoint of the line segment is located at point (2, −3). The coordinates of the other endpoint are

   A. (4, 1)

   B. (−2, 3)

   C. (10, 13)

   D. (−2, −11)

14. If the point (−1, 2) is the midpoint of the line segment with endpoints that are $(a, -4)$ and $(-7, b)$, then the respective values of a and b are

   A. 1 and 6   **B.** 3 and 7

   C. 5 and 8   **D.** 7 and 9

AG2.2 develop the formula for the length of a line segment, and use this formula to solve problems

FINDING THE LENGTH OF A LINE SEGMENT

Finding the length of a line segment is useful in many aspects of analytical geometry. In order to determine the distance between points A and B, it is necessary to calculate the length of line segment AB. Consider the points $A(x_1, y_1)$ and $B(x_2, y_2)$, and build a right triangle as shown below.

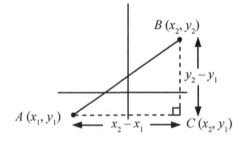

Let d represent the length of line segment AB.

Use the Pythagorean theorem to derive an expression for d.

$d^2 = (AC)^2 + (BC)^2$

$d^2 = (x_2 - x_1)^2 + (y_2 - y_1)^2$

$d = \sqrt{(x_2 - x_1)^2 + (y_2 - y_1)^2}$

USING THE DISTANCE FORMULA

In general, the length of the line segment with endpoints $A(x_1, y_1)$ and $B(x_2, y_2)$ is given by the following formula:

$$d = \sqrt{(x_2 - x_1)^2 + (y_2 - y_1)^2}$$

Example

Determine the length of the line segment with endpoints $A(3, 6)$ and $B(-2, -1)$. Express the answer as an exact value.

Substitute the endpoint values into the distance formula.

$$d = \sqrt{(x_2 - x_1)^2 + (y_2 - y_1)^2}$$
$$= \sqrt{(-2 - 3)^2 + (-1 - 6)^2}$$
$$= \sqrt{(-5)^2 + (-7)^2}$$
$$= \sqrt{25 + 49}$$
$$d = \sqrt{74}$$

The length of the line segment AB is $\sqrt{74}$ units.

Example

A fishing boat sends a distress signal from a location given by the coordinates $(200, 180)$. An ocean freighter at coordinates $(170, 240)$ and a cruise ship at coordinates $(230, 180)$ pick up the distress signal. Which ship is closer to the fishing boat?

In order to determine which of the two ships is closer to the fishing boat, begin by finding the distance from each boat to the fishing boat using the distance formula.

$$d = \sqrt{(x_2 - x_1)^2 + (y_2 - y_1)^2}$$

The distance between the ocean freighter and the fishing boat:

$$= \sqrt{(200 - 170)^2 + (180 - 240)^2}$$
$$= \sqrt{(30)^2 + (-60)^2}$$
$$= \sqrt{900 + 3600}$$
$$= \sqrt{4500} \approx 67.082$$

The distance between the cruise ship and the fishing boat:

$$= \sqrt{(200 - 230)^2 + (180 - 145)^2}$$
$$= \sqrt{(-30)^2 + (35)^2}$$
$$= \sqrt{900 + 1\ 225}$$
$$= \sqrt{2125} \approx 46.098$$

The cruise ship is approximately 21 units closer to the fishing boat than the ocean freighter.

----

15. Given two points $A(0, 5)$ and $B(-3, 1)$, what is the length of line segment AB?
    A. 2   B. 3
    C. 4   D. 5

16. If the distance between point $(1, 1)$ and point $(a, -3)$ is 5, one possible value of a is
    A. 2   B. 3
    C. 4   D. 10

17. The distance between point A and point B is 10 units on a coordinate grid. If point B lies on the y-axis and point A is at $(-6, 8)$, then two possible sets of coordinates for point B are
    A. $(0, 0)$ and $(0, 16)$
    B. $(0, 0)$ and $(16, 0)$
    C. $(0, -8)$ and $(0, 8)$
    D. $(-8, 0)$ and $(8, 0)$

Numerical Response

18. Given $A(3, 1)$, $B(5, -2)$, and $C(-3, -5)$, the perimeter of triangle ABC is _____. (correct to one decimal place)

AG2.3 develop the equation for a circle with centre (0, 0) and radius r, by applying the formula for the length of a line segment;

DEVELOPING THE EQUATION OF A CIRCLE

A **circle** is a set of points in a plane equidistant from a given point (the centre).

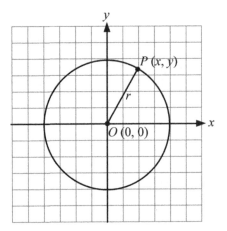

Since any point on the circle can be represented by the ordered pair $P(x, y)$, the distance P to the centre, $(0, 0)$, is the radius, r. Using the distance formula yields the following result:

Length of line segment PO:

$$= \sqrt{(x_2 - x_1)^2 + (y_2 - y_1)^2}$$
$$= \sqrt{(x - 0)^2 + (y - 0)^2}$$
$$= \sqrt{x^2 + y^2} = r$$

Therefore, $x^2 + y^2 = r^2$ when both sides of the equation $\sqrt{x^2 + y^2} = r$ are squared.

The equation of a circle with centre $(0, 0)$ and radius r is $x^2 + y^2 = r^2$.

Example

Using the distance formula, determine the equation of the circle with centre $(0, 0)$ that passes through the point $(-2, 7)$.

$$d = \sqrt{(x_2 - x_1)^2 + (y_2 - y_1)^2}$$
$$= \sqrt{(-2 - 0)^2 + (7 - 0)^2}$$
$$= \sqrt{4 + 49}$$
$$= \sqrt{53}$$

Recall that $x^2 + y^2 = r^2$.

Thus,
$$x^2 + y^2 = (\sqrt{53})^2$$
$$x^2 + y^2 = 53$$

Therefore, the equation $x^2 + y^2 = 53$ describes a circle with centre $(0, 0)$ and passing through the point $(-2, 7)$.

19. What is the equation of a circle with a radius of 8 units and a centre located at the origin?

    A. $x^2 + y^2 = 64$

    B. $x^2 - y^2 = 64$

    C. $x^2 + y^2 = 8$

    D. $x^2 - y^2 = 8$

Use the following information to answer the next question.

A circle with centre $(0, 0)$ and a diameter with endpoints (a, b) and (c, d) is shown.

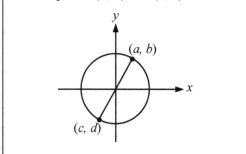

20. The equation of this circle could be written as

A. $x^2 + y^2 = \dfrac{(a-b)+(c-d)}{2}$

B. $x^2 + y^2 = \dfrac{(a-b)+(c-d)}{4}$

C. $x^2 + y^2 = \dfrac{(a-c)^2+(b-d)^2}{2}$

D. $x^2 + y^2 = \dfrac{(a-c)^2+(b-d)^2}{4}$

AG2.4 determine the radius of a circle with centre $(0, 0)$, given its equation; write the equation of a circle with centre $(0, 0)$, given the radius; and sketch the circle, given the equation in the form $x^2 + y^2 = r^2$

DETERMINING THE RADIUS OF A CIRCLE

Recall that the equation of a circle with centre $(0, 0)$ and radius r is $x^2 + y^2 = r^2$. Knowing this, you can do the following:

- Determine the radius r of a particular circle written in the form $x^2 + y^2 = r^2$.
- Write the equation of a circle with centre $(0, 0)$, given its radius r.
- On a Cartesian plane, sketch a given circle written in the form $x^2 + y^2 = r^2$.

Example

Determine the radius of the circle defined by the equation $x^2 + y^2 = 81$.

Since the equation $x^2 + y^2 = r^2$ represents a circle with centre $(0, 0)$ and radius r, it follows that:
$r^2 = 81$
$r = \sqrt{81} = 9$

Thus, the radius of the circle $x^2 + y^2 = 81$ is 9 units.

___

Example

A circle has its centre at $(0, 0)$ and a diameter of 6 units. Write the equation of the circle, and then sketch the circle on a Cartesian plane.

Since the diameter is twice the length of the radius, the radius of the circle is 3 units. In order to write the equation of the circle, substitute 3 for r in the equation $x^2 + y^2 = r^2$.
$x^2 + y^2 = (3)^2$
$x^2 + y^2 = 9$

Thus, the equation of the circle with centre $(0, 0)$ and a diameter of 6 units is $x^2 + y^2 = 9$.

The circle defined by the equation $x^2 + y^2 = 9$ has a centre of $(0, 0)$ and a radius of 3 units. You can choose the ordered pairs $(0, 3)$, $(0, -3)$, $(3, 0)$, and $(-3, 0)$ to help sketch the circle. The circle is sketched below.

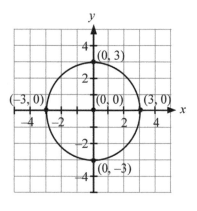

The diagram illustrates a circle sketched on a Cartesian plane.

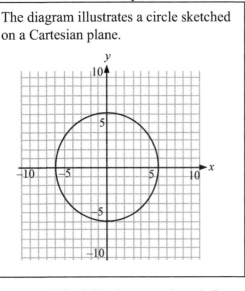

21. Which of the following equations defines this circle?

   A. $x^2 + y^2 = 25$

   B. $x^2 + y^2 = 36$

   C. $x^2 + y^2 = 100$

   D. $x^2 + y^2 = 144$

The diagram illustrates Mrs. Carter's circular flower bed, sketched on a Cartesian plane.

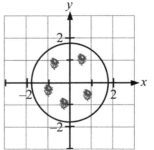

The equation that defines the outside edge of Mrs. Carter's flower bed is $x^2 + y^2 = 2.89$, where the radius is expressed in metres.

22. If Mrs. Carter decides to place a border around her circular flower bed, then the minimum length of the required border material, to the nearest tenth, is

   A. 5.3 m   **B.** 9.1 m

   C. 10.7 m   **D.** 18.2 m

Numerical Response

23. A circle is defined by the equation $x^2 + y^2 = 18$. The length of the radius of this circle, to the nearest tenth, is _____ units.

AG2.5 solve problems involving the slope, length, and midpoint of a line segment.

SOLVING LINE SEGMENT PROBLEMS

Often, certain analytical geometry problems can be solved using a combination of concepts such as slope, length, and midpoint of a line segment.

Example

Determine the equation of the right bisector of line segment AB with endpoints $A(-2, 6)$ and $B(4, -3)$.

Solution

Step 1

Determine the slope of line segment AB by applying the slope formula.

$$m = \frac{y_2 - y_1}{x_2 - x_1}$$
$$= \frac{6 - (-3)}{-2 - 4}$$
$$= \frac{9}{-6}$$
$$= -\frac{3}{2}$$

Step 2

Determine the slope of the right bisector of line segment AB.

The right bisector of line segment AB has a slope of $\frac{2}{3}$ since it is perpendicular to AB (the negative reciprocal of $-\frac{3}{2}$ is $\frac{2}{3}$).

Step 3

Determine the midpoint of line segment AB by applying the midpoint formula.

$$M_{AB} = \left(\frac{x_1 + x_2}{2}, \frac{y_1 + y_2}{2}\right)$$
$$= \left(\frac{-2 + 4}{2}, \frac{6 + (-3)}{2}\right)$$
$$= \left(\frac{2}{2}, \frac{3}{2}\right)$$
$$= \left(1, \frac{3}{2}\right)$$

Step 4

Determine the equation of the right bisector, by using the point-slope form of the equation of a line, $y = m(x - x_1) + y_1$.

Since the slope of the right bisector is $\frac{2}{3}$ and the right bisector will pass through the point $\left(1, \frac{3}{2}\right)$, substitute $\frac{2}{3}$ for m and $\left(1, \frac{3}{2}\right)$ for (x_1, y_1) in the equation.

$$y = m(x - x_1) + y_1$$
$$y = \frac{2}{3}(x - 1) + \frac{3}{2}$$
$$y = \frac{2}{3}x - \frac{2}{3} + \frac{3}{2}$$
$$y = \frac{2}{3}x + \frac{5}{6}$$

The equation of the right bisector of line segment AB is $y = \frac{2}{3}x + \frac{5}{6}$.

Example

To the nearest hundredth, determine the shortest distance from the point $(2, 1)$ to the line defined by the equation $y = -x + 7$.

Solution

The shortest distance from a point to a line is the perpendicular distance from that point to the line.

Line segment AD passes through the point $(2, 1)$ and is perpendicular to $y = -x + 7$.

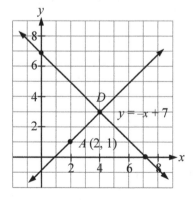

Analytic Geometry

Copyright Protected

Step 1

Determine the slope of the perpendicular line segment AD.

The slope of the line $y = -x + 7$ is -1.

Thus, the slope of AD is 1 (the negative reciprocal of -1).

Step 2

Determine the equation that defines line segment AD.

Apply the point slope formula of a line using the point $(2, 1)$ and the slope of 1.

$y = m(x - x_1) + y_1$
$y = 1(x - 2) + 1$
$y = x - 2 + 1$
$y = x - 1$

The equation of line segment AD is $y = x - 1$.

Step 3

Determine the point of intersection.

The intersection point D can be found by solving this system of two linear equations.

(1) $y = -x + 7$
(2) $y = x - 1$

Solve for x by substituting the expression for y in equation (2) into equation (1).

$x - 1 = -x + 7$
$2x - 1 = 7$
$2x = 8$
$x = 4$

Substitute 4 into equation (2) to find the y-coordinate of point D.

$y = x - 1$
$y = (4) - 1$
$y = 3$

The intersection point D is $(4, 3)$.

Step 4

Determine the distance from $(2, 1)$ to $(4, 3)$ by applying the distance formula.

$d = \sqrt{(x_2 - x_1)^2 + (y_2 - y_1)^2}$
$d = \sqrt{(4 - 2)^2 + (3 - 1)^2}$
$d = \sqrt{(2)^2 + (2)^2}$
$d = \sqrt{4 + 4}$
$d = \sqrt{8}$

To the nearest hundredth, $d \approx 2.83$.

The shortest distance from the point $(2, 1)$ to the line defined by the equation $y = -x + 7$ is approximately 2.83 units.

24. To the nearest whole number, what is the horizontal distance between the point $(4, -7)$ and the line $y = -\dfrac{1}{3}x + 2$?

A. 5 units
B. 9 units
C. 23 units
D. 34 units

Use the following information to answer the next question.

The vertices of triangle ABC are $A(-3, -4)$, $B(1, 4)$, and $C(3, 0)$, as shown in the diagram.

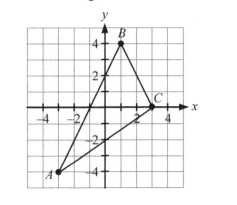

25. To the nearest tenth, the perimeter of the triangle formed by joining the midpoints of each side of the triangle shown is

A. 7.7 units
B. 10.3 units
C. 12.9 units
D. 20.6 units

26. To the nearest hundredth, the shortest distance from the point $(4, 1)$ to the line $y = 2x - 12$ is

A. 2.24 units
B. 6.47 units
C. 9.20 units
D. 10.05 units

Use the following information to answer the next multipart question.

27. A diameter of a circle has endpoints $A(-2, 3)$ and $B(4, 11)$.

Open Response

a) Determine the coordinates of the centre of the circle. Show your work.

b) Verify that the radius of the circle is 5 units in length. Show your work.

c) Verify that the point $P(-3, 10)$ is on the circle. Show your work.

AG3.1 determine, through investigation some characteristics and properties of geometric figures

INVESTIGATING CHARACTERISTICS AND PROPERTIES OF TRIANGLES AND QUADRILATERALS

Characteristics and properties of geometric figures can be derived by using a variety of methods. Possible methods could include the use of grid paper, paper folding or the use of technology such as a graphing calculator or dynamic geometry software. This lesson will restrict the focus to the examination of triangles and, quadrilaterals and their related properties.

INVESTIGATION 1: CHARACTERISTICS OF TRIANGLES

Recall the following triangle characteristics and properties:

- A **right triangle** is a triangle that contains an angle of 90°.
- When each side of a triangle is equal in length, the triangle is defined as an **equilateral triangle**.
- When exactly two sides of a triangle are equal in length, the triangle is defined as an **isosceles triangle**.
- When each side of a triangle is different in length, the triangle is defined as a **scalene triangle**.

Consider triangle ABC with vertices $A(2, 1)$, $B(4, 0)$ and $C(5, 7)$, as shown.

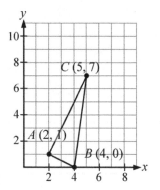

Step 1:

Determine the slope of each side of the triangle by applying the slope formula $m = \dfrac{y_2 - y_1}{x_2 - x_1}$.

$$m_{AB} = \frac{0 - 1}{4 - 2}$$
$$= -\frac{1}{2}$$

$$m_{AC} = \frac{7 - 1}{5 - 2}$$
$$= \frac{6}{3}$$
$$= 2$$

$$m_{BC} = \frac{7 - 0}{5 - 4}$$
$$= \frac{7}{1}$$
$$= 7$$

Step 2:

Determine if side AB and BC are perpendicular. The slopes of sides AB and AC are negative reciprocals. Observe that $-\dfrac{1}{2} \times 2 = -1$.

Since $m_{AB} \times m_{AC} = -1$, side AB is perpendicular to side AC, and $\angle A = 90°$.

A **right triangle** is a triangle that contains an angle of 90°. Therefore, $\triangle ABC$ is a right triangle.

Now consider triangle ABC with vertices $A(-4, 6)$, $B(-4, 1)$ and $C(0.33, 3.5)$, as shown.

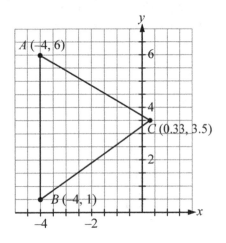

To determine if $\triangle ABC$ is an equilateral triangle, calculate the length of each side of the triangle by applying the distance formula,
$$d = \sqrt{(x_2 - x_1)^2 + (y_2 - y_1)^2}.$$

$$d_{AB} = \sqrt{(-4 - (-4))^2 + (1 - 6)^2}$$
$$= \sqrt{0 + 25}$$
$$= 5 \text{ units}$$

$$d_{BC} = \sqrt{(0.33 - (-4))^2 + (3.5 - 1)^2}$$
$$= \sqrt{18.7489 + 6.25}$$
$$\approx \sqrt{25}$$
$$\approx 5 \text{ units}$$

$$d_{AC} = \sqrt{(0.33 - (-4))^2 + (3.5 - 6)^2}$$
$$= \sqrt{18.7489 + 6.25}$$
$$\approx \sqrt{25}$$
$$\approx 5 \text{ units}$$

Observe that the length of each given line segment is the same ($d_{AB} = d_{BC} = d_{AC}$).

A triangle, where all three sides are equal is defined as an **equilateral triangle**

From further similar investigations involving other triangles, the following observations and triangle definitions can also be concluded:

1. **Observation:** In triangle ABC the length of line segment AB and the length of line segement AC are equal: $d_{AB} = d_{AC}$.**Definition:** A triangle with exactly two sides equal in length is defined as an **isosceles triangle**

2. **Observation:** In triangle ABC the length of each of the line segments AB, BC and AC is different: $d_{AB} \neq d_{BC} \neq D_{AC}$**Definition:** A triangle with three sides of different lengths is defined as a **scalene triangle**

Example

Line segments AB and BC intersect at B.
Line segments AC and AB intersect at A.
Line segments AC and BC intersect at C.

If $AB = 4$ cm, $BC = 7$ cm, and $AC = 4$ cm, then what type of geometric figure is formed from these line segments?

Solution

Since there are three line segments, the figure is a triangle.

Since $AB = AC = 4$, the triangle is an isosceles triangle. (Two sides of the triangle are equal in length.)

INVESTIGATION 2: CHARACTERISTICS OF QUADRILATERALS

Through investigation, recall the following quadrilateral characteristics and properties:

- A **rectangle** is a quadrilateral in which opposite sides are parallel to one another and equal in length, and adjacent sides are perpendicular to one another.
- When opposite sides of a quadrilateral are equal in length and have equal slopes, the quadrilateral is called a **parallelogram**.
- It can be shown that the diagonals of a parallelogram bisect each other.
- When all the sides of a quadrilateral are equal in length and opposite sides have equal slopes, the quadrilateral is called a **rhombus**.
- A quadrilateral in which all four sides are equal in length, opposite sides are parallel, and adjacent sides are perpendicular is called a **square**.
- A quadrilateral in which the slope of exactly one pair of opposite sides is equal is called a **trapezoid**.

Consider quadrilateral $ABCD$ with vertices $A(-2, 3)$, $B(-2, -1)$, $C(6, -1)$ and $D(6, 3)$ as shown.

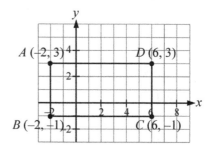

Step 1:
Determine the length of each side of the quadrilateral by applying the distance formula, $d = \sqrt{(x_2 - x_1)^2 + (y_2 - y_1)^2}$.

$$d_{AB} = \sqrt{(-2 - (-2))^2 + (-1 - 3)^2}$$
$$= \sqrt{0 + 16}$$
$$= \sqrt{16}$$
$$= 4 \text{ units}$$

$$d_{BC} = \sqrt{(-2 - 6)^2 + (-1 - (-1))^2}$$
$$= \sqrt{64 + 0}$$
$$= \sqrt{64}$$
$$= 8 \text{ units}$$

$$d_{CD} = \sqrt{(6 - 6)^2 + (3 - (-1))^2}$$
$$= \sqrt{0 + 16}$$
$$= \sqrt{16}$$
$$= 4 \text{ units}$$

$$d_{AD} = \sqrt{(6 - (-2))^2 + (3 - 3)^2}$$
$$= \sqrt{64 + 0}$$
$$= \sqrt{64}$$
$$= 8 \text{ units}$$

Observe that line segments AB and CD are equal in length, and line segments BC and AD are equal in length. $d_{AB} = d_{CD}$ and $d_{BC} = d_{AD}$.

Step 2:
Determine the slope of each side of the quadrilateral by applying the slope formula, $m = \dfrac{y_2 - y_1}{x_2 - x_1}$.

$$m_{AB} = \frac{-1 - 3}{-2 - (-2)}$$
$$= -\frac{4}{0}$$
$$= \text{undefined}$$

$$m_{BC} = \frac{-1 - (-1)}{4 - (-4)}$$
$$= \frac{0}{8}$$
$$= 0$$

$$m_{CD} = \frac{3 - (-1)}{6 - 6}$$
$$= \frac{4}{0}$$
$$= \text{undefined}$$

$$m_{AD} = \frac{3 - 3}{6 - (-2)}$$
$$= \frac{0}{8}$$
$$= 0$$

Observe that line segments AB and CD have the same slope, and line segments BC and AD have the same slope. Thereofre, the opposite sides of the quadrilateral are parallel to each other since they have equal slopes.

Note that the slope of line segment AB and the slope of line segment BC are negative reciprocals of each other. As well, the slope of line segment CD is the negative reciprocal of the slope of line segment AD. Therefore, the adjacent line segments are perpendicular.

A **rectangle** is a quadrilateral in which opposite sides are parallel to one another and equal in length, and the adjacent sides are perpendicular to one another.

Now consider quadrilateral $ABCD$ with vertices $A(-2, 3)$, $B(-4, -1)$, $C(4, -1)$ and $D(6, 3)$, as shown.

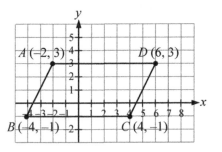

Step 1:
Determine the length of each side of the quadrilateral by applying the distance formula, $d = \sqrt{(x_2 - x_1)^2 + (y_2 - y_1)^2}$.

$$d_{AB} = \sqrt{(-4 - (-2))^2 + (-1 - 3)^2}$$
$$= \sqrt{4 + 16}$$
$$= \sqrt{20} \text{ units}$$

$$d_{BC} = \sqrt{(4 - (-4))^2 + (-1 - (-1))^2}$$
$$= \sqrt{64 + 0}$$
$$= \sqrt{64}$$
$$= 8 \text{ units}$$

$$d_{CD} = \sqrt{(6 - 4)^2 + (3 - (-1))^2}$$
$$= \sqrt{4 + 16}$$
$$= \sqrt{20} \text{ units}$$

$$d_{AD} = \sqrt{(6 - (-2))^2 + (3 - 3)^2}$$
$$= \sqrt{64 + 0}$$
$$= \sqrt{64}$$
$$= 8 \text{ units}$$

Observe that line segments AB and CD are equal in length, and line segments BC and AD are equal in length.
$$d_{AB} = d_{CD} \text{ and } d_{BC} = D_{AD}$$

Step 2:

Determine the slope of each side of the quadrilateral y applying the slope formula, $m = \dfrac{y_2 - y_1}{x_2 - x_1}$.

$$m_{AB} = \frac{-1 - 3}{-4 - (-2)}$$
$$= \frac{-4}{-2}$$
$$= 2$$

$$m_{BC} = \frac{-1 - (-1)}{4 - (-4)}$$
$$= \frac{0}{8}$$
$$= 0$$

$$m_{CD} = \frac{3 - (-1)}{6 - 4}$$
$$= \frac{4}{2}$$
$$= 2$$

$$m_{AD} = \frac{3 - 3}{6 - (-2)}$$
$$= \frac{0}{8}$$
$$= 0$$

Observe that line segments AB and CD have equal slopes. As well, line segments BC and AD have equal slopes. Therefore, AB is parallel to CD and BC is parallel to AD.

When opposite sides of a quadrilateral are equal in length and have equal slopes, the quadrilateral is called a **parallelogram**.

It can be shown that the diagonals of a parallelogram **bisect** each other. Consider quadrilateral $ABCD$ with vertices $A(-2, 3)$, $B(-4, -1)$, $C(4, -1)$ and $D(6, 3)$, as shown. Line segments AC and BD are the diagonals of quadrilateral $ABCD$. Using the midpoint formula $M = \left(\dfrac{x_1 + x_2}{2}, \dfrac{y_1 + y_2}{2} \right)$ calculate the midpoint of each diagonal.

$$M_{AC} = \left(\frac{-2 + 4}{2}, \frac{3 + (-1)}{2} \right)$$
$$= (1, 1)$$

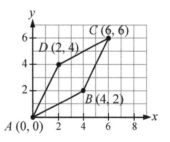

$$M_{BD} = \left(\frac{-4 + 6}{2}, \frac{-1 + 3}{2} \right)$$
$$= (1, 1)$$

Since $M_{AC} = M_{BD}$ the diagonals AC and BD bisect each other.

Given quadrilateral $ABCD$ with vertices $A(0, 0)$, $B(4, 2)$, $C(6, 6)$ and $D(2, 4)$ as shown. **Step 1:** Determine the length of each side of the quadrilateral by applying the distance formula, $d = \sqrt{(x_2 - x_1)^2 + (y_2 - y_1)^2}$.

$$d_{AB} = \sqrt{(4-0)^2 + (2-0)^2}$$
$$= \sqrt{16+4}$$
$$= \sqrt{20} \text{ units}$$

$$d_{BC} = \sqrt{(6-4)^2 + (6-2)^2}$$
$$= \sqrt{4+16}$$
$$= \sqrt{20} \text{ units}$$

$$d_{CD} = \sqrt{(6-2)^2 + (6-4)^2}$$
$$= \sqrt{16+4}$$
$$= \sqrt{20} \text{ units}$$

$$d_{AD} = \sqrt{(2-0)^2 + (4-0)^2}$$
$$= \sqrt{4+16}$$
$$= \sqrt{20} \text{ units}$$

Observe that the length of each line segment is the same: $d_{AB} = d_{BC} = d_{CD} = d_{AD}$

Step 2:

Determine the slope of each side of the quadrilateral by applying the slope formula, $m = \dfrac{y_2 - y_1}{x_2 - x_1}$.

$$m_{AB} = \frac{2-0}{4-0}$$
$$= \frac{2}{4}$$
$$= \frac{1}{2}$$

$$m_{BC} = \frac{6-2}{6-4}$$
$$= \frac{4}{2}$$
$$= 2$$

$$m_{CD} = \frac{4-6}{2-6}$$
$$= \frac{-2}{-4}$$
$$= \frac{1}{2}$$

$$m_{AD} = \frac{4-0}{2-0}$$
$$= \frac{4}{2}$$
$$= 2$$

Observe that line segments AB and CD have equal slopes. As well, line segments BC and AD have equal slopes. Therefore, AB is parallel to CD and BC is parallel to AD.

When all the sides of a quadrilateral are equal in length and opposite sides have equal slopes, the quadrilateral is a **rhombus**.

Further similar investigations give the following observations and quadrilateral defintions.

Observations

- In quadrilateral $ABCD$, the length of line segments AB, BC, CD and AD are equal: $d_{AB} = d_{BC} = d_{CD} = d_{AD}$.
- The slope of AB is equal to the slope of CD and the slope of BC is equal to the slope of AD. Therefore, the opposite sides of the quadrilateral $ABCD$ are paralllel.
- The slope of AB is the negative receiprocal of the slope of BC, and the slope of AD is the negative reciprocal of CD. Adjacent sides of the quadrilateral $ABCD$ are perpendicular.

Definition

- A quadrilateral in which all four sides are equal in length and opposite sides are parallel and adjacent sides are perpendicular is called a **square**

Observations

- In quadrilateral $ABCD$ the slope of the line segment AB is equal to the slope of line segment CD. The slope of the line segment BC is not equal to the slope of line segment AD.

Defintion

- A quadrilateral in which the slope of exactly one pair of opposite sides is equal is called a **trapezoid**

28. In triangle PQR, line segment PT intersects the midpoint of line segment QR, forming a right angle at point T. Line segment PT is classified as the perpendicular

   A. radius   **B.** bisector

   C. diagonal   **D.** connector

Use the following information to answer the next question.

Martha draws a quadrilateral with the following properties:

- The opposite sides are equal.
- The opposite angles are equal.
- The diagonals bisect each other at 90°.

29. The quadrilateral that Martha draws is a

    A. parallelogram   **B.** rectangle

    C. trapezoid   **D.** square

AG3.2 verify, using algebraic techniques and analytic geometry, some characteristics of geometric figures

DETERMINING THE SHAPE OF GEOMETRIC FIGURES USING ANALYTICAL GEOMETRY

The shapes of geometric figures can be determined and verified using both algebraic and geometric techniques. An algebraic verification may require the use of previously developed definitions, formulas, or theorems. Geometric verification often involves sketching by hand or using dynamic geometric software.

Example

Verify that triangle ABC with vertices $A(2, 3)$, $B(6, 1)$, and $C(5, 4)$ is an isosceles triangle.

Solution

To verify that triangle ABC is isosceles, determine the lengths of each of the three sides of the triangle, and show that exactly two sides have the same length. Recall the distance formula $d = \sqrt{(x_2 - x_1)^2 + (y_x - y_1)^2}$.

Length of side AB:
$$\begin{aligned} d_{AB} &= \sqrt{(6-2)^2 + (1-3)^2} \\ &= \sqrt{16+4} \\ &= \sqrt{20} \text{ units} \end{aligned}$$

Length of side BC:
$$\begin{aligned} d_{BC} &= \sqrt{(5-6)^2 + (4-1)^2} \\ & \sqrt{1+9} \\ & \sqrt{10} \text{ units} \end{aligned}$$

Length of side AC:
$$\begin{aligned} d_{AC} &= \sqrt{(5-2)^2 + (4-3)^2} \\ &= \sqrt{9+1} \\ &= \sqrt{10} \text{ units} \end{aligned}$$

Since the length of side BC is equal to the length of side AC, triangle ABC is isosceles. It is important to note that if all three sides of triangle ABC were the same length, triangle ABC would be an equilateral triangle.

Example

Verify that the quadrilateral with vertices $A(1, 1)$, $B(6, 1)$, $C(9, 5)$, and $D(4, 5)$ is a rhombus.

Solution

In order to verify that quadrilateral $ABCD$ is a rhombus, determine the length and then the slope of each side of the quadrilateral.

Step 1

Calculate the length of each side of the quadrilateral. Apply the distance formula $d = \sqrt{(x_2 - x_1)^2 + (y_2 - y_1)^2}$.

$$d_{AB} = \sqrt{(6 - 1)^2 + (1 - 1)^2}$$
$$= \sqrt{5^2 + 0^2}$$
$$= \sqrt{25}$$
$$= 5 \text{ units}$$

$$d_{BC} = \sqrt{(9 - 6)^2 + (5 - 1)^2}$$
$$= \sqrt{3^2 + 4^2}$$
$$= \sqrt{9 + 16}$$
$$= \sqrt{25}$$
$$= 5 \text{ units}$$

$$d_{CD} = \sqrt{(4 - 9)^2 + (5 - 5)^2}$$
$$= \sqrt{(-5)^2 + 0^2}$$
$$= \sqrt{25}$$
$$= 5 \text{ units}$$

$$d_{AD} = \sqrt{(4 - 1)^2 + (5 - 1)^2}$$
$$= \sqrt{3^2 + 4^2}$$
$$= \sqrt{9 + 16}$$
$$= \sqrt{25}$$
$$= 5 \text{ units}$$

Notice that all four sides of the quadrilateral are equal.

Step 2

Determine the slope of each side of the quadrilateral by applying the slope formula $m = \dfrac{y_2 - y_1}{x_2 - x_1}$.

$$m_{AB} = \frac{1 - 1}{6 - 1}$$
$$= \frac{0}{5}$$
$$= 0$$

$$m_{DC} = \frac{5 - 5}{9 - 4}$$
$$= \frac{0}{5}$$
$$= 0$$

Observe that $m_{AB} = m_{DC}$.

$$m_{BC} = \frac{5 - 1}{9 - 6}$$
$$= \frac{4}{3}$$

$$m_{AD} = \frac{5 - 1}{4 - 1}$$
$$= \frac{4}{3}$$

Observe that $m_{BC} = m_{AD}$.

The quadrilateral has sides of equal length, and its opposite sides are parallel (opposite sides have equal slopes). Since its adjacent sides are not perpendicular (slopes are not negative reciprocals of each other), the quadrilateral is a rhombus.

Example

Verify that quadrilateral *KLMN* with vertices $K(1, 3)$, $L(5, -1)$, $M(1, -5)$, and $N(-3, -1)$ is a square.

Solution

In order to verify that quadrilateral *KLMN* is a square, determine the length of each side, the slope of each side, and whether adjacent sides are perpendicular.

Step 1

Calculate the length of each side of the quadrilateral by applying the distance formula $d = \sqrt{(x_2 - x_1)^2 + (y_2 - y_1)^2}$.

Length of side *KL*:

$$\begin{aligned} d_{KL} &= \sqrt{(5 - 1)^2 + (-1 - 3)^2} \\ &= \sqrt{(4)^2 + (-4)^2} \\ &= \sqrt{16 + 16} \\ &= \sqrt{32} \end{aligned}$$

Length of *LM*:

$$\begin{aligned} d_{LM} &= \sqrt{((1 - 5)^2) + (-5 - (-1))^2} \\ &= \sqrt{(-4)^2 + (-4)^2} \\ &= \sqrt{16 + 16} \\ &= \sqrt{32} \end{aligned}$$

Length of *MN*:

$$\begin{aligned} d_{MN} &= \sqrt{(-3 - 1)^2 + (-1 - (-5))^2} \\ &= \sqrt{(-4)^2 + 4^2} \\ &= \sqrt{16 + 16} \\ &= \sqrt{32} \end{aligned}$$

Length of *KN*:

$$\begin{aligned} d_{KN} &= \sqrt{(-3 - 1)^2 + (-1 - 3)^2} \\ &= \sqrt{(-4)^2 + (-4)^2} \\ &= \sqrt{16 + 16} \\ &= \sqrt{32} \end{aligned}$$

All four sides of the quadrilateral are equal.

Step 2

Determine the slope of each side of the quadrilateral by applying the slope formula $m = \dfrac{y_2 - y_1}{x_2 - x_1}$.

$$\begin{aligned} m_{KL} &= \frac{-1 - 3}{5 - 1} \\ &= -\frac{4}{4} \\ &= -1 \end{aligned}$$

$$\begin{aligned} m_{LM} &= \frac{-5 - (-1)}{1 - 5} \\ &= \frac{-4}{-4} \\ &= 1 \end{aligned}$$

$$\begin{aligned} m_{MN} &= \frac{-1 - (-5)}{-3 - 1} \\ &= \frac{4}{-4} \\ &= -1 \end{aligned}$$

$$\begin{aligned} m_{KN} &= \frac{-1 - 3}{-3 - 1} \\ &= \frac{-4}{-4} \\ &= 1 \end{aligned}$$

Since line segments *KL* and *MN* have the same slope, they are parallel. As well, line segments *LM* and *KN* have the same slope, so they are parallel.

Step 3

Determine if the adjacent sides are perpendicular.

Perpendicular lines have negative reciprocal slopes: $m_1 \times m_2 = -1$.

KL and *LM* are adjacent sides.

$$\begin{aligned} m_{KL} \times m_{LM} &= -1 \times 1 \\ &= -1 \end{aligned}$$

MN and *KN* are adjacent sides.

$$\begin{aligned} m_{MN} \times m_{KN} &= -1 \times 1 \\ &= -1 \end{aligned}$$

The adjacent line segments are perpendicular. Therefore, quadrilateral *KLMN* is a square since all its sides are equal, the opposite sides are parallel, and the adjacent sides are perpendicular.

Analytic Geometry

Example

Verify that triangle *DEF* with vertices *D*(3, 5), *E*(5, 2), and *F*(8, 4) is a right triangle.

Solution

To verify that triangle *DEF* is a right triangle, show that either ∠*D*, ∠*E*, or ∠*F* is a right angle. An angle is a right angle when the two sides forming the angle are perpendicular to one another. If two sides of a triangle are perpendicular to one another, their respective slopes are negative reciprocals of each other $(m_1 \times m_2 = -1)$. Therefore, determine the slope of each side of triangle *DEF*, and show that one side of the triangle is perpendicular to another side of the triangle.

Determine the slope of each side of triangle *DEF* by applying the slope formula

$$m = \frac{y_2 - y_1}{x_2 - x_1}.$$

Slope of *DE*:

$$m = \frac{2 - 5}{5 - 3}$$

$$m = \frac{-3}{2}$$

Slope of *DF*:

$$m = \frac{4 - 5}{8 - 3}$$

$$m = \frac{-1}{5}$$

Slope of *EF*:

$$m = \frac{4 - 2}{8 - 5}$$

$$m = \frac{2}{3}$$

The slope of side *DE* is the negative reciprocal of the slope of side *EF* $\left(\frac{-3}{2} \times \frac{2}{3} = \frac{-6}{6} = -1\right)$.

Therefore, side *DE* is perpendicular to side *EF*.

It follows that ∠*E* = 90° and triangle *DEF* is a right triangle.

---

30. If points *P*(2, 4), *Q*(6, 1), and *R*(−1, 0) are the vertices of a triangle, then the triangle is

    A. a right triangle

    B. a scalene triangle

    C. an equilateral triangle

    D. a right isosceles triangle

Use the following information to answer the next question.

Points *J*(−1, 3), *K*(3, −2), and *L* (5, 1) are plotted on the grid shown. Point *N* lies on the *y*-axis so that line *LN* is perpendicular to line *JK*..

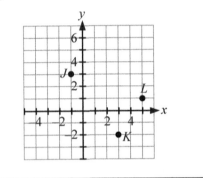

31. What are the coordinates of point *N*?

    A. (0, 3)   **B.** (0, −3)

    C. $\left(0, \dfrac{29}{4}\right)$ **D.** $\left(0, \dfrac{15}{4}\right)$

Numerical Response

32. The graph of a particular line passes through the ordered pairs (3, 7) and (5, 15). The graph of a line that is perpendicular to this line could pass through the ordered pairs (*a*, −6) and (−2, −5). The value of *a* is _____.

AG3.3 plan and implement a multi-step strategy that uses analytic geometry and algebraic techniques to verify a geometric property

VERIFYING PROPERTIES OF TRIANGLES AND QUADRILATERALS

The use of analytical geometry to verify properties of triangles and quadrilaterals often requires a multi-step approach.

Use these general steps to verify properties in any given problem:

1. Sketch the given information on a Cartesian plane.
2. Apply the appropriate formulas such as distance, midpoint, and slope.
3. State the solution to the given problem.

Example

The vertices of $\triangle ABC$ are $A(2, 5)$, $B(-4, -1)$, and $C(1, -1)$. Segment DE is formed by connecting the midpoint D of side AB and the midpoint E of side AC.

In the given triangle, verify that segment DE is parallel to and half the length of segment BC.

Solution

Step 1

Draw a sketch to represent the given information.

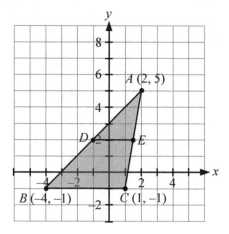

Step 2

Determine the coordinates of the midpoints D and E.

Apply the midpoint formula

$$M = \left(\frac{x_1 + x_2}{2}, \frac{y_1 + y_2}{2}\right).$$

$$D = M_{AB} = \left(\frac{2 + (-4)}{2}, \frac{5 + (-1)}{2}\right)$$
$$= \left(\frac{-2}{2}, \frac{4}{2}\right)$$
$$= (-1, 2)$$

$$E = M_{AC} = \left(\frac{2 + 1}{2}, \frac{5 + (-1)}{2}\right)$$
$$= \left(\frac{3}{2}, \frac{4}{2}\right)$$
$$= \left(\frac{3}{2}, 2\right)$$

Step 3

Determine the slope of segment DE and segment BC.

Apply the slope formula $m = \dfrac{y_2 - y_1}{x_2 - x_1}$.

$$m_{DE} = \frac{2 - 2}{-1 - \left(\frac{3}{2}\right)}$$
$$= \frac{0}{-\frac{5}{2}}$$
$$= 0$$

$$m_{BC} = \frac{-1 - (-1)}{1 - (-4)}$$
$$= \frac{0}{5}$$
$$= 0$$

Therefore, $m_{DE} = m_{BC} = 0$.

Step 4

Determine the length of segments *DE* and *BC*.

Apply the distance formula

$d = \sqrt{(x_2 - x_1)^2 + (y_2 - y_1)^2}.$

$$d_{DE} = \sqrt{\left(\frac{3}{2} - (-1)\right)^2 + (2 - 2)^2}$$

$$= \sqrt{\left(\frac{5}{2}\right)^2 + (0)^2}$$

$$= \sqrt{\frac{25}{4}}$$

$$= \frac{5}{2} \text{ units}$$

$$d_{BC} = \sqrt{(1 - (-4))^2 + (-1 - (-1))^2}$$

$$= \sqrt{(5)^2 + (0)^2}$$

$$= \sqrt{25}$$

$$= 5 \text{ units}$$

Notice that $d_{DE} = \frac{1}{2}d_{BC}$.

Since the slope of *DE* is equal to the slope of *BC* and the length of *DE* is one-half the length of *BC*, it is verified that segment *DE* is parallel to and half the length of segment *BC*.

Example

The vertices of a parallelogram are $A(-2, 4)$, $B(2, -1)$, $C(-2, -4)$, and $D(-6, 1)$.

Verify that the diagonals of the given parallelogram *ABCD* bisect each other.

Solution

Step 1

Draw a sketch to represent the given information.

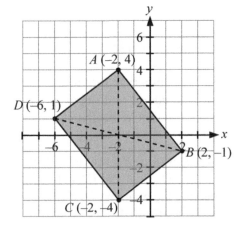

The diagonals of the parallelogram are line segments *AC* and *BD*.

If the diagonals bisect each other, then line segments *AC* and *BD* will have the same midpoint.

Step 2

Determine the coordinates of the midpoint of *AC* and the coordinates of the midpoint of *BD*.

Apply the midpoint formula

$$M = \left(\frac{x_1 + x_2}{2}, \frac{y_1 + y_2}{2}\right).$$

$$M_{AC} = \left(\frac{-2 + (-2)}{2}, \frac{4 + (-4)}{2}\right)$$

$$= \left(\frac{-4}{2}, \frac{0}{2}\right)$$

$$= (-2, 0)$$

$$M_{BD} = \left(\frac{2 + (-6)}{2}, \frac{-1 + 1}{2}\right)$$

$$= \left(\frac{-4}{2}, \frac{0}{2}\right)$$

$$= (-2, 0)$$

Since line segments *AC* and *BD* have the same midpoint $(-2, 0)$, the diagonals of quadrilateral *ABCD* bisect each other.

Use the following information to answer the next question.

Alex is asked to verify that the diagonals of the quadrilateral with vertices $(5, 4)$, $(7, 1)$, $(-4, -2)$, and $(-2, -5)$ are equal in length. He labelled the vertices $A(5, 4)$, $B(7, 1)$, $C(-4, -2)$, and $D(-2, -5)$ and made use of the distance formula $d = \sqrt{(x_2 - x_1)^2 + (y_2 - y_1)^2}$. He followed these steps:

Alex's Solution

Step 1

$d_{AC} = d_{BD}$

Step 2

$\sqrt{(5 - (-4))^2 + (4 - (-2))^2}$
$= \sqrt{(-2 - 7)^2 + (-5 - 1)^2}$

Step 3

$\sqrt{(9)^2 + (2)^2} = \sqrt{(-9)^2 + (-2)^2}$

Step 4

$\sqrt{85} = \sqrt{93}$

33. In which step was Alex's first error?
    A. Step 1   **B.** Step 2
    C. Step 3   **D.** Step 4

Use the following information to answer the next question.

A line segment has endpoints $A(-8, 6)$ and $B(4, 6)$. Krystal is asked to verify that a particular point is on the perpendicular bisector of AB.

34. Which of the following points is a possible point that Krystal could be asked to verify?
    A. $(-4, 6)$ **B.** $(-2, 14)$
    C. $(6, -2)$ **D.** $(14, -4)$

Use the following information to answer the next question.

Three points are collinear if they are on the same line.

35. Which of the following methods could **not** be used in order to determine if the points $A(-9, -2)$, $B(-6, 5)$, and $C(0, 19)$ are collinear?
    A. Verify that the slope of segment AB is equal to the slope of segment BC.

    B. Verify that the slope of segment AC is equal to the slope of segment AB.

    C. Verify that the midpoint of line segment AB is equal to the midpoint of line segment BC.

    D. Verify that the distance from point A to C is equal to the distance from point A to B plus the distance from point B to C.

*Use the following information to
answer the next multipart question.*

36. In the diagram shown, *AD* is parallel
to *BC*, and *AB* is parallel to *CD*.

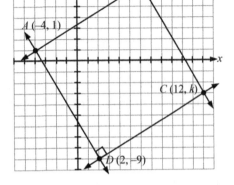

| Open Response |

a) Algebraically, determine the value of *k* in
the diagram. Show your work.

b) Determine algebraically the value of *n* in
the diagram. Show your work.

c) If *n* = 6 and *k* = −3, verify that
quadrilateral *ABCD* is a square. Show
your work.

ANSWERS AND SOLUTIONS
ANALYTIC GEOMETRY

1. **B**	10. **D**	18. **20.6**	27. **a) OR**	34. **B**
2. **D**	11. **a) OR**	19. **A**	**b) OR**	35. **C**
3. **B**	**b) OR**	20. **D**	**c) OR**	36. **a) OR**
4. **C**	12. **A**	21. **B**	28. **B**	**b) OR**
5. **B**	13. **D**	22. **C**	29. **D**	**c) OR**
6. **15**	14. **C**	23. **4.2**	30. **D**	
7. **D**	15. **D**	24. **C**	31. **B**	
8. **B**	16. **C**	25. **B**	32. **2**	
9. **D**	17. **A**	26. **A**	33. **A**	

1. B

In $Ax + By = 29$, substitute 2 for x and -5 for y.
This gives $2A - 5B = 29$.

Then substitute -5 for x and -2 for y.
This gives $-5A - 2B = 29$.
Now, solve as a system.

$$(1) \qquad 2A - 5B \quad = \quad 29$$
$$(2) \qquad -5A - 2B \quad = \quad 29$$

Subtract the equations.
$$(1) \times 2 \qquad 4A - 10B = 58$$
$$\underline{(2) \times 5 \quad -25A - 10B = 145}$$
$$29A = -87$$
$$A = -3$$

2. D

A vertical line can intersect other lines, thus, producing a solution to a system of equation.

3. B

If the lines are parallel, they must have the same slope.

For $-9x + 6y = 10$:

Add $9x$ to both sides.
$6y = 9x + 10$

Divide both sides by 6.
$$y = \frac{9x}{6} + \frac{10}{6}$$

Reduce fractions.
$$y = \frac{3}{2}x + \frac{5}{3}$$

For $Ax - 8y = 15$:

Subtract Ax from both sides.
$-8y = -Ax + 15$

Divide both sides by -8.
$$y = \frac{Ax}{8} + \left(-\frac{15}{8}\right)$$

Thus, the coefficients of x (the slope) must be equal.

$$\frac{3}{2} = \frac{A}{8}$$

Cross multiply.
$2A = 24$

Solve for A.
$A = 12$

4. C

Step 1
Label the equations, and choose which variable is to be eliminated.
  ① $8x + 3y = -41$
  ② $6x - 5y = -9$
Eliminate the y-value so that the x-value can be found.

Step 2

Eliminate y by addition.

Multiply equation ① by 5 and equation ② by 3.

$5 \times$ ① $8x + 3y = -41$
$\qquad 40x + 15y = -205$
$3 \times$ ② $6x - 5y = -9$
$\qquad 18x - 15y = -27$

- Let $40x + 15y = -205$ represent equation ③.
- Let $18x - 15y = -27$ represent equation ④.

Step 3

Add equations ③ and ④ to eliminate y.

③ $40x + 15y = -205$
④ $\underline{18x - 15y = -27}$
$\qquad 58x + 0y = -232$

Step 4

Solve for x.

$58x + 0y = -232$
$\qquad 58x = -232$
$\qquad\quad x = -4$

5. B

Step 1

Label the equations.

① $\quad x + y = 365$
② $\quad 3x + 2y = 925$

Step 2

Multiply both sides of equation (1) by 2.

$2 \times$ ① $2x + 2y = 730$
$\qquad$ ② $3x + 2y = 925$

Step 3

Subtract the two equations, and solve for x.

$2x + 2y = 730$
$\underline{3x + 2y = 925}$
$-x + 0y = -195$
$x = 195$

Step 4

Substitute 195 for x in one of the equations.

In this case, use equation (1).

$\quad x + y = 365$
$195 + y = 365$

Step 5

Solve for y.

$195 + y = 365$
$\qquad\quad y = 170$

Rebecca must replace x with 195 and y with 170 in both equations.

6. 15

To have an infinite number of solutions, the equations must be equivalent.

For the equation $-16x - 20y = 12$, divide both sides by -4 to get $4x + 5y = -3$.

For the equation $12x + Ky = -9$, divide both sides by 3 to get $4x + \dfrac{K}{3}y = -3$.

The coefficients for x are both 4, and the constant terms are equal. Therefore, the coefficients of y must also be equal.

Thus, $\dfrac{K}{3} = 5$.

Multiply both sides by 3.
$K = 15$

For the given system of linear equations to have an infinite number of solutions, the value of K is 15.

7. D

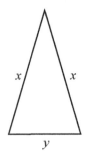

x is the length of each of the two equal sides.

y is the length of the base.

Create a system showing the two cases.

(1) $2x + y = 71$

(2) $y = 2x - 1$

Add 1 and subtract y from both sides.

$1 = 2x - y$

Thus, the system is as shown:

$2x + y = 71$

$2x - y = 1$

8. B

It is given that a represents the number of adult tickets sold and b represents the number of student tickets sold. It follows that $7a + 5b = 880$ is the equation showing income from sales, and $b = 3a$ is the equation showing the number of student tickets as three times the number of adult tickets.

9. D

Noel's graph starts at a higher point on the y-axis, indicating that there is an initial membership fee that must be paid. Steve has a better deal for the first 12 visits, since y-values are lower when x is between 0 and 12.

Both gyms cost the same for 13 visits. The fitness gym that Noel uses is most cost-effective after 13 visits, since the y-values are lower when x is greater than 13; therefore, it is false that Steve's gym would be the most cost-effective.

10. D

Let x = the number of pens purchased
Let y = the number of pencils purchased.

Create a system showing the two cases.
(1) $2x + 8y = 5.20$
(2) $3x + 4y = 5.80$

Multiply equation (2) by 2, then subtract the equations solving for x.
$2x + 8y = 5.20$
$6x + 8y = 11.60$
$-4x = -6.40$
$x = 1.60$

Thus, one pen costs $1.60.

11. a) OR

$I = Prt$
Substitute $2\ 500$ for P, 0.042 for r, and 1 for t.
$I = \$2\ 500 \times 0.042 \times 1$
$I = \$105$

Ken will earn $105 in interest at the end of the first year of his investment.

b) OR

Let x = the amount of money Ken invested at 4%.

Let y = the amount of money Ken invested at 3.5%.

Change percentages to decimals.
4% = 0.04 and 3.5% = 0.035
(1) $x + y = 6\ 000$
(2) $0.04x = 30 + 0.035y$

Equation (2) can be rewritten as
$40x = 30\ 000 + 35y$ when each term is multiplied by 1 000. Next, subtract 35 from both sides to get equation (2) as $40x - 35y = 30\ 000$.

Equation (1) and (2) can be solved by using the method of elimination as shown.

$$
\begin{array}{r}
35 \times (1)\ \ 35x + 35y = 210\ 000 \\
(2)\ \ 40x - 35y = 30\ 000 \\
\hline
35 \times (1) + (2)\ \ \ \ \ \ \ \ 75x = 240\ 000 \\
x = 3\ 200
\end{array}
$$

The value of y can be determined by substituting $3\ 200$ for x in equation (1) as follows:
$x + y = 6\ 000$
$3\ 200 + y = 6\ 000$
$y = 2\ 800$

Ken invested $3\ 200 at 4% and $2\ 800 at 3.5%.

12. A

Step 1
Determine the coordinates of point A and B.

Looking at the graph point A is at the coordinates $(-4, -1)$ and point B is at the coordinates $(6, 5)$.

Step 2
Determine the midpoint (x, y), using the midpoint formula $(x, y) = \left(\dfrac{x_1 + x_2}{2}, \dfrac{y_1 + y_2}{2}\right)$.

Let $(x_1, y_1) = (-4, -1)$ and $(x_2, y_2) = (6, 5)$.

Substitute the values into the midpoint formula, and simplify.
$$(x, y) = \left(\dfrac{x_1 + x_2}{2}, \dfrac{y_1 + y_2}{2}\right)$$
$$(x, y) = \left(\dfrac{-4 + 6}{2}, \dfrac{-1 + 5}{2}\right)$$
$$(x, y) = \left(\dfrac{2}{2}, \dfrac{4}{2}\right)$$
$$(x, y) = (1, 2)$$

Therefore, the midpoint of the line segment AB is $(1, 2)$.

13. D

Let (x, y) be the other endpoint.

Using the midpoint formula:

$$\dfrac{6 + x}{2} = 2 \qquad \dfrac{5 + y}{2} = -3$$

Multiply both sides of each equation by 2.

$6 + x = 4 \qquad 5 + y = -6$

Solve for x.   Solve for y.

$x = -2 \qquad\quad y = -11$

The other endpoint is $(-2, -11)$.

14. C

The point $(-1, 2)$ is the midpoint of the line segment with endpoints that are $(a, -4)$ and $(-7, b)$.
The values of a and b are

$$(-1, 2) = \left(\frac{a + (-7)}{2}, \frac{-4 + b}{2}\right)$$

$$\therefore -1 = a + \frac{-7}{2}, \qquad 2 = \frac{-4 + b}{2}$$

$$a + (-7) = -2, \qquad 4 = -4 + b$$
$$a - 7 = -2, \qquad b = 4 + 4$$
$$a = 7 - 2 = 5, \quad b = 8$$

Hence, the values of a and b are 5 and 8, respectively.

15. D

The length of line segment AB can be calculated using the distance formula.

$$d = \sqrt{(x_2 - x_1)^2 + (y_2 - y_1)^2}$$

Use $A(0, 5)$ as point 1 and $B(-3, 1)$ as point 2.

$$d(\overline{AB}) = \sqrt{(-3 - 0)^2 + (1 - 5)^2}$$

$$AB = \sqrt{9 + 16} = \sqrt{25}$$

$$AB = 5$$

The length of line segment AB is 5 units.

16. C

Using the distance formula:

$$d = \sqrt{(1 - a)^2 + (1 - (-3))^2}$$

$$5 = \sqrt{(1 - a)^2 + 4^2}$$

$$5 = \sqrt{(1 - a)^2 + 16}$$

Square both sides.

$$25 = (1 - a)^2 + 16$$

Subtract 16 from both sides.

$$9 = (1 - a)^2$$

Take the square root of both sides.

$$\pm 3 = 1 - a$$

$$\begin{array}{ll} 3 = 1 - a & -3 = 1 - a \\ 2 = -a & \text{or} \quad -4 = -a \end{array}$$

Solve for a in both cases.
$-2 = a$, or $4 = a$

Since distance must be a positive value, one possible solution for a is 4.

17. A

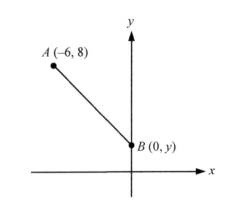

Using the distance formula:

$$d_{AB} = \sqrt{(-6 - 0)^2 + (8 - y)^2}$$

$$10 = \sqrt{(-6)^2 + (8 - y)^2} \text{ (Note: } d_{AB} \text{ is 10 as given)}$$

$$10 = \sqrt{36 + (8 - y)^2}$$

Square both sides.

$$100 = 36 + (8 - y)^2$$

Subtract 36 from both sides.

$$64 = (8 - y)^2$$

Take the square root of both sides.
$$\pm 8 = 8 - y$$

Solve for y in both cases.
$$\begin{array}{ll} 8 = 8 - y & -8 = 8 - y \\ 0 = -y & \text{or } -16 = -y \\ 0 = y & 16 = y \end{array}$$

Point B could be $(0, 0)$ or $(0, 16)$ using the two possible solutions for y.

18. 20.6

Perimeter of triangle $ABC = \overline{AB} + \overline{AC} + \overline{BC}$
Use the distance formula.

$$d = \sqrt{(x_2 - x_1)^2 + (y_2 - y_1)^2}$$

$$d(\overline{AB}) = \sqrt{(5 - 3)^2 + (-2 - 1)^2}$$
$$= \sqrt{4 + 9}$$
$$= \sqrt{13}$$

$$d(\overline{AC}) = \sqrt{(-3 - 3)^2 + (-5 - 1)^2}$$
$$= \sqrt{36 + 36} = \sqrt{72}$$

$$d(\overline{BC}) = \sqrt{(-3 - 5)^2 + (-5 + 2)^2}$$
$$= \sqrt{64 + 9} = \sqrt{73}$$

The perimeter of triangle ABC
$$= d(\overline{AB}) + d(\overline{AC}) + d(\overline{BC})$$
$$= \sqrt{13} + \sqrt{72} + \sqrt{73}$$
$$= 20.6 \text{ units}$$

19. A

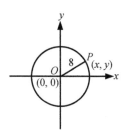

Let any point on the circumference of the circle be $P(x, y)$.

The radius of the circle is OP.

$$\Rightarrow (OP) = 8 \text{ units}$$
$$\Rightarrow \sqrt{(x - 0)^2 + (y - 0)^2} = 8$$
$$\Rightarrow x^2 + y^2 = 64$$

The circle that has a radius of 8 units with its centre located at the origin has an equation of $x^2 + y^2 = 64$.

20. D

Determine an expression for the radius, r, in the equation of a circle given by the equation $x^2 + y^2 = r^2$.

Recall that the radius of a circle is $\frac{1}{2}$ the diameter.

Use the distance formula to determine the diameter of this circle.

$$d = \sqrt{(x_2 - x_1)^2 + (y_2 - y_1)^2}$$
$$d = \sqrt{(a - c)^2 + (b - d)^2}$$

Therefore, the radius will be

$$= \frac{\sqrt{(a - c)^2 + (b - d)^2}}{2}$$

If $x^2 + y^2 = r^2$ is the equation of a circle with its centre at $(0, 0)$, substitute the expression for the radius into this equation.

$$x^2 + y^2 = \left(\frac{\sqrt{(a - c)^2 + (b - d)^2}}{2}\right)^2$$
$$x^2 + y^2 = \frac{(a - c)^2 + (b - d)^2}{4}$$

Therefore, the equation of this circle could be

$$x^2 + y^2 = \frac{(a - c)^2 + (b - d)^2}{4}.$$

21. B

In the diagram, the radius of the circle is 6 units, and the centre of the circle is at $(0, 0)$. In order to write the equation of the circle, substitute 6 for r in the equation $x^2 + y^2 = r^2$.

$$x^2 + y^2 = (6)^2$$
$$x^2 + y^2 = 36$$

Thus, the equation that defines the circle with centre $(0, 0)$ and a radius of 6 units is $x^2 + y^2 = 36$.

22. C

The minimum length of the required border can be found by determining the circumference of the circle. Recall that circumference (C) is equal to $2\pi r$. To determine the circumference of the flower bed, identify the measure of the radius of the flower bed.

Since the equation $x^2 + y^2 = r^2$ represents a circle with centre $(0, 0)$ and radius r, it follows that for the equation $x^2 + y^2 = 2.89$, the value of r^2 is 2.89.

Solve for r.

$$r^2 = 2.89$$
$$r = \sqrt{2.89}$$
$$= 1.7 \text{ m}$$

Now, substitute 1.7 for r in the circumference formula.

$$C = 2\pi r$$
$$C = 2\pi(1.7)$$
$$C \approx 10.681 \text{ m}$$

Therefore, the minimum length of the required border material, rounded to the nearest tenth of a metre, is 10.7 m.

23. 4.2

Since the equation $x^2 + y^2 = r^2$ represents a circle with centre $(0, 0)$ and radius r, it follows that:

$$r^2 = 18$$
$$r = \sqrt{18} = 4.2$$

Thus, the radius of the circle $x^2 + y^2 = 18$ is 4.2 units.

24. C

Step 1

Determine the point where the horizontal line from point $(4, -7)$ intersects the line defined by the equation $y = -\dfrac{1}{3}x + 2$.

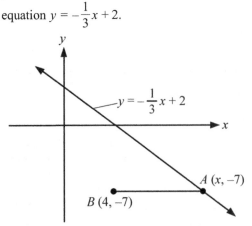

For point A on the line to be horizontally-aligned with point $B(4, -7)$, it must have the same y-coordinate. Therefore, point A must have an ordered pair of the form $(x, -7)$.

To determine the x-coordinate of the point of intersection, substitute -7 for y in the equation of the line $y = -\dfrac{1}{3}x + 2$, and solve for x.

$$-7 = -\frac{1}{3}x + 2$$
$$-9 = -\frac{1}{3}x$$
$$27 = x$$

Therefore, the point of intersection A occurs at $(27, -7)$.

Step 2

Determine the horizontal distance from point $A(4, -7)$ to point $B(27, -7)$ using the distance formula.

$$d = \sqrt{(x_2 - x_1)^2 + (y_2 - y_1)^2}$$
$$d = \sqrt{(4 - 27)^2 + (-7 - (-7))^2}$$
$$d = \sqrt{(-23)^2 + (-7 + 7)^2}$$
$$d = \sqrt{(-23)^2 + (0)^2}$$
$$d = 23$$

Thus, the horizontal distance is 23 units.

25. B

First, find all the midpoints.

$$M_{AB} = \left(\frac{-3 + 1}{2}, \frac{-4 + 4}{2}\right) = (-1, 0)$$

$$M_{AC} = \left(\frac{-3 + 3}{2}, \frac{-4 + 0}{2}\right) = (0, -2)$$

$$M_{BC} = \left(\frac{1 + 3}{2}, \frac{4 + 0}{2}\right) = (2, 2)$$

Let these midpoints be $P(-1, 0)$, $Q(0, -2)$, and $R(2, 2)$.

Now, find the distances of PQ, PR, and QR.

$$d_{PQ} = \sqrt{(-1 - 0)^2 + (0 - (-2))^2}$$
$$d_{PQ} = \sqrt{(-1)^2 + 2^2}$$
$$d_{PQ} = \sqrt{5}$$
$$d_{PQ} = 2.24$$

$$d_{PR} = \sqrt{(-1 - 2)^2 + (0 - 2)^2}$$
$$d_{PR} = \sqrt{(-3)^2 + (-2)^2}$$
$$d_{PR} = \sqrt{13}$$
$$d_{PR} = 3.61$$

$$d_{QR} = \sqrt{(0 - 2)^2 + (-2 - 2)^2}$$
$$d_{QR} = \sqrt{(-2)^2 + (-4)^2}$$
$$d_{QR} = \sqrt{20}$$
$$d_{QR} = 4.47$$

Thus, the perimeter is $2.24 + 3.61 + 4.47 = 10.32$ or 10.3 units.

26. A

The shortest distance from a point to a line is the perpendicular distance from the point to the line.

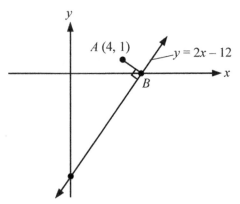

In the given graph, the line segment AB is perpendicular to the line $y = 2x - 12$.

Step 1
Determine the slope of the perpendicular line segment AB.

The slope, m, of the line $y = 2x - 12$ is 2 (coefficient of x).

The slope of AB (as shown in the diagram) is $-\frac{1}{2}$.

It is the negative reciprocal of 2.

Step 2
Determine the equation that defines line segment AB.

Apply the point slope formula of a line using the point $(4, 1)$ and the slope of $-\frac{1}{2}$.

$$y = m(x - x_1) + y_1$$
$$y = -\frac{1}{2}(x - 4) + 1$$
$$y = -\frac{1}{2}x + \frac{4}{2} + 1$$
$$y = -\frac{1}{2}x + 3$$

The equation of line segment AB is $y = -\frac{1}{2}x + 3$.

Step 3
Determine the point of intersection B.

The point of intersection B can be determined by solving the system involving the two equations.

1. $y = 2x - 12$

2. $y = -\frac{1}{2}x + 3$

Solve by substitution.
$$-\frac{1}{2}x + 3 = 2x - 12$$

Multiply both sides by 2.
$$-x + 6 = 4x - 24$$
$$6 = 5x - 24$$
$$30 = 5x$$
$$6 = x$$

Substitute 6 for x into the equation $y = 2x - 12$ to find the y-coordinate of point B.
$$y = 2(6) - 12$$
$$y = 0$$

The point of intersection B is $(6, 0)$.

Step 4
Determine the distance from $A(4, 1)$ to $B(6, 0)$ by applying the distance formula.

$$d_{AB} = \sqrt{(x_2 - x_1)^2 + (y_2 - y_1)^2}$$
$$= \sqrt{(4 - 6)^2 + (1 - 0)^2}$$
$$= \sqrt{(-2)^2 + (1)^2}$$
$$= \sqrt{4 + 1}$$
$$= \sqrt{5}$$

To the nearest hundredth, $d_{AB} \approx 2.24$.

The shortest distance from $(4, 1)$ to the line $y = 2x - 12$ is approximately 2.24 units.

27. **a) OR**

The centre of the circle can be found by determining the midpoint of the diameter as shown:

$$m = \left(\frac{x_1 + x_2}{2}, \frac{y_1 + y_2}{2}\right)$$
$$m_{AB} = \left(\frac{-2 + 4}{2}, \frac{3 + 11}{2}\right)$$
$$m_{AB} = (1, 7)$$

The coordinates of the centre of the circle are $(1, 7)$.

b) OR

The radius is half the length of the diameter. The length of the diameter can be determined by applying the distance formula as shown:

$$d = \sqrt{(x_2 - x_1)^2 + (y_2 - y_1)^2}$$
$$d_{AB} = \sqrt{(4 - (-2))^2 + (11 - 3)^2}$$
$$d_{AB} = \sqrt{(6)^2 + (8)^2}$$
$$d_{AB} = \sqrt{36 + 64}$$
$$d_{AB} = \sqrt{100}$$
$$d_{AB} = 10$$

Since the diameter is 10 units in length, the radius is 5 units in length.

c) OR

If the point $P(-3, 10)$ is on the circle, then the distance from the centre, C, of the circle to this point must be 5 units in length. Verify this by applying the distance formula as shown:

$$d = \sqrt{(x_2 - x_1)^2 + (y_2 - y_1)^2}$$

Recall the centre of the circle is at $(1, 7)$.

$$d_{CP} = \sqrt{(-3 - 1)^2 + (10 - 7)^2}$$

$$d_{CP} = \sqrt{(-4)^2 + (3)^2}$$

$$d_{CP} = \sqrt{16 + 9}$$

$$d_{CP} = \sqrt{25}$$

$$d_{CP} = 5$$

Since CP is 5 units in length, point P must be on the circle.

28. B

A line segment that bisects any side of a triangle and makes a right angle at the midpoint is known as the perpendicular bisector of that side of the triangle. Thus, line segment PT is the perpendicular bisector of side QR.

29. D

A quadrilateral in which all four sides (both sets of opposite sides) are equal in length, the opposite sides are parallel, and the adjacent sides are perpendicular is called a square. Only in a square will the diagonals bisect each other at $90°$

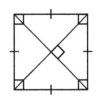

30. D

Step 1

Sketch a diagram

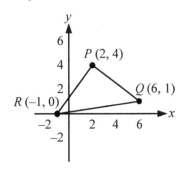

Step 2

Calculate the slope of each side of the triangle.

Apply the slope formula $m = \dfrac{y_2 - y_1}{x_2 - x_1}$.

$$m_{PQ} = \frac{4 - 1}{2 - 6}$$
$$= -\frac{3}{4}$$

$$m_{PR} = \frac{4 - 0}{2 - (-1)}$$
$$= \frac{4}{3}$$

$$m_{RQ} = \frac{0 - 1}{-1 - 6}$$
$$= \frac{-1}{-7}$$
$$= \frac{1}{7}$$

Since the slopes of PQ and PR are negative reciprocals, there is a right angle at P.

Step 3

Calculate the length of each side of the triangle. Apply the distance formula

$$d = \sqrt{(x_2 - x_1)^2 + (y_2 - y_1)^2}.$$

$$d_{PQ} = \sqrt{(2 - 6)^2 + (4 - 1)^2}$$
$$= \sqrt{(-4)^2 + 3^2}$$
$$= \sqrt{25}$$
$$= 5 \text{ units}$$

$$d_{PR} = \sqrt{(2 - (-1))^2 + (4 - 0)^2}$$
$$= \sqrt{3^2 + 4^2}$$
$$= \sqrt{25}$$
$$= 5 \text{ units}$$

$$d_{RQ} = \sqrt{(6 - (-1))^2 + (1 - 0)^2}$$
$$= \sqrt{7^2 + 1^2}$$
$$= \sqrt{50} \text{ units}$$

Therefore, $PQ = PR$. The triangle is an isosceles triangle since the lengths of two sides are equal. $\triangle PQR$ is a right isosceles triangle.

31. B

Step 1

Find the slope of JK.

$$m_{JK} = \frac{-2 - 3}{3 - (-1)} = -\frac{5}{4}$$

Therefore, because LN is perpendicular to JK, the slope of LN must be $\dfrac{4}{5}$, which is the negative reciprocal of $-\dfrac{5}{4}$.

Step 2

Find the coordinates of point N.

Let N be the point $(0, y)$ because N is on the y-axis. Use the slope formula to determine the y-coordinate of N.

$$\frac{y_2 - y_1}{x_2 - x_1} = m$$

Substitute $m = \frac{4}{5}$ for the slope and points L $(5, 1)$ and $N(0, y)$.

$$\frac{y - 1}{0 - 5} = \frac{4}{5}$$

$$\frac{y - 1}{-5} = \frac{4}{5}$$

$$5(y - 1) = 4(-5)$$

$$5y - 5 = -20$$

$$5y = -15$$

$$y = -3$$

The coordinates of point N are $(0, -3)$.

32. 2

Begin by finding the slope of the given line segment.

$$m = \frac{y_2 - y_1}{x_2 - x_1}$$

$$m = \frac{15 - 7}{5 - 3}$$

$$m = \frac{8}{2} = 4$$

Since the lines are perpendicular to one another, their respective slopes are negative reciprocals of each other $(m_1 \times m_2 = -1)$.

Therefore, the slope of the line perpendicular to the line that passes through the given points is $-\frac{1}{4}$.

Use the slope formula again for the perpendicular line.

$$m = \frac{y_2 - y_1}{x_2 - x_1}$$

$$m = \frac{-5 - (-6)}{-2 - a}$$

$$m = \frac{-5 + 6}{-2 - a} = \frac{1}{-2 - a}$$

Since the slope is $-\frac{1}{4}$,

$$\frac{1}{-2 - a} = -\frac{1}{4}$$

$$4 = -(-2 - a)$$

$$4 = 2 + a$$

$$2 = a$$

The value of a is 2.

33. A

The first error occurs in step 1 because the student is asked to verify that the *diagonals* of the quadrilateral are equal in length. Alex's solution is attempting to verify that the opposite sides of the quadrilateral are equal in length.

As shown in the sketch, the diagonals are line segments AD and BC and not AC and BD.

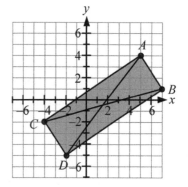

34. B

Step 1

Determine the midpoint of line segment AB since the perpendicular bisector will pass through this point.

$$M_{AB} = \left(\frac{x_1 + x_2}{2}, \frac{y_1 + y_2}{2}\right)$$

$$M_{AB} = \left(\frac{-8 + 4}{2}, \frac{6 + 6}{2}\right)$$

$$M_{AB} = \left(\frac{-4}{2}, \frac{12}{2}\right)$$

$$M_{AB} = (-2, 6)$$

Step 2

The perpendicular bisector must be a vertical line passing through the point $(-2, 6)$. All points on the vertical line will be equidistant from either endpoint. Therefore, the x-coordinate of any ordered pair on the perpendicular bisector must have a value of -2. The sketch illustrates the preceding statements.

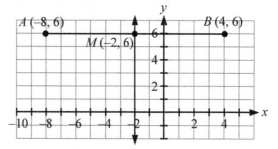

Step 3

The only possible point that can be verified geometrically will be the point $(-2, 14)$, since it will also be on the line $x = -2$, which is the equation of the perpendicular bisector of segment AB.

Step 4

Verify algebraically that $d_{PA} = d_{PB}$ by applying the distance formula, $d = \sqrt{(x_2 - x_1)^2 + (y_2 - y_1)^2}$.

Substitute -2 for x and 14 for y for point P. As well, substitute $A(-8, 6)$ and $B(4, 6)$ in the distance formula to determine if $d_{PA} = d_{PB}$.

$$\sqrt{(x - (-8))^2 + (y - 6)^2} = \sqrt{(x - 4)^2 + (y - 6)^2}$$
$$\sqrt{(-2 - (-8))^2 + (14 - 6)^2} = \sqrt{(-2 - 4)^2 + (14 - 6)^2}$$
$$\sqrt{6^2 + 8^2} = \sqrt{(-6)^2 + 8^2}$$
$$\sqrt{36 + 64} = \sqrt{36 + 64}$$
$$\sqrt{100} = \sqrt{100}$$
$$10 = 10$$

Therefore, since $d_{PA} = d_{PB}$, the point $(-2, 14)$ is a possible point on the perpendicular bisector of AB.

35. C

Step 1

Graph the given points, $A(-9, -2)$, $B(-6, 5)$, and $C(0, 19)$, and draw a line to connect each segment, AB and BC.

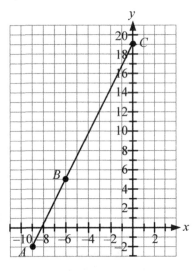

Step 2

The method of determining the slope of each segment can be used to prove that the points are collinear since the slope of a line is constant. Using the graph, the slope of segments AB, BC, and AC are all $m = \dfrac{7}{3}$

Step 3

The method of finding the distance from point A to C compared to the sum of the distances from A to B and B to C can be used to show the points are collinear. A basic ruler can be used for this.

Step 4

The method of determining the midpoint of each segment can not be used to prove that the three points are collinear. There is no guarantee that the three chosen points are equally spaced apart since any three points along the line can be used to test for a collinear relationship.

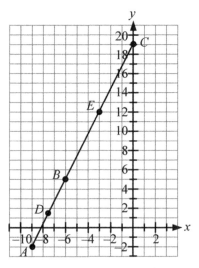

The midpoint of line segment AB (point D on the graph) is not equal to the midpoint of line segment BC (point E on the graph).

36. a) OR

AD is perpendicular to DC given that $\angle ADC = 90°$. The value of k can be determining by making use of the slope formula, $m = \dfrac{y_2 - y_1}{x_2 - x_1}$.

Slope of $AD = \dfrac{-9 - 1}{2 - (-4)}$

$= \dfrac{-10}{6}$

$= \dfrac{-5}{3}$

Slope of $DC = \dfrac{k - (-9)}{12 - 2}$

$= \dfrac{k + 9}{10}$

Since $AD \perp DC$,

$\dfrac{3}{5} = \dfrac{k + 9}{10}$ (The negative reciprocal of $\dfrac{-5}{3}$ is $\dfrac{3}{5}$.)

Cross multiply.
$5k + 45 = 30$
$5k = -15$
$k = -3$

The value of k is -3.

b) OR

The value of n can be found given that AD is parallel to BC and by making use of the slope formula.

Slope of $AD = -\dfrac{5}{3}$ as determined above.

Slope of $BC = \dfrac{7 - (-3)}{n - 12}$, since $k = -3$.

$= \dfrac{7 + 3}{n - 12}$

$= \dfrac{10}{n - 12}$

Since AD is parallel to BC, it follows that

$\dfrac{-5}{3} = \dfrac{10}{n - 12}$

Cross multiply.
$-5n + 60 = 30$
$-5n = -30$
$\quad n = 6$

The value of $n = 6$.

c) OR

Verify that quadrilateral $ABCD$ is a square by showing that each side of quadrilateral $ABCD$ is equal in length. The length of each side can be determined by using the distance formula.

$d = \sqrt{(x_2 - x_1)^2 + (y_2 - y_1)^2}$

$d_{AB} = \sqrt{(6 - (-4))^2 + (7 - 1)^2}$ Recall $n = 6$.

$d_{AB} = \sqrt{(10)^2 + (6)^2}$

$d_{AB} = \sqrt{100 + 36}$

$d_{AB} = \sqrt{136}$

$d_{BC} = \sqrt{(12 - 6)^2 + (-3 - 7)^2}$ Recall $k = -3$.

$d_{BC} = \sqrt{(6)^2 + (-10)^2}$

$d_{BC} = \sqrt{36 + 100}$

$d_{BC} = \sqrt{136}$

$d_{CD} = \sqrt{(2 - 12)^2 + (-9 - (-3))^2}$

$d_{CD} = \sqrt{(-10)^2 + (-6)^2}$

$d_{CD} = \sqrt{100 + 36}$

$d_{CD} = \sqrt{136}$

$d_{AD} = \sqrt{(2 - (-4))^2 + (-9 - 1)^2}$

$d_{AD} = \sqrt{(6)^2 + (-10)^2}$

$d_{AD} = \sqrt{36 + 100}$

$d_{AD} = \sqrt{136}$

Since $d_{AB} = d_{BC} = d_{CD} = d_{AD}$, quadrilateral $ABCD$ is a square.

UNIT TEST — ANALYTIC GEOMETRY

Use the following information to answer the next question.

A System of Linear Equations
$4x + 2y = 20$
$x - 3y = 12$

1. The value of x in the solution to the system is

   A. -6 B. -2

   C. 6   D. 18

Use the following information to answer the next question.

The given system of linear equations can be solved using the elimination method. To eliminate y by addition, the first equation is multiplied by 3.
$-3x - 4y = -2$
$5x + 6y = 4$

2. The second equation must be multiplied by

   A. -4   B. -2

   C. 2   D. 4

3. The value of y in the solution to the system of linear equations $x + y = 1$ and $5x - 2y = -16$ is

   A. 3   B. -2

   C. -3 D. -7

Use the following information to answer the next question.

The solution to the system of linear equations $x - \dfrac{1}{3}y = 2$ and $3x + 2y - 24 = 0$ is obtained using the method of substitution.

4. A possible substitution that could be made to solve this system is to replace

   A. x with $\dfrac{y + 2}{2}$

   B. x with $1 + 2y$

   C. y with $1 - 2x$

   D. y with $\dfrac{24 - 3x}{2}$

Use the following information to answer the next question.

A system of linear equations is given.
$11y = -ax + 4$
$3y = -45x + 13$

Numerical Response

5. To the nearest whole number, what is the value of a if the system has no solutions? _____

Use the following information to answer the next question.

To make a special blend of two teas, a store owner wants to mix Orange Blossom tea, selling at $6.40 per kilogram, with Red Dragon tea, selling at $7.20 per kilogram. He will sell 10 kg of the blended tea at $6.72 per kilogram. If he lets x represent the number of kilograms of Orange Blossom tea and y represent the number of kilograms of Red Dragon tea, he will be able to find out how much of each type of tea he needs for the blend.

6. The system of linear equations that can be solved to determine the amounts of tea needed to make the blended tea is

   A. $x + y = 10$
   $6.40x + 7.20y = 6.72$

   B. $6.40x + 7.20y = 10$
   $x + y = 6.72$

   C. $x + y = 10$
   $6.40x + 7.20y = 67.20$

   D. $6.40x + 7.20y = 10$
   $6.40x + 7.20 = 67.20$

Use the following information to answer the next question.

The sum of the present ages of Samantha and Jocelyn is 22 years. In four years, Samantha will be twice as old as Jocelyn.

7. If x represents the present age of Samantha and y represents the present age of Jocelyn, then the system of linear equations that could be solved in order to determine the present age of each girl is

   A. $x + y = 22$ and $x - 2y = 4$

   B. $x + y = 22$ and $x = 2(y - 4)$

   C. $x + y = 22$ and $x = 2(y + 4)$

   D. $x + y = 22$ and $2x - y = -4$

8. Two numbers have a sum of 80. If the larger number is 10 more than the smaller, then the smaller number is

   A. 30   B. 35

   C. 50   D. 55

Use the following information to answer the next multipart question.

9. Crates of oranges have a different mass depending on the number of oranges in the crate. A crate contains 18 larger oranges, each with a mass of 0.15 kg.

   Open Response

   a) If the crate has a mass of 0.50 kg, what is the total mass of the crate of oranges?

   b) Set up a system of two linear equations involving two variables, and then use this system to solve the following problem. Show your work.

   A crate of 48 smaller oranges has a total mass of 6.75 kg. When 12 oranges are removed, the total mass becomes 5.25 kg. If each orange has the same mass, determine the mass of the crate and the mass of a smaller orange.

10. The point $M(2, 4)$ is at the midpoint of the line segment, where $A(8, 4)$ and $B(x, y)$. The coordinates of point B are

    A. $(-4, 4)$ B. $(4, -4)$

    C. $(4, 5)$ D. $(5, 4)$

Use the following information to answer the next question.

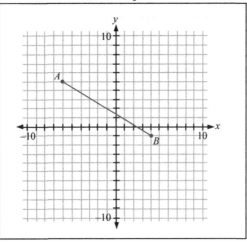

11. The midpoint of line segment *AB* is
  A. $(-1, 2)$ **B.** $(-2, 1)$
  C. $(2, 1)$ **D.** $(-1, 1)$

Use the following information to answer the next question.

Points $C(4.2, -1.9)$ and $D(-3.6, -6.7)$ are the endpoints of line segment *CD*.

12. Which of the following expressions represents the length of line segment *CD*?
  A. $\sqrt{(4.2 + 3.6)^2 + ((-1.9) - 6.7)^2}$
  B. $\sqrt{(4.2 - (-1.9))^2 + ((-3.6) - (6.7))^2}$
  C. $\sqrt{(4.2 - (-6.7))^2 + ((-1.9) - (-3.6))^2}$
  D. $\sqrt{(4.2 - (-3.6))^2 + ((-1.9) - (-6.7))^2}$

13. The distance formula can **best** be derived by
  A. applying the concept of $\dfrac{\text{rise}}{\text{run}}$
  B. applying the Pythagorean theorem
  C. determining how far each of two given points is from the origin
  D. placing two given points on a coordinate system and then measuring the distance between the two points with a ruler

Numerical Response

14. Point *A* is 10 km west of point *B*, point *C* is 30 km north of point *B*, and point *D* is 20 km east of point *C*. What is the distance from *A* to *D*?

_____

(To the nearest tenth)

Use the following information to answer the next question.

A circle with a centre of $(0, 0)$ and passing through the point $(3, 4)$ is shown.

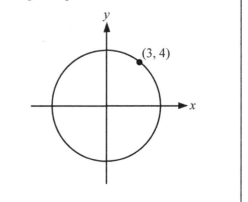

15. Another point that this circle will pass through is
  A. $(-5, 5)$ **B.** $(0, 25)$
  C. $(4, -5)$ **D.** $(-4, -3)$

Two concentric circles are shown in the diagram.

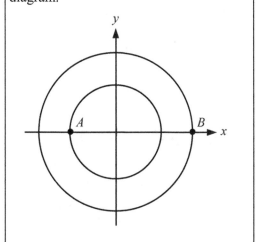

16. If the smaller circle is defined by the equation $x^2 + y^2 = 9$ and the larger circle is defined by the equation $x^2 + y^2 = 25$, then the distance from point A to point B is

   A. 2 units   B. 8 units

   C. 16 units   D. 34 units

A circle has its centre at $(0, 0)$, and a diameter that is 16 units in length.

17. The equation that defines this circle is

   A. $x^2 + y^2 = 8$

   B. $x^2 + y^2 = 16$

   C. $x^2 + y^2 = 64$

   D. $x^2 + y^2 = 256$

The diagram illustrates Mrs. Ruby's circular flower bed, sketched on a Cartesian plane.

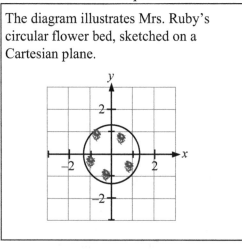

Numerical Response

18. The equation that defines the outside edge of Mrs. Ruby's flower bed is $x^2 + y^2 = 1.44$, where the radius is expressed in metres. So the flowers do not become root-bound, the minimum area allocated to each flower is 0.09 m^2. The maximum number of flowers Mrs. Ruby can plant in her flower bed is

19. To the nearest tenth, the vertical distance between the point $(-5, -4)$ and the line $2x + 3y + 15 = 0$ is

   A. 1.0 units   B. 2.3 units

   C. 3.3 units   D. 5.7 units

20. If a line segment has endpoints at points $C(-5, -4)$ and $D(1, 1)$, then the equation of the perpendicular bisector of the line segment CD will be

   A. $y = \dfrac{-6}{5}x - \dfrac{39}{10}$

   B. $y = \dfrac{5}{6}x - 4$

   C. $y = \dfrac{-6}{5}x + 4$

   D. $y = -\dfrac{5}{6}x + \dfrac{1}{6}$

Open Response

21. To the nearest tenth, determine the shortest distance between point $P(-4, 8)$ and point $Q(-9, -7)$. Show your work.

Open Response

22. To the nearest tenth, determine the shortest distance between point $P(-4, 8)$ and the line defined by the equation $y = 2x + 1$. Show your work.

23. In which of the following types of quadrilaterals do the diagonals **not** bisect each other?

   A. Square   **B.** Rectangle

   C. Trapezoid   **D.** Parallelogram

24. The points $P(-4, 0)$, $Q(0, \sqrt{48})$, and $R(4, 0)$ are the vertices of triangle PQR. If the length of side PQ is 8 units, then $\triangle PQR$ is

   A. a scalene triangle

   B. an isosceles triangle

   C. a right angle triangle

   D. an equilateral triangle

25. Which of the following pairs of equations represents a pair of perpendicular lines?

   A. $y = x - 4$ and $y = x + \dfrac{1}{4}$

   B. $y = 75x$ and $y = -75x$

   C. $y = -3x + 7$ and $y = -\dfrac{1}{3}x + 4$

   D. $y = 4x - 5$ and $y = -\dfrac{1}{4}x + 5$

Numerical Response

26. Two of the vertices of $\triangle ABC$ are $A(6, 5)$ and $B(8, 4)$. If $\angle ABC = 90°$, then vertex C could be the ordered pair $(d, -2)$. The value of d is _____.

Use the following information to answer the next question.

Jody and Brittany are asked to verify that $\triangle ABC$ with vertices $A(-3, 1)$, $B(-1, 5)$, and $C(5, 2)$ is a right triangle with $\angle ABC = 90°$. Each student's partial solution is shown below.

Jody's Partial Solution

It is given that $\angle ABC = 90°$. In order to verify that $\triangle ABC$ is a right triangle, it is necessary to verify that segments AB and BC are perpendicular.

Step 1:

Slope of $AB = \dfrac{5 - 1}{-1 - (-3)} = \dfrac{4}{2} = 2$

Step 2:

Slope of $BC = \dfrac{2 - 5}{5 - (-1)} = \dfrac{-3}{6}$

Brittany's Partial Solution

It is given that $\angle ABC = 90°$. In order to verify that $\triangle ABC$ is a right triangle, it is necessary to show that $(AB)^2 + (BC)^2 = (AC)^2$.

Step 1:

$AB = \sqrt{(-1 - (-3))^2 + (5 - 1)^2}$
$AB = \sqrt{(2)^2 + (4)^2}$
$AB = \sqrt{20}$

Step 2:

$BC = \sqrt{(5 - (-1))^2 + (2 - 5)^2}$
$BC = \sqrt{(6)^2 + (-3)^2}$
$BC = \sqrt{45}$

Step 3:

$AC = \sqrt{(5 - (-3))^2 + (2 - 1)^2}$

27. Which of the following statements is **true** with respect to the partial solution obtained by each of the two students?

  A. Both girls have a correct partial solution.

  B. Both girls have an incorrect partial solution.

  C. Jody has a correct partial solution, and Brittany has an incorrect partial solution.

  D. Jody has an incorrect partial solution, and Brittany has a correct partial solution.

28. The vertices of a parallelogram are $A(-4, -2)$, $B(-1, 2)$, $C(8, 6)$, and $D(6, 2)$. Which of the following methods could be used to determine that the diagonals AC and BD bisect each other?

  A. Verify that segment AC is perpendicular to segment BD.

  B. Verify that segment AC and segment BD have the same midpoint.

  C. Verify that the slope of segment AC is equal to the slope of segment BD.

  D. Verify that the length of segment AC is equal to the length of segment BD.

Use the following information to answer the next multipart question.

29. The vertices of a quadrilateral are $A(7, 6)$, $B(11, 2)$, $C(3, -6)$, and $D(1, 4)$.

Open Response

a) Sketch the quadrilateral on the following grid.

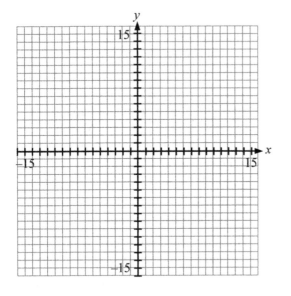

b) Determine the midpoint of each side of the quadrilateral. Show your work.

c) Verify that the quadrilateral formed by joining the four midpoints is a parallelogram.

ANSWERS AND SOLUTIONS — UNIT TEST

1. C	8. B	14. 42.4	21. OR	28. B
2. C	9. a) OR	15. D	22. OR	29. a) OR
3. A	b) OR	16. B	23. C	b) OR
4. D	10. A	17. C	24. D	c) OR
5. 165	11. A	18. 50	25. D	
6. C	12. D	19. B	26. 5	
7. A	13. B	20. A	27. A	

1. C

Solve as a system.

(1) $4x + 2y = 20$
(2) $x - 3y = 12$

(1) × 3 $12x + 6y = 60$
(2) × 2 $\underline{2x - 6y = 24}$
                        $14x = 84$
                              $x = 6$

2. C

Step 1
Label the equations.
① $3x - 4y = -2$
② $5x + 6y = 4$

Step 2
Multiply equation① by 3.
$3 × $ ① $-9x - 12y = -6$

Step 3
Determine the value by which the second equation must be multiplied.
In order to use addition to eliminate y, the coefficient of y in equation ② must be 12.
This can be obtained by multiplying equation ② by 2.

3. A

(1) $x + y = 1$
(2) $3x - 2y = -16$
(1) × 5 $5x + 5y = 5$
(2) $\underline{5x - 2y = -16}$
                        $7y = 21$
                          $y = 3$

4. D

Isolate the equation $3x + 2y - 24 = 0$ for y.
$3x + 2y - 24 = 0$
            $2y = 24 - 3x$
              $y = \dfrac{24 - 3x}{2}$

Thus, y could be replaced with $\dfrac{24 - 3x}{2}$.

5. 165

In order to have no solution, the lines must be parallel; they must have the same slope.

Step 1
Rewrite the equation $3y = -45x + 13$ in the slope-intercept form $y = mx + b$.
$3y = -45x + 13$
$y = \dfrac{-45x + 13}{3}$
$y = -15x + \dfrac{13}{3}$

For the line represented by this equation, the slope is -15.

Step 2
Rewrite the equation $11y = -ax + 4$ in the slope-intercept form $y = mx + b$.
$11y = -ax + 4$
$y = \dfrac{-ax + 4}{11}$
$y = -\dfrac{a}{11}x + \dfrac{4}{11}$

For the line represented by this equation, the slope is $\dfrac{-a}{11}$.

Step 3
Equate the slope from $y = -15x + \dfrac{13}{3}$ and the slope from $y = -\dfrac{a}{11}x + \dfrac{4}{11}$.

$-\dfrac{a}{11} = -15$
$-a = -165$
$a = 165$

If the system has no solutions, the value of a is 165.

6. C

Step 1
Create an equation for the total weight of the two blends.
① $x + y = 10$

Step 2

Create an equation for the total amount of sales.

- Let $6.40x$ be the amount made on the Orange Blossom tea.
- Let $7.20y$ be the amount made on the Red Dragon tea.
- The amount made on the blended tea is \$67.20 $(6.72 \times 10 = 67.20)$.

② $6.40x + 7.20y = 67.20$

This system of linear equations can be solved to determine the amounts of tea needed.

① $\qquad x + y = 10$
② $6.40x + 7.20y = 67.20$

7. A

Step 1

Write an equation to express the sum of their ages.
$x + y = 22$

Step 2

Write the equation to express their ages in four years.

- $x + 4 \to$ Samantha's age in 4 years
- $y + 4 \to$ Jocelyn's age in 4 years

Samantha is twice as old as Jocelyn in 4 years.
$x + 4 = 2(y + 4)$

Expand.
$x + 4 = 2y + 8$

Subtract 4 and $2y$ from both sides.
$$x + 4 = 2y + 8$$
$$x - 2y + 4 - 4 = 2y - 2y + 8 - 4$$
$$x - 2y = 4$$

The system is as shown:
① $\quad x + y = 22$
② $\quad x - 2y = 4$

8. B

Let x be the larger number.
Let y be the smaller number.

The numbers have a sum of 80.
(1) $x + y = 80$
The larger number is 10 more than the smaller.
(2) $x = y + 10$
Substitute $y + 10$ for x in (1).
$y + 10 + y = 80$
Simplify.
$2y + 10 = 80$
Subtract 10 from both sides.
$2y = 70$
Solve for y.
$y = 35$
Thus, the smaller number is 35.

9. a) OR

The total mass of the larger oranges is $18 \times 0.15 = 2.7$ kg. Therefore, the total mass of the crate of oranges is $2.7 + 0.50 + 3.2$ kg.

b) OR

Let $x =$ the mass of the crate.

Let $y =$ the mass of a smaller orange.

Thus, (1) $x + 48y = 6.75$
When 12 oranges are removed, 36 oranges remain.
(2) $x + 36y = 5.25$

Equations (1) and (2) can be solved by using the method of elimination as shown:

(1) $\qquad x + 48y = 6.75$
(2) $\qquad \underline{x + 36y = 5.25}$
(1) − (2) $\qquad 12y = 1.50$
$\qquad\qquad\qquad y = 0.125$

The value of x can be determined by substituting 0.125 for y in either equation (1) or (2). Using equation (1) has the following result:
$$x + 48y = 6.75$$
$$x + 48(0.125) = 6.75$$
$$x + 6 = 6.75$$
$$x = 0.75$$
The mass of the crate is 0.75 kg, and the mass of a smaller orange is 0.125 kg.

10. A

Using the midpoint formula:

$$\frac{8 + x}{2} = 2 \text{ and } \frac{4 + y}{2} = 4$$

Multiply both equations by 2.
$8 + x = 4$ and $4 + y = 8$

Solve for x and y.
$x = -4$ and $y = 4$

Thus, coordinates of point B are $(-4, 4)$.

11. A

Point A is at $(-6, 5)$.
Point B is at $(4, -1)$.
Use the midpoint formula.

$$M_{AB} = \left(\frac{x_1 + x_2}{2}, \frac{y_1 + y_2}{2} \right)$$

$$M_{AB} = \left(\frac{-6 + 4}{2}, \frac{5 + (-1)}{2} \right)$$

$$M_{AB} = (-1, 2)$$

12. D

Use the distance formula
$$d = \sqrt{(x_2 - x_1)^2 + (y_2 - y_1)^2}.$$

Substitute the values from points C and D into the formula.

$$d = \sqrt{(4.2 - (-3.6))^2 + ((-1.9) - (-6.7))^2}.$$

13. B

The distance formula is an application of the Pythagorean theorem.

14. 42.4

Set up a coordinate system where point B is represented by the origin.
Then, A is at $(-10, 0)$, C is at $(0, 30)$, and D is at $(20, 30)$.
Find the distance between $(-10, 0)$ and $(20, 30)$.
Recall that the distance between two points (x_1, y_1) and (x_2, y_2) is given by the formula
$$d(\overline{AD}) = \sqrt{(x_2 - x_1)^2 + (y_2 - y_1)^2}.$$
Use $A(-10, 0)$ as point 1 and $D(20, 30)$ as point 2.
$$d(\overline{AD}) = \sqrt{(20 + 10)^2 + (30 - 0)^2}$$
$$= \sqrt{(30)^2 + (30)^2} = \sqrt{900 + 900}$$
$$= \sqrt{1800} = 30\sqrt{2}$$
$$= 30 \times 1.414$$
$$= 42.4$$
The distance between A and D is 42.4 km.

15. D

The distance between the centre $(0, 0)$ and the point $(3, 4)$ is the radius of the circle. Find the length of the radius using the distance formula.
$$d = \sqrt{(x_2 - x_1)^2 + (y_2 - y_1)^2}$$
$$= \sqrt{(3 - 0)^2 + (4 - 0)^2}$$
$$= \sqrt{9 + 16}$$
$$= \sqrt{25}$$
$$= 5$$

Since the radius of the circle is 5 units, the distance from the centre to any other point on the circle must also be 5 units.

Determine the distance from the centre to each of the other points provided in each choice.

Choice A: For the point $(-5, 5)$:
$$d = \sqrt{(-5 - 0)^2 + (5 - 0)^2}$$
$$= \sqrt{25 + 25}$$
$$= \sqrt{50}$$
$$\cong 7.1$$

Choice B: For the point $(0, 25)$:
$$d = \sqrt{(0 - 0)^2 + (25 - 0)^2}$$
$$= \sqrt{0 + 625}$$
$$= \sqrt{625}$$
$$= 25$$

Choice C: For the point $(4, -5)$:
$$d = \sqrt{(4 - 0)^2 + (-5 - 0)^2}$$
$$= \sqrt{16 + 25}$$
$$= \sqrt{41}$$
$$\cong 6.4$$

Choice D: For the point $(-4, -3)$:
$$d = \sqrt{(-4 - 0)^2 + (-3 - 0)^2}$$
$$= \sqrt{16 + 9}$$
$$= \sqrt{25}$$
$$= 5$$

Since the point $(-4, -3)$ is 5 units from the centre, it is another point that this circle will pass through.

16. B

Since the equation $x^2 + y^2 = r^2$ represents a circle with centre of $(0, 0)$ and radius r, it follows that:
Smaller circle:
$$r^2 = 9$$
$$r = \sqrt{9} = 3$$

Larger circle:
$$r^2 = 25$$
$$r = \sqrt{25} = 5$$

Thus, the radii of the circles $x^2 + y^2 = 9$ and $x^2 + y^2 = 25$ are 3 and 5 units, respectively.

Label the diagram as follows:

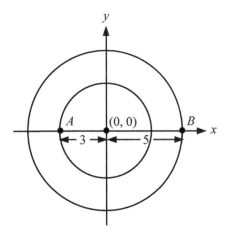

As the diagram shows, the distance from point A to point B can be found by adding the two radii together. Therefore, the distance from point A to point B is 8 units ($3 + 5 = 8$).

17. C

The equation of a circle is given by $x^2 + y^2 = r^2$.

Since the diameter is twice the length of the radius, the radius of the circle is 8 units.

To write the equation of the circle, substitute 8 for r in the equation $x^2 + y^2 = r^2$.
$$x^2 + y^2 = (8)^2$$
$$x^2 + y^2 = 64$$

Thus, the equation that defines a circle with its centre at $(0, 0)$ and a diameter of 16 units is $x^2 + y^2 = 64$.

18. 50

To determine the maximum number of flowers Mrs. Ruby can plant, first determine the total area of the flower bed. Recall that the area of a circle is $A = \pi r^2$. To solve, find the value of the radius of the flower bed. Since the equation $x^2 + y^2 = r^2$ represents a circle with a centre of $(0, 0)$ and a radius r, it follows that for the equation $x^2 + y^2 = 1.44$:
$$r^2 = 1.44$$
$$r = \sqrt{1.44} = 1.2 \text{ m}$$

Now, substitute 1.2 for r in the area formula for a circle, and solve for the area, A.
$$A = \pi r^2$$
$$A = \pi (1.2)^2$$
$$A = 1.44\pi$$
$$A \cong 4.5 \text{ m}^2$$

Since the minimum area allocated to each flower is 0.09 m^2, divide the total area of the flower bed by the minimum area of each flower.
$$\frac{4.5 \text{ m}^2}{0.09 \text{ m}^2} = 50$$

Therefore, the maximum number of flowers Mrs. Ruby can plant in her flower bed is 50.

19. B

For a point A on the line to be vertically-aligned with the given point, it must have the same x-coordinate as $B(-5, -4)$. Therefore, point A is $(-5, y)$.

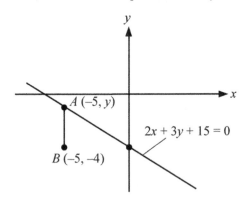

Step 1
Determine the y-coordinate of point A.
Since A is a point on the line, it satisfies the equation of the line. Substitute -5 for x in the equation of the line $2x + 3y + 15 = 0$, and solve for y.
$$2(-5) + 3y + 15 = 0$$
$$-10 + 3y + 15 = 0$$
$$3y + 5 = 0$$
$$3y = -5$$
$$y = -\frac{5}{3}$$

Step 2

Determine the length of AB by applying the distance formula.

$$d = \sqrt{(x_2 - x_1)^2 + (y_2 - y_1)^2}$$

$$d = \sqrt{(-5 - (-5))^2 + \left(-4 - \left(-\frac{5}{3}\right)\right)^2}$$

$$d = \sqrt{(-5 + 5)^2 + \left(-4 + \frac{5}{3}\right)^2}$$

$$d = \sqrt{(0)^2 + \left(-\frac{7}{3}\right)^2}$$

$$d = \frac{7}{3}$$

The vertical distance is $\frac{7}{3}$ or 2.3 units, to the nearest tenth.

20. A

Using the slope formula, find the slope of CD.

$$m = \frac{-4 - 1}{-5 - 1}$$

$$m = \frac{-5}{-6}$$

$$m = \frac{5}{6}$$

The slope of the perpendicular bisector will be $\frac{-6}{5}$, which is the negative reciprocal of $\frac{5}{6}$.

Find the midpoint of CD.

$$M_{CD} = \left(\frac{-5 + 1}{2}, \frac{-4 + 1}{2}\right)$$

$$M_{CD} = \left(-2, \frac{-3}{2}\right)$$

The perpendicular bisector of CD has a slope of $\frac{-6}{5}$ and passes through the point $\left(-2, \frac{-3}{2}\right)$.

Using the point-slope form, find the equation of this line.

$$y = m(x - x_1) + y_1$$

$$y = \frac{-6}{5}(x - (-2)) - \frac{3}{2}$$

$$y = -\frac{6}{5}(x + 2) - \frac{3}{2}$$

$$y = -\frac{6}{5}x - \frac{12}{5} - \frac{3}{2}$$

Use a common denominator.

$$y = -\frac{6}{5}x - \frac{24}{10} - \frac{15}{10}$$

$$y = -\frac{6}{5}x - \frac{39}{10}$$

21. OR

The shortest distance from point P to point Q is a line segment and can be determined by applying the distance formula as shown:

$$d = \sqrt{(x_2 - x_1)^2 + (y_2 - y_1)^2}$$

$$d_{PQ} = \sqrt{(-9 - (-4))^2 + (-7 - 8)^2}$$

$$d_{PQ} = \sqrt{(-5)^2 + (-15)^2}$$

$$d_{PQ} = \sqrt{25 + 225}$$

$$d_{PQ} = \sqrt{250}$$

$$d_{PQ} \approx 15.81$$

To the nearest tenth, the distance between point P and point Q is 15.8 units.

22. OR

The shortest distance from point P to the line $y = 2x + 1$ is the length of the line segment PQ, where point Q is on the line $y = 2x + 1$ and PQ is perpendicular to the line $y = 2x + 1$.

The first step is to determine the equation of PQ. The slope of the line $y = 2x + 1$ is 2 (the coefficient of x).

Therefore, the slope of PQ is $-\frac{1}{2}$ (since PQ is perpendicular to the line $y = 2x + 1$). The equation of line segment PQ can be found by applying the point-slope formula as shown below.

$$y = m(x - x_1) + y_1$$

Substitute $-\frac{1}{2}$ for m, -4 for x_1, and 8 for y_1.

$$y = -\frac{1}{2}(x - (-4)) + 8$$

$$y = -\frac{1}{2}(x + 4) + 8$$

$$y = -\frac{1}{2}x - 2 + 8$$

$$y = -\frac{1}{2}x + 6$$

Multiply each term by 2.

$$2y = -x + 12$$
$$2y = -x + 12$$
$$x + 2y = 12$$

The next step is to determine the coordinates of point Q by solving the system of linear equations $y = 2x + 1$ and $x + 2y = 12$. Solve this system of equations by using the method of substitution as follows:

(1) $\quad y = 2x + 1$
(2) $x + 2y = 12$

Substitute $2x + 1$ for y in equation (2).

$x + 2(2x + 1) = 12$

$\quad x + 4x + 2 = 12$

$\quad\quad 5x + 2 = 12$

$\quad\quad\quad 5x = 10$

$\quad\quad\quad\quad x = 2$

The value of y can be determined by substituting 2 for x in equation (1).

$(1)\, y = 2x + 1$

$\quad y = 2(2) + 1$

$\quad y = 4 + 1$

$\quad y = 5$

Thus, the coordinates of point Q are $(2, 5)$.

Finally, determine the distance from point P to point Q by using the distance formula as shown:

$$d = \sqrt{(x_2 - x_1)^2 + (y_2 - y_1)^2}$$

$$d_{PQ} = \sqrt{(2 - (-4))^2 + (5 - 8)^2}$$

$$d_{PQ} = \sqrt{(6)^2 + (-3)^2}$$

$$d_{PQ} = \sqrt{36 + 9}$$

$$d_{PQ} = \sqrt{45}$$

$$d_{PQ} \approx 6.71$$

To the nearest tenth, the shortest distance from point P to the line $y = 2x + 1$ is 6.7 units.

23. C

The diagonals of parallelograms, rectangles, and squares bisect each other. In a trapezoid, they do not bisect each other.

24. D

Step 1

Sketch the diagram.

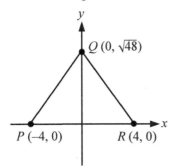

Step 2

Calculate the length of each side of the triangle using the distance formula.

$d_{PQ} = 8$ (given)

$d_{RQ} = \sqrt{(0 - 4)^2 + (\sqrt{48} - 0)^2}$

$d_{RQ} = \sqrt{(-4)^2 + (\sqrt{48})^2}$

$d_{RQ} = \sqrt{16 + 48}$

$d_{RQ} = \sqrt{64}$

$d_{RQ} = 8$

$d_{PR} = \sqrt{(4 - (-4))^2 + (0 - 0)^2}$

$\quad\quad = \sqrt{64}$

$\quad\quad = 8$

$d_{PR} = 8$ (the horizontal distance from P to R)

All three sides are 8 units long. The triangle is equilateral.

Step 3

Distractor Rationale

Distractor C

Equilateral triangles have equal angles → 60°.

$\triangle PQR$ is not right angled

25. D

For two lines to be perpendicular, their slopes must be negative reciprocals of each other.

The slopes are negative reciprocals only in choice **D**

$y = 4x - 5$ and $y = -\dfrac{1}{4}x + 5$. The two slopes are 4 and $-\dfrac{1}{4}$.

26. 5

Begin by finding the slope of the given line segment AB.

$$m = \frac{y_2 - y_1}{x_2 - x_1}$$

$$m = \frac{4 - 5}{8 - 6} = \frac{-1}{2}$$

Since the line segments AB and BC form a 90° or are perpendicular to one another, their respective slopes are negative reciprocals of each other $(m_1 \times m_2 = -1)$.

Therefore, the slope of the line segment perpendicular to the line segment AB is 2.

Use the slope formula again for the perpendicular line segment BC.

$$m = \frac{y_2 - y_1}{x_2 - x_1}$$

$$m = \frac{-2 - 4}{d - 8} = \frac{-6}{d - 8}$$

Since the slope is 2,

$$\frac{-6}{d - 8} = 2$$

$$-6 = 2(d - 8)$$

$$-6 = 2d - 16$$

$$10 = 2d$$

$$\frac{10}{2} = d$$

$$5 = d$$

The value of d is 5.

27. A

In order to verify that $\triangle ABC$ is a right triangle using the fact that $\angle ABC = 90°$, there are two main methods.

Method 1:
Verify that segments AB and BC are perpendicular by using the slope formula $m = \frac{y_2 - y_1}{x_2 - x_1}$ to determine the slopes of line segments AB and BC.

Step 1
Determine the slope of $AB = \frac{5 - 1}{-1 - (-3)} = \frac{4}{2} = 2$

Step 2
Determine the slope of
$BC = \frac{2 - 5}{5 - (-1)} = \frac{-3}{6} = -\frac{1}{2}$

Note that $2 \times -\frac{1}{2} = -1$. Since $m_1 \times m_2 = -1$, line segments AB and BC are perpendicular.

Method 2:
Verify the Pythagorean theorem for this triangle, such that $(AB)^2 + (BC)^2 = (AC)^2$.

Use the distance formula $d = \sqrt{(x_2 - x_1)^2 + (y_2 - y_1)^2}$ to determine the distance of each of the line segments.

Step 1
$$AB = \sqrt{(-1 - (-3))^2 + (5 - 1)^2}$$
$$AB = \sqrt{(2)^2 + (4)^2}$$
$$AB = \sqrt{20}$$

Step 2
$$BC = \sqrt{(5 - (-1))^2 + (2 - 5)^2}$$
$$BC = \sqrt{(6)^2 + (-3)^2}$$
$$BC = \sqrt{45}$$

Step 3
$$AC = \sqrt{(5 - (-3))^2 + (2 - 1)^2}$$
$$AC = \sqrt{(8)^2 + (1)^2}$$
$$AC = \sqrt{65}$$

Step 4
Substitute the distance values into $(AB)^2 + (BC)^2 = (AC)^2$.
$$(\sqrt{20})^2 + (\sqrt{45})^2 = (\sqrt{65})^2$$
$$20 + 45 = 65$$
$$65 = 65$$

Since the Pythagorean theorem has been verified for this triangle, it is a right triangle.

When the full solutions are compared with the partial student solutions, both girls have a correct partial solution.

28. B

A sketch of the parallelogram is shown.

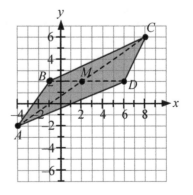

The diagram shows that the diagonals of the parallelogram are line segments AC and BD. If the diagonals bisect each other, then line segments AC and BD will have the same midpoint M. Therefore, the procedure in which you must verify that segment AC and segment BD have the same midpoint could be used to determine if the diagonals bisect each other.

29. a) OR

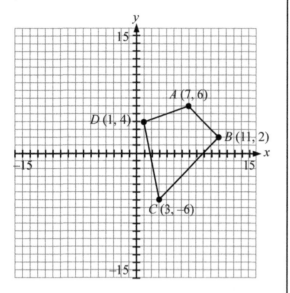

b) OR

The midpoint of each side of the quadrilateral can be determined by applying the midpoint formula

$$M = \left(\frac{x_1 + x_2}{2}, \frac{y_1 + y_2}{2} \right).$$

$$M_{AB} = \left(\frac{7 + 11}{2}, \frac{6 + 2}{2} \right) \quad M_{BC} = \left(\frac{11 + 3}{2}, \frac{2 + (-6)}{2} \right)$$

$$M_{AB} = \left(\frac{18}{2}, \frac{8}{2} \right) \quad\quad M_{BC} = \left(\frac{14}{2}, \frac{-4}{2} \right)$$

$$M_{AB} = (9, 4) \quad\quad\quad M_{BC} = (7, -2)$$

$$M_{CD} = \left(\frac{3 + 1}{2}, \frac{-6 + 4}{2} \right) \quad M_{DA} = \left(\frac{1 + 7}{2}, \frac{4 + 6}{2} \right)$$

$$M_{CD} = \left(\frac{4}{2}, \frac{-2}{2} \right) \quad\quad M_{DA} = \left(\frac{8}{2}, \frac{10}{2} \right)$$

$$M_{CD} = (2, -1) \quad\quad\quad M_{DA} = (4, 5)$$

c) OR

Step 1

Determine the midpoints of each side of the quadrilateral.

The midpoint of each side of the quadrilateral can be determined by applying the midpoint formula,

$$M = \left(\frac{x_1 + x_2}{2}, \frac{y_1 + y_2}{2} \right).$$

$$M_{AB} = \left(\frac{7 + 11}{2}, \frac{6 + 2}{2} \right)$$

$$= \left(\frac{18}{2}, \frac{8}{2} \right)$$

$$= (9, 4)$$

$$M_{BC} = \left(\frac{11 + 3}{2}, \frac{2 + (-6)}{2} \right)$$

$$= \left(\frac{14}{2}, \frac{-4}{2} \right)$$

$$= (7, -2)$$

$$M_{CD} = \left(\frac{3 + 1}{2}, \frac{-6 + 4}{2} \right)$$

$$= \left(\frac{4}{2}, \frac{-2}{2} \right)$$

$$= (2, -1)$$

$$M_{DA} = \left(\frac{1 + 7}{2}, \frac{4 + 6}{2} \right)$$

$$= \left(\frac{8}{2}, \frac{10}{2} \right)$$

$$= (4, 5)$$

Step 2

Denote the midpoint of AB as P, the midpoint of BC as Q, the midpoint of CD as R, and the midpoint of DA as T.

$$M_{AB} = P = (9, 4)$$

$$M_{BC} = Q = (7, -2)$$

$$M_{CD} = R = (2, -1)$$

$$M_{DA} = T = (4, 5)$$

Step 3

In order to verify that $PQRT$ is a parallelogram, use the slope formula ($m = \dfrac{y_2 - y_1}{x_2 - x_1}$) to show that side PT is parallel to side QR and that side RT is parallel to side PQ.

Determine if side PT is parallel to side QR.

$$m_{PT} = \frac{5 - 4}{4 - 9}$$
$$= \frac{1}{-5}$$
$$= -\frac{1}{5}$$

$$m_{QR} = \frac{-1 - (-2)}{2 - 7}$$
$$= \frac{-1 + 2}{2 - 7}$$
$$= \frac{1}{-5}$$
$$= -\frac{1}{5}$$

Since $m_{PT} = m_{QR}$, side PT is parallel to side QR.

Step 4

Determine if side RT is parallel to side PQ.

$$m_{RT} = \frac{5 - (-1)}{4 - 2}$$
$$= \frac{5 + 1}{2}$$
$$= \frac{6}{2}$$
$$= 3$$

$$m_{PQ} = \frac{-2 - 4}{7 - 9}$$
$$= \frac{-6}{-2}$$
$$= 3$$

Since $m_{RT} = m_{PQ}$, side RT is parallel to side PQ.

The opposite sides of quadrilateral $PQRT$ are parallel; therefore, when the midpoints of quadrilateral $ABCD$ are joined, a parallelogram ($PQRT$) is formed.

NOTES

Trigonometry

TRIGONOMETRY

Table of Correlations					
Specific Expectation	**Practice Questions**	**Unit Test Questions**	**Practice Test 1**	**Practice Test 2**
TR1 Investigating Similarity and Solving Problems Involving Similar Triangles				
TR1.1	*verify, through investigation the properties of similar triangles*	1, 2	1		
TR1.2	*describe and compare the concepts of similarity and congruence*	3, 4	2		
TR1.3	*solve problems involving similar triangles in realistic situations*	5, 6, 7	3, 4	33, 34	33, 34
TR2 Solving Problems Involving the Trigonometry of Right Triangles				
TR2.1	*determine, through investigation the relationship between the ratio of two sides in a right triangle and the ratio of the two corresponding sides in a similar right triangle, and define the sine, cosine, and tangent ratios*	8, 9	5		
TR2.2	*determine the measures of the sides and angles in right triangles, using the primary trigonometric ratios and the Pythagorean theorem*	10, 11, 12, 13	6, 7, 8, 9	35, 36	35
TR2.3	*solve problems involving the measures of sides and angles in right triangles in real life applications using the primary trigonometric ratios and the Pythagorean theorem.*	14, 15, 16, 17, 18a, 18b	10, 11, 12, 13, 14a, 14b	37, 38, 39	36a, 36b
TR3 Solving Problems Involving the Trigonometry of Acute Triangles				
TR3.1	*explore the development of the sine law within acute triangles*	19, 20	15	40	37
TR3.2	*explore the development of the cosine law within acute triangles*	21, 22	16	41	38
TR3.3	*determine the measures of sides and angles in acute triangles, using the sine law and the cosine law*	23, 24, 25, 26, 27	17, 18, 19, 20	42	39, 40
TR3.4	*solve problems involving the measures of sides and angles in acute triangles*	28, 29, 30, 31, 32a, 32b	21, 22, 23, 24a, 24b	43a, 43b	41, 42, 43

VERIFYING THE PROPERTIES OF SIMILAR TRIANGLES

Through investigation, the following properties of similar triangles can be verified.

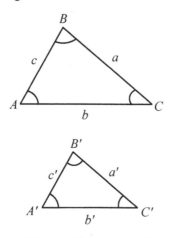

- **Corresponding angles** are equal.

  $\angle A = \angle A'$

  $\angle B = \angle B'$

  $\angle C = \angle C'$

- **Corresponding sides** have proportional lengths.

  $\dfrac{a}{a'} = \dfrac{b}{b'} = \dfrac{c}{c'}$

Example

Triangle *ABC* is similar to triangle *DEF*, as shown.

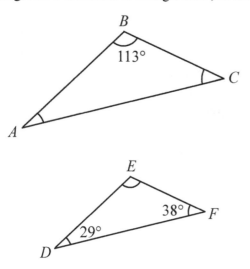

What is the value of $\angle A - \angle C + \angle E$?

Since corresponding angles are equal, it follows that $\angle A = \angle D$, $\angle B = \angle E$, and $\angle C = \angle F$. From the diagram, $\angle D = 29° = \angle A$, $\angle F = 38° = \angle C$, and $\angle B = 113° = \angle F$. Therefore, substitute these values into $\angle A - \angle C + \angle E$ to get $29° - 38° + 113° = 104°$.

━━━━━━━━━━━━━━

1. To guarantee that $\triangle ABC$ is similar to $\triangle DEF$, a student can verify that $\angle A = \angle D$ and that

   A. $\angle C = \angle F$

   B. *AB* is proportional to *DE*

   C. *BC* is proportional to *EF*

   D. $\angle B + \angle C = \angle E + \angle F$

2. Which of the following statements is **true** for similar triangles?

   A. The measure of corresponding sides are equal in length.

   B. Similar triangles always have the same shape and the same size.

   C. The ratio of corresponding sides is equal to the ratio of corresponding angles.

   D. The ratio of corresponding sides are equal and the measure of corresponding angles are equal.

COMPARING SIMILARITY AND CONGRUENCE

Two triangles are **congruent** if all pairs of corresponding sides and angles are equal. That means the triangles are exactly the same size, but may have a different orientation.

　　　　　　　　Trigonometry

The sign for congruent is ≅ .

There are three methods to verifying congruency:

1. SSS: If all three sides of one triangle are equal to the corresponding sides of the other triangle.

2. SAS: If any two sides and the angle contained within them is equal to the corresponding sides and contained angle of the other triangle.

3. ASA: If any two angles and the side contained within them is equal to the corresponding angles and contained side of the other triangle.

Example
Prove triangle $ABC \cong \triangle DEF$.
Side *AB* is equal in length to corresponding side *EF*.
Side *AC* is equal in length to corresponding side *ED*.
Side *BC* is equal in length to corresponding side *DF*.
All three sides of triangle *ABC* are equal to the corresponding sides of triangle *DEF*.
Therefore, by SSS, $\triangle ABC \cong \triangle DEF$.

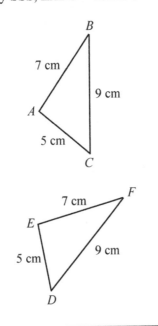

Similar triangles have the same shape, but not necessarily the same size. Two triangles are similar if the measures of the corresponding angles are equal or if the ratios of the corresponding sides are equal.
The symbol for similar is ~ .

Example
The diagram below shows how two triangles can be used to find the width of a river.

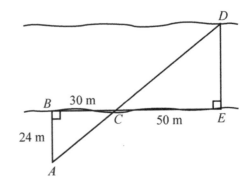

Determine the length of the river at *DE*.

$\angle ABC = \angle CED = 90°$
$\angle ACB = \angle DCE$ (Opposite angles are equal.)
If two sets of angles in two triangles are equal, then the third set must also be equal .
Therefore, all corresponding angles are equal, so $\triangle ABC \sim \triangle DEC$.

Since the triangles are similar, it follows that the ratio of the corresponding sides must also be equal.

$$\frac{DE}{AB} = \frac{CE}{CB}$$

$$\frac{DE}{24 \text{ m}} = \frac{50 \text{ m}}{30 \text{ m}}$$

$$DE = \frac{(24 \text{ m})(50 \text{ m})}{30 \text{ m}}$$

$$DE = \frac{1200 \text{ m}}{30 \text{ m}}$$

$DE = 40$ m
The width of the river at *DE* is 40 m.

3. What is the length of side *y*?

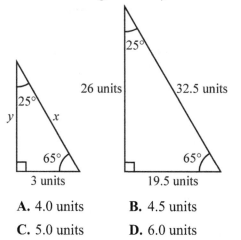

26 units   32.5 units

A. 4.0 units   B. 4.5 units

C. 5.0 units   D. 6.0 units

4. The two given triangles can be described as congruent because

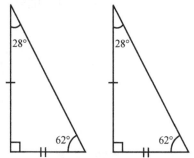

A. all of their corresponding angles are equal

B. they each contain a 90° angle

C. the sum of the angles in each triangle is 180° angle

D. all of their corresponding angles and sides are equal

TR1.3 solve problems involving similar triangles in realistic situations

SOLVING PROBLEMS USING SIMILAR TRIANGLES

Similar triangles are often used to solve problems in realistic situations.

Example

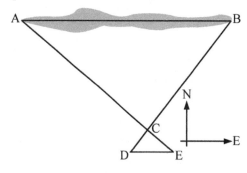

To determine the distance from A to B across a lake, two triangles are drawn as shown. The following distances were measured: DE = 412 m, DC = 260 m, BC = 1 264 m, and CE = 308 m. Also, AB is parallel to DE.

What is the distance across the lake to the nearest metre?
Using properties of geometry, it is given that AB|| DE.
Therefore, lines AE and DB act as transversals across these parallel lines. This means that ∠A = ∠E and ∠B = ∠D (which form opposite interior angles in both cases).
Thus,
∠C = ∠C

∠A = ∠E

∠B = ∠D
It follows that △ABC~△EDC.

Trigonometry

Draw the two triangles with the same orientation, and label them with the given distances as shown.

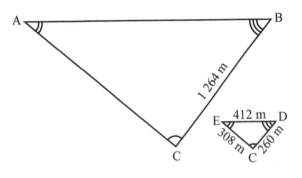

Since $\triangle ABC \sim \triangle EDC$,

$$\frac{BC}{DC} = \frac{AC}{EC} = \frac{AB}{ED}$$

Substitute the given distances into this equation.

$$\frac{1\ 264\ m}{260\ m} = \frac{AC}{308\ m} = \frac{AB}{412\ m}$$

Since all three of these ratios are equal, equate the first and last to get $\frac{1\ 264\ m}{260\ m} = \frac{AB}{412\ m}$.

$$AB = \frac{1\ 264\ m}{260\ m} \times 412\ m = 2\ 002.95\ m$$

Therefore, the distance from point A to point B across the lake is 2 003 m.

Use the following information to answer the next question.

The diagram shows shadows cast by a tree and a statue at the same point in time.

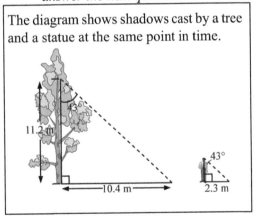

5. To the nearest tenth of a metre, how tall is the statue?

   A. 2.2 m   **B.** 2.5 m

   C. 4.5 m   **D.** 11.7 m

Use the following information to answer the next question.

A triangular field is drawn on a map. The lengths of the sides of the field on the map are 5 cm, 7 cm, and 8 cm. The actual length of the shortest side of the field is 125 m.

6. What is the length of the longest side of the field?

   A. 143 m   **B.** 175 m

   C. 200 m   **D.** 243 m

Use the following information to answer the next question.

Two lookout bridges *AB* and *CD* are built across a pond as shown in the diagram.

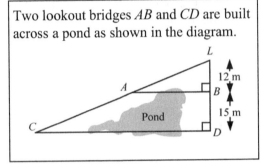

Numerical Response

7. If bridge *AB* is 30 m in length, then what is the length of bridge *CD*? Round the answer to one decimal place.

TR2.1 determine, through investigation the relationship between the ratio of two sides in a right triangle and the ratio of the two corresponding sides in a similar right triangle, and define the sine, cosine, and tangent ratios

PRIMARY TRIGONOMETRIC RATIOS

Through investigation, you can determine the relationship between the ratios of the lengths of two sides in a right triangle relative to an angle other than the right angle. Recall that a right triangle is a triangle containing a 90° angle. A triangle can be labelled with respect to ∠A as follows:

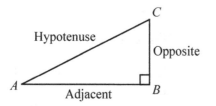

- The **hypotenuse** is the longest side and is always across from the 90° angle.
- The **opposite** side is always the side across from the given angle.
- The **adjacent** side is the side next to the given angle, and shorter than the hypotenuse.

When you compare the lengths of the different sides of similar right triangles that hold the same acute angle, investigation will show that the ratios of the lengths of the three sides will remain the same, regardless of the right triangles that are chosen. This is summarized in the following illustration:

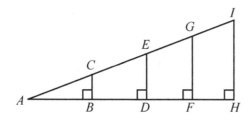

Given the acute angle A, it follows that:

- $\dfrac{BC}{AC} = \dfrac{DE}{AE} = \dfrac{FG}{AG} = \dfrac{HI}{AI} = \dfrac{\text{opposite}}{\text{hypotenuse}}$

- $\dfrac{AB}{AC} = \dfrac{AD}{AE} = \dfrac{AF}{AG} = \dfrac{AH}{AI} = \dfrac{\text{adjacent}}{\text{hypotenuse}}$

- $\dfrac{BC}{AB} = \dfrac{DE}{AD} = \dfrac{FG}{AF} = \dfrac{HI}{AH} = \dfrac{\text{opposite}}{\text{adjacent}}$

These ratios are known as the primary trigonometric ratios.

$$\text{Sine ratio: } \sin A = \frac{\text{opposite}}{\text{hypotenuse}}$$

$$\text{Cosine ratio: } \cos A = \frac{\text{adjacent}}{\text{hypotenuse}}$$

$$\text{Tangent ratio: } \tan A = \frac{\text{opposite}}{\text{adjacent}}$$

To remember these ratios, think of this mnemonic: SOH CAH TOA.

Example
Write the three primary trigonometric ratios for angle θ.

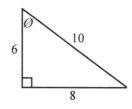

Begin by labelling the triangle as follows:

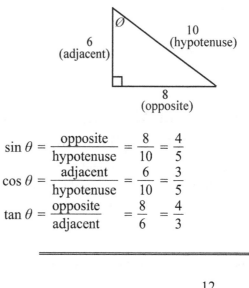

$$\sin \theta = \frac{\text{opposite}}{\text{hypotenuse}} = \frac{8}{10} = \frac{4}{5}$$

$$\cos \theta = \frac{\text{adjacent}}{\text{hypotenuse}} = \frac{6}{10} = \frac{3}{5}$$

$$\tan \theta = \frac{\text{opposite}}{\text{adjacent}} = \frac{8}{6} = \frac{4}{3}$$

8. In a right triangle, if $\cos \theta = \dfrac{12}{13}$ and $\tan \theta = \dfrac{5}{12}$, what is the value of $\sin \theta$?

A. $\dfrac{5}{13}$ **B.** $\dfrac{5}{12}$

C. 1   **D.** $\dfrac{12}{5}$

Use the following information to answer the next question.

In the given triangle, tan 72° = 3.078.

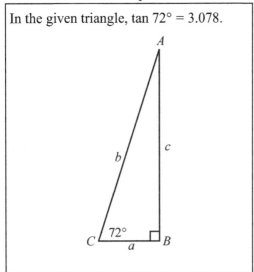

9. Which of the following ratios is equal to 3.1?

A. $\dfrac{a}{c}$	**B.** $\dfrac{c}{a}$
C. $\dfrac{b}{a}$	**D.** $\dfrac{a}{b}$

TR2.2 determine the measures of the sides and angles in right triangles, using the primary trigonometric ratios and the Pythagorean theorem

DETERMINING THE MEASURES OF SIDES AND ANGLES IN RIGHT TRIANGLES

The primary trigonometric ratios and the Pythagorean theorem are mathematical tools that can be used to determine the value of an unknown side or angle in a right triangle.

Example
Determine the measure of the indicated angle to the nearest tenth of a degree.

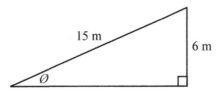

Begin by labelling the triangle as follows:

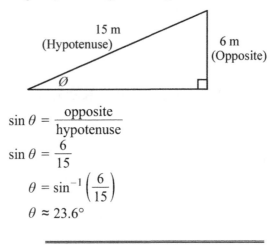

$$\sin \theta = \frac{\text{opposite}}{\text{hypotenuse}}$$
$$\sin \theta = \frac{6}{15}$$
$$\theta = \sin^{-1}\left(\frac{6}{15}\right)$$
$$\theta \approx 23.6°$$

SOLVING A TRIANGLE

Solving a triangle involves determining all the unknown sides and angles of a triangle. In order to solve a triangle, it is common to use the Pythagorean theorem, the rule that the sum of the angles in a triangle equals 180°, and the trigonometric ratios.

Example
Solve the following triangle.

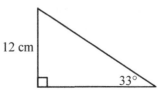

Begin by labelling the unknown sides and angles as follows:

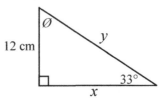

$90° + 33° + \theta = 180°$
$\theta = 57°$

Next, the length of x can be calculated using the tangent ratio.

$\tan \theta = \dfrac{\text{opposite}}{\text{adjacent}}$

$\tan 33° = \dfrac{12}{x}$

$x\tan 33° = 12$

$x = \dfrac{12}{\tan 33°}$

$x \approx 18.5 \text{ cm}$

The final side, y, can be determined either by using the Pythagorean theorem or by using a trigonometric ratio.

Using the Pythagorean theorem:
$c^2 = a^2 + b^2$
$y^2 = 12^2 + x^2$
$y^2 = 12^2 + \left(\dfrac{12}{\tan 33°}\right)^2$
$y = \sqrt{12^2 + \left(\dfrac{12}{\tan 33°}\right)^2}$
$y \approx 22.0 \text{ cm}$

Using the sine ratio:

$\sin \theta = \dfrac{\text{opposite}}{\text{hypotenuse}}$

$\sin 33° = \dfrac{12}{y}$

$y\sin 33° = 12$

$y = \dfrac{12}{\sin 33°}$

$y \approx 22.0 \text{ cm}$

Use the following information to answer the next question.

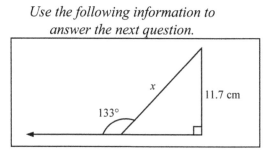

10. What is the length of side x to the nearest tenth?

    A. 8.0 cm   **B.** 8.6 cm

    C. 16.0 cm   **D.** 17.2 cm

11. If the hypotenuse of a right triangle is 90 cm and a second side is 45 cm, then what is the length of the third side to the nearest whole number?

    A. 78 cm   **B.** 80 cm

    C. 82 cm   **D.** 85 cm

Use the following information to answer the next question.

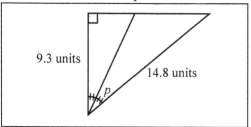

12. What is the measure of angle p to the nearest tenth?

    A. 16.5°   **B.** 25.5°

    C. 33.0°   **D.** 51.0°

Use the following information to answer the next question.

A diagram of two right angle triangles is shown.

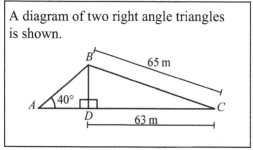

Numerical Response

13. Correct to the nearest tenth metre, the length of side AB is _____ m.

TR2.3 solve problems involving the measures of sides and angles in right triangles in real life applications using the primary trigonometric ratios and the Pythagorean theorem.

Solving Problems by Applying the Primary Trigonometric Ratios and the Pythagorean Theorem

The primary trigonometric ratios and the Pythagorean theorem can be used to solve problems involving the measures of sides and angles in real-life applications. When solving these types of problems, recall these key definitions:

- The **angle of elevation** is up from the horizontal.
- The **angle of depression** is down from the horizontal.

Example
A cat watches a bird in a tree. The bird is at an angle of elevation of 40° from the cat. If the cat is 7.1 m from the base of the tree, how high up in the tree is the bird?

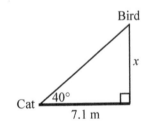

$\tan 40° = \dfrac{x}{7.1}$
$x = 7.1 \tan 40°$
$x \approx 6.0$ m
The bird is 6.0 m from the ground.

Example
Lexi is standing in her yard. She sees a cat sitting directly west of her. Directly east of her is a dog. Lexi's eye level is 1.48 m high. To look directly at where the cat is sitting, she looks down at an angle of depression of 30°. To the dog, the angle of depression is 25°. How far apart are the cat and dog?

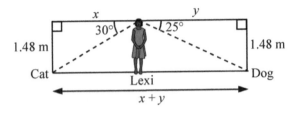

Notice that $x + y$ at eye level will be the same as $x + y$ on the ground.
The distance between the cat and dog = $x + y$.

$\tan 30° = \dfrac{1.48}{x}$

$x = \dfrac{1.48}{\tan 30°}$

$\tan 25° = \dfrac{1.48}{y}$

$y = \dfrac{1.48}{\tan 25°}$

distance $= x + y$
$= \dfrac{1.48}{\tan 30°} + \dfrac{1.48}{\tan 25°}$
≈ 5.74 m

The cat and the dog are 5.74 m apart.

Use the following information to answer the next question.

A telephone pole is kept vertical by two wires that run from the top of the pole to the ground as illustrated in the given diagram. The wire closest to the pole measures 13.2 m in length and makes an angle of 36° with the ground. The other wire measures 15.8 m in length.

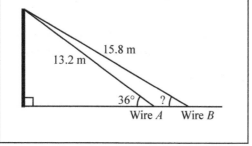

14. Correct to the nearest degree, what is the angle between wire B and the ground?

    A. 29°   B. 31°

    C. 45°   D. 57°

Use the following information to answer the next question.

Each wall of a new style of tent is 3.5 m long and the angle between the tent wall and the ground is 47° when the centre pole is erected.

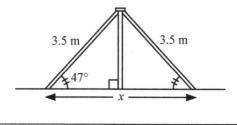

15. What is the width, x, of the tent at its base, rounded to the nearest tenth of a metre?

    A. 2.4 m   B. 2.6 m

    C. 4.8 m   D. 5.2 m

Use the following information to answer the next question.

Two buildings are 40 m apart, as illustrated in the given diagram. From a point at the top of the shorter building, the angle of elevation to the top of the taller building is 37°. From the same point, the angle of depression to the foot of the taller building is 26°.

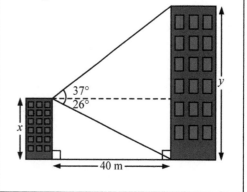

16. Rounded to the nearest tenth of a metre, the height y of the taller building is

    A. 52.8 m   B. 51.4 m

    C. 49.7 m   D. 27.1 m

Use the following information to answer the next question.

The given map shows routes that Marrah often takes to get to school. Every Friday afternoon, Marrah goes from school to the café before going home.

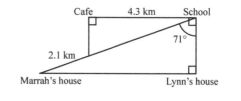

17. How far does Marrah have to travel to get home from school if she first stops at the café?

    A. 1.5 km   B. 4.3 km

    C. 5.8 km   D. 7.9 km

Trigonometry

Use the following information to answer the next multipart question.

18. A ladder sits between two trees at a point 3.5 m from the base of the first tree. The ladder makes an angle of 70° with the ground when its top is placed against that tree. If the ladder is turned and its top is placed against the second tree with the foot of the ladder remaining in the same location, the ladder makes an angle of 66°, as shown in the diagram.

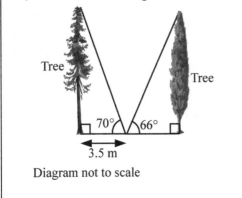

Tree

Tree

70° 66°

3.5 m

Diagram not to scale

Open Response

a) What is the length of the ladder to the nearest tenth of a metre?

b) To the nearest tenth of a metre, what is the distance between the bases of the two trees?

TR3.1 explore the development of the sine law within acute triangles

DEVELOPING THE SINE LAW

Any triangle that is not a right-angled triangle is called an **oblique triangle**.

The primary trigonometric ratios can only be applied to solve for a side or an angle of a right triangle, so a new procedure needs to be developed when presented with an oblique triangle. The primary trigonometric ratios are used to develop a new method called the sine law.

Consider $\triangle ABC$.

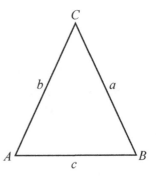

Side BC is opposite angle A and can be denoted by a. Similarly, side AC can be denoted by b, and side AB can be denoted by c.

Draw DC perpendicular to AB in order to form two right triangles, as shown.

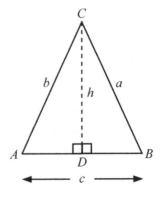

DC is the height, h, of $\triangle ABC$.

There are now two right triangles: $\triangle ADC$ and $\triangle BDC$. Applying the primary trigonometric sine ratio for angle A and angle B gives $\sin A = \dfrac{h}{b}$ and $\sin B = \dfrac{h}{a}$.

Solving for h in each case gives $h = b\sin A$ and $h = a\sin B$.

Since the value of h is identical for $\triangle ADC$ and $\triangle BDC$, $b\sin A = a\sin B$.

The equation $b\sin A = a\sin B$ can be rewritten as $\dfrac{a}{\sin A} = \dfrac{b}{\sin B}$. If a line perpendicular to AC is drawn and the same steps are followed, the equation $\dfrac{a}{\sin A} = \dfrac{c}{\sin C}$ can also be generated.

Combining the derived results gives the equation $\dfrac{a}{\sin A} = \dfrac{b}{\sin B} = \dfrac{c}{\sin C}$. This equation is called the sine law. The sine law can be illustrated by examining each of the following triangles.

The sine law can also be written as $\dfrac{\sin A}{a} = \dfrac{\sin B}{b} = \dfrac{\sin C}{c}$.

Example

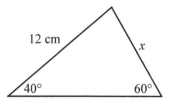

Since the side measuring x cm is opposite the 40°angle, and the side measuring 12 cm is opposite the 60°angle, the following equation is generated:
$$\frac{12}{\sin 60°} = \frac{x}{\sin 40°}.$$

Example

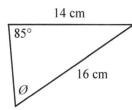

Since the side measuring 14 cm is opposite angle θ, and the side measuring 16 cm is opposite the 85°angle, the following equation is generated:
$$\frac{14}{\sin \theta} = \frac{16}{\sin 85°}.$$

Example

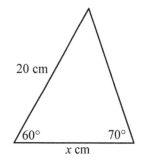

Recall that the sum of the interior angles of a triangle is equal to 180°. Therefore, the angle opposite the side measuring x cm is equal to $180° - 60° - 70° = 50°$. Since the side measuring 20 cm is opposite the 70° angle, the following equation is generated:
$$\frac{x}{\sin 50°} = \frac{20}{\sin 70°}.$$

Use the following information to answer the next question.

A student drew the diagram shown in order to derive the law of sines.

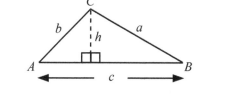

19. If the student correctly determined that $\sin A = \dfrac{h}{b}$ and $\sin B = \dfrac{h}{a}$, then which of the following equations is correct?

   A. $h = \dfrac{b\sin A}{a\sin B}$

   B. $h = \dfrac{a\sin A}{b\sin B}$

   C. $b\sin B = a\sin A$

   D. $b\sin A = a\sin B$

20. For which of the following triangles can the equation $\dfrac{80}{\sin 50°} = \dfrac{65}{\sin x°}$ be used to determine the measure of angle x?

A.

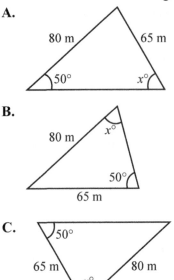

80 m

65 m

50°

$x°$

B.

80 m

$x°$

50°

65 m

C.

50°

65 m

80 m

$x°$

D.

65 m

$x°$

50°

80 m

TR3.2 explore the development of the cosine law within acute triangles

DEVELOPING THE COSINE LAW

Some oblique triangles cannot be solved directly using the law of sines. A new procedure can be developed by applying the Pythagorean theorem and the cosine ratio.

Consider $\triangle ABC$.

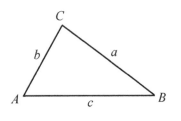

C

b

a

A

c

B

In $\triangle ABC$, draw a segment DC perpendicular to AB to form two right triangles. Recall that DC is the height, h, of $\triangle ABC$. Denote side AD by x. It follows that side $DB = c - x$ as illustrated in the following diagram.

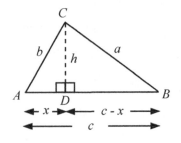

C

b h a

A D B

x $c - x$

c

Apply the Pythagorean theorem to both $\triangle ADC$ and $\triangle BDC$.

In $\triangle ADC$, $b^2 = x^2 + h^2$ or $b^2 - x^2 = h^2$.

In $\triangle BDC$, $a^2 = h^2 + (c - x)^2$.

Substitute $b^2 - x^2$ for h^2 in the equation $a^2 = h^2 + (c - x)^2$.

$a^2 = b^2 - x^2 + (c - x)^2$

Expand $(c - x)^2$.

$a^2 = b^2 - x^2 + c^2 - 2cx + x^2$

Collect like terms.

$a^2 = b^2 + c^2 - 2cx$

Also, in $\triangle ADC$, $\cos A = \dfrac{x}{b}$ or $b\cos A = x$.

By substituting $b\cos A$ for x in the equation $a^2 = b^2 + c^2 - 2cx$, the equation becomes $a^2 = b^2 + c^2 - 2bc\cos A$. This equation is called the Cosine Law.

Similar equations can be derived that involve $\cos B$ and $\cos C$:

$b^2 = a^2 + c^2 - 2ac\cos B$

$c^2 = a^2 + b^2 - 2ab\cos C$

The Cosine Law can be used to calculate the measure of an angle in a triangle when the lengths of all three sides of the triangle are known. In this case, one of the following forms of the law of cosines is useful.

$\cos A = \dfrac{b^2 + c^2 - a^2}{2bc}$

$\cos B = \dfrac{a^2 + c^2 - b^2}{2ac}$

$\cos C = \dfrac{a^2 + b^2 - c^2}{2ab}$

The Cosine Law can be illustrated by examining each of the following triangles.

Example

This example illustrates the use of the Cosine Law when a side length is unknown.

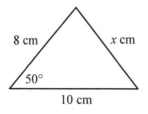

Since the side measuring x cm is opposite the $50°$ angle, $x^2 = 8^2 + 10^2 - 2(8)(10)\cos 50°$.

————————————

Example

This example illustrates the use of the Cosine Law when the measure of an angle is unknown.

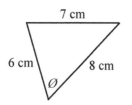

Since the angle measuring θ is opposite the side measuring 7 cm, $\cos \theta = \dfrac{6^2 + 8^2 - 7^2}{2(6)(8)}$.

————————————

21. The equation $\cos x° = \dfrac{15^2 + 20^2 - 17^2}{2(15)(20)}$ applies to which of the following acute triangles?

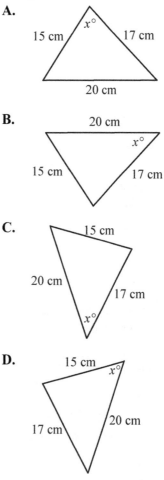

Trigonometry

Use the following information to answer the next question.

Acute $\triangle PQR$ is given.

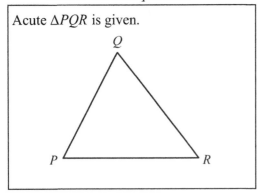

22. Which of the following equations correctly represents the law of cosines with respect to $\triangle PQR$?

A. $\dfrac{QR}{\cos P} = \dfrac{PQ}{\cos R}$

B. $\dfrac{PR}{\cos P} = \dfrac{QR}{\cos Q}$

C. $(PQ)^2 = (PR)^2 + (QR)^2 - 2(PR)(QR)\cos Q$

D. $(QR)^2 = (QP)^2 + (PR)^2 - 2(QP)(PR)\cos P$

TR3.3 determine the measures of sides and angles in acute triangles, using the sine law and the cosine law

APPLYING THE SINE AND COSINE LAWS

The law of sines and the law of cosines can both be used to determine either a missing side length or a missing angle measure in an acute triangle, provided that at least three other measures are given.

APPLYING THE SINE LAW

The sine law should be used when a pair of measures, such as a side with its corresponding opposite angle, is given. The measure to be calculated then depends on what the third known measure is:

- If another side length is given, the measure of the angle opposite the given side can be calculated.
- If the measure of another angle is given, the length of the side opposite the given angle can be calculated.

Example

In $\triangle ABC$, $\angle A = 40°$, $\angle B = 60°$, and $AC = 18$ cm. Determine the length of side BC to the nearest tenth.

Solution

Draw a sketch of the given triangle, and place the indicated measurements in the appropriate locations.

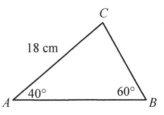

Since a pair of measures is given, apply the sine law: $\dfrac{a}{\sin A} = \dfrac{b}{\sin B} = \dfrac{c}{\sin C}$

The side measuring 18 cm is opposite the $60°$ angle, and side BC is opposite the $40°$ angle. Thus,

$$\frac{BC}{\sin 40°} = \frac{18}{\sin 60°}$$
$$BC(\sin 60°) = 18(\sin 40°)$$
$$\frac{BC(\sin 60°)}{\sin 60°} = \frac{18(\sin 40°)}{\sin 60°}$$
$$BC = \frac{18(\sin 40°)}{\sin 60°}$$
$$BC \approx 13.36 \text{ cm}$$

Rounded to the nearest tenth of a centimetre, the measure of side BC is 13.4 cm.

Example

In $\triangle DEF$, $\angle D = 48°$, $EF = 27$ cm, and $DF = 32$ cm. Determine the measure of $\angle E$ to the nearest tenth.

Solution

Draw a sketch of the given triangle, and place the indicated measurements in the appropriate locations.

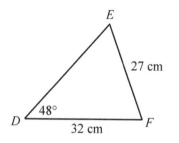

Since a side and its corresponding opposite angle are given, apply the sine law.

The side measuring 27 cm is opposite the 48° angle, and the side measuring 32 cm is opposite $\angle E$. Thus,

$$\frac{27}{\sin 48°} = \frac{32}{\sin E}$$
$$27(\sin E) = 32(\sin 48°)$$
$$\frac{27(\sin E)}{27} = \frac{32(\sin 48°)}{27}$$
$$\sin E = \frac{32(\sin 48°)}{27}$$
$$\angle E = \sin^{-1}\left(\frac{32(\sin 48°)}{27}\right)$$
$$\angle E \approx 61.73°$$

Rounded to the nearest tenth of a degree, the measure of $\angle E$ is 61.7°.

APPLYING THE COSINE LAW

The cosine law should be used when no measures of a known pair are given. The measure to be calculated then depends on these given measures:

• If the measures of all three sides of the triangle are given, the measures of any of the angles can be calculated.
• If the measures of two sides of the triangle and the measure of the angle contained between those sides are given, the measure of the unknown side can be calculated.

Example

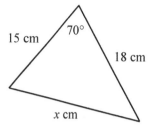

Determine the value of x to the nearest tenth of a centimetre.

Solution

Since two sides of the triangle and the angle contained between those sides are given, apply the cosine law in the form $a^2 = b^2 + c^2 - 2bc \cos A$.

The side measuring x cm is opposite the 70° angle. Thus,

$$x^2 = 15^2 + 18^2 - 2(15)(18)\cos 70°$$
$$x^2 \approx 225 + 324 - 184.69$$
$$x^2 \approx 364.310$$
$$x \approx \sqrt{364.31}$$
$$x \approx 19.09$$

Rounded to the nearest tenth of a centimetre, the measure of side x is 19.1 cm.

Trigonometry

Example

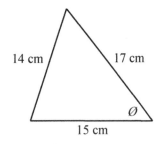

14 cm / 17 cm

15 cm

Ø

Determine the measure of angle θ to the nearest tenth.

Solution

The lengths of all three sides of the triangle are given; therefore, apply the law of cosines in the form $\cos A = \dfrac{b^2 + c^2 - a^2}{2bc}$.

The side measuring 14 cm is opposite angle θ, so the measure of angle θ is

$$\cos \theta = \frac{17^2 + 15^2 - 14^2}{2(17)(15)}$$

$$\cos \theta = \frac{289 + 225 - 196}{510}$$

$$\cos \theta = \frac{318}{510}$$

$$\theta = \cos^{-1}\left(\frac{318}{510}\right)$$

$$\theta \approx 51.43°$$

Rounded to the nearest tenth of a degree, the measure of angle θ is 51.4°.

Use the following information to answer the next question.

Triangle *ABC* has sides measuring 17 m, 23 m, and 24 m.

23. Correct to the nearest degree, what is the measure of the angle opposite the side measuring 23 m?

   A. 35°   **B.** 42°

   C. 66°   **D.** 72°

Use the following information to answer the next question.

A student is asked to determine the length of side *x* in the given diagram.

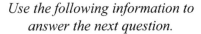

80°

37 m / 37 m

40°

x

24. Which of the following equations can the student use in order to solve for the length of side *x*?

   A. $\sin 40° = \dfrac{37}{x}$

   B. $\dfrac{x}{\sin 40°} = \dfrac{37}{\sin 80°}$

   C. $x^2 = 37^2 + 37^2 - 2(37)(37)\cos(80°)$

   D. $x^2 = 37^2 + 37^2 - 2(37)(37)\cos(40°)$

Use the following information to answer the next question.

ΔLMN

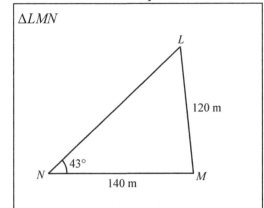

L

120 m

43°

N

140 m

M

25. To the nearest degree, what is the measure of angle *M*?

   A. 84°   **B.** 72°

   C. 53°   **D.** 36°

Use the following information to answer the next question.

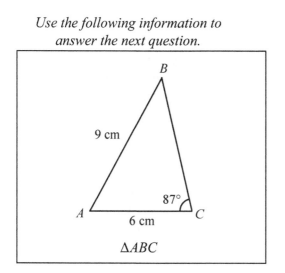

△*ABC*

26. Correct to the nearest degree, what is the measure of ∠*B*?

   A. 87°   **B.** 42°

   C. 40°   **D.** 34°

Use the following information to answer the next question.

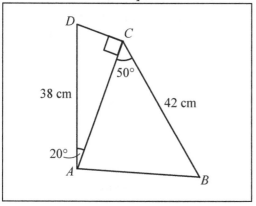

Numerical Response

27. Correct to the nearest centimetre, the perimeter of △*ABC* is _____ cm.

SOLVING PROBLEMS BY APPLYING THE SINE AND COSINE LAWS

Problems involving acute triangles can be solved by following these general steps:

1. Read the problem carefully. Determine which measures are given and which measure needs to be calculated.
2. If a diagram is not given, draw a sketch to represent the situation presented in the problem.
3. Examine the diagram or sketch to decide whether to apply the sine law or the cosine law. If calculating an unknown side length, apply the cosine law in a side-angle-side situation; otherwise, apply the sine law. If calculating an unknown angle measure, apply the cosine law in a side-side-side situation; otherwise, apply the sine law.
4. Make substitutions into the appropriate formula, and use correct algebraic steps to solve for the unknown value. Avoid or minimize rounding until the last step.
5. Check your calculations.
6. Write a concluding statement.

Trigonometry

Some of these problem-solving suggestions are put to use in the following four problems.

Example

A radar tracking station locates two boats: a fishing boat at a distance of 3.4 km from the tracking station, and a passenger ferry at a distance of 5.6 km from the tracking station. From the tracking station, the angle between the line of sight to the two boats is 86°. Determine the distance between the two boats to the nearest tenth of a kilometre.

Solution

Draw a diagram representing the situation. Let x represent the distance between the two boats.

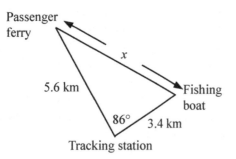

Since the problem is a side-angle-side situation, apply the cosine law. Side x is opposite the 86° angle; therefore, solve for x as follows:

$a^2 = b^2 + c^2 - 2bc\cos A$
$x^2 = 5.6^2 + 3.4^2 - 2(5.6)(3.4)\cos 86°$
$x^2 \approx 31.36 + 11.56 - 2.66$
$x^2 \approx 40.26$
$x \approx \sqrt{40.26}$
$x \approx 6.345$ km

The distance between the fishing boat and the passenger ferry, to the nearest tenth of a kilometre, is 6.3 km.

Example

Two points, A and B, are separated by a body of water. Line AC is measured to be 600 m in length. A measuring device is used to determine that $\angle BAC = 49°$ and $\angle ACB = 68°$. To the nearest tenth of a metre, what is the distance between points A and B?

Solution

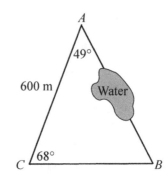

Since the problem is not a side-angle-side situation, apply the sine law. Side AB is opposite the 68° angle, and side AC (600 m) is opposite angle B. The measure of $\angle B$ is $180° - 49° - 68° = 63°$. Now, solve for AB as follows:

$$\frac{AB}{\sin 68°} = \frac{600}{\sin 63°}$$
$$AB\sin 63° = 600\sin 68°$$
$$\frac{AB\sin 63°}{\sin 63°} = \frac{600\sin 68°}{\sin 63°}$$
$$AB = \frac{600\sin 68°}{\sin 63°}$$
$$AB \approx 624.362 \text{ m}$$

The distance between points A and B, to the nearest tenth of a kilometre, is 624.4 km.

Example

To display the Stanley Cup, staff at a hockey arena roped off a triangular area and installed a security camera, as illustrated in the given diagram.

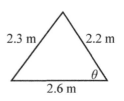

The security camera, located at θ, moves continuously between the two ropes, which measure 2.2 m and 2.6 m, respectively.

To the nearest tenth of a degree, determine the measure of angle θ.

Solution

Since this is a side-side-side situation, apply the cosine law. Angle θ is opposite the side measuring 2.3 m, so solve for θ as follows:

$$\cos A = \frac{b^2 + c^2 - a^2}{2bc}$$
$$\cos \theta = \frac{2.6^2 + 2.2^2 - 2.3^2}{2(2.6)(2.2)}$$
$$\cos \theta = \frac{6.76 + 4.84 - 5.29}{11.44}$$
$$\cos \theta = \frac{6.31}{11.44}$$
$$\theta \approx 56.525°$$

To the nearest tenth of a degree, the measure of angle θ is 56.5°.

Example

During hockey practice, players performed the following drill: Player A passed the puck to player B, who was 12 m away. Player B redirected the puck at an angle of 40° to player C. Player C then passed the puck back to player A, who was standing 9 m away.

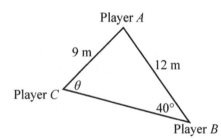

To the nearest degree, determine the measure of angle θ.

Solution

Since it is not a side-side-side situation, apply the sine law. The side measuring 9 m is opposite the 40° angle, and the side measuring 12 m is opposite angle θ. Solve for θ as follows:

$$\frac{9}{\sin 40°} = \frac{12}{\sin \theta}$$
$$9\sin \theta = 12\sin 40°$$
$$\frac{9\sin \theta}{9} = \frac{12\sin 40°}{9}$$
$$\sin \theta = \frac{12\sin 40°}{9}$$
$$\theta \approx 58.99°$$

The measure of angle θ, to the nearest degree, is 59°.

Use the following information to answer the next question.

A power station is situated on a cliff h metres above a river. A surveyor maps out a triangle across the river with measurements as indicated in the diagram shown.

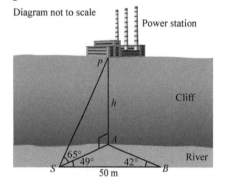

From the surveyor's position at S, the angle of elevation to the base of the power station is 65°.

28. To the nearest metre, what is the height of the cliff, h?

   A. 72 m   **B.** 81 m

   C. 95 m   **D.** 121 m

Use the following information to answer the next question.

A golfer at point *T* on the given diagram wishes to sink his golf ball in a hole directly on the other side of a pond at point *H*. The golfer has two options. He can play two low-risk shots (one from point *T* to point *A* and another from point *A* to point *H*) or he can play a high-risk shot and attempt to shoot directly from point *T* to point *H*.
The golfer estimates that the distance from point *T* to point *A* is 175 m, the measure of angle *ATH* is 45°, and the measure of angle *TAH* is 95°.

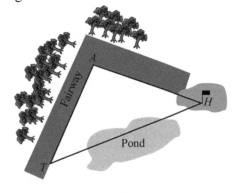

Open Response

29. To the nearest metre, what is the distance from point *T* to point *H*?

Use the following information to answer the next question.

The Royal Caribbean, the Norwegian, and the Princess cruise ships are moored in the harbour off George Town, Grand Cayman. The distance between the Norwegian and the Princess is 250 m. The angle formed by the Royal Caribbean, the Princess, and the Norwegian is 85°, and the angle formed by the Royal Caribbean, the Norwegian, and the Princess is 24° as shown in the diagram.

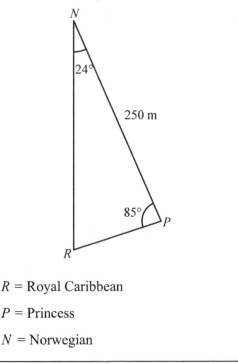

R = Royal Caribbean

P = Princess

N = Norwegian

30. Correct to the nearest metre, what is the distance between the Royal Caribbean and the Norwegian cruise ships?
    A. 237 m   B. 263 m
    C. 581 m   D. 612 m

A golf course engineer designs a fairway that curves to the right. In golf terms, this is called a dog-leg right. The designer places four reference points on his sketch of the hole. Reference point T is at the starting location, A and B are at each side of the dog leg, and point G is where the hole is, as shown in the diagram.

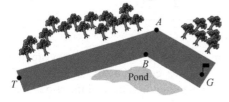

In the sketch, distance TA = 240 m, distance TB = 210 m, $\angle ATB$ = 10°, $\angle GAB$ = 68°, and $\angle GBA$ = 84°.

31. Rounded to the nearest metre, the distance of BG is

A. 46 m   B. 53 m

C. 97 m   D. 104 m

32. Danny is in a 90 m high watchtower. Lily and Bryan are out searching for clues in regards to the route taken by an escaped prisoner. Lily radios to Danny that she has found some evidence and estimates that she is 350 m from the base of the watchtower. Danny radios this information to Bryan, who estimates that from this location, the angle of elevation to the top of the watchtower is 20°. Danny estimates that the angle from Bryan to the base of the watchtower to Lily is 85°, as shown in the diagram.

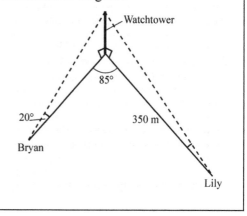

Open Response

a) To the nearest metre, how far is Bryan from the base of the watchtower?

b) To the nearest metre, how far apart are Bryan and Lily?

ANSWERS AND SOLUTIONS
TRIGONOMETRY

1. A	8. A	15. C	21. D	28. A
2. D	9. B	16. C	22. D	29. OR
3. A	10. C	17. D	23. C	30. B
4. D	11. A	18. a) OR	24. C	31. C
5. B	12. B	b) OR	25. A	32. a) OR
6. C	13. 24.9	19. D	26. B	b) OR
7. 67.5	14. A	20. B	27. 111	

1. A

In similar triangles, corresponding angles are equal. If two angles of one triangle are identical to two angles in another triangle, the third angle of both triangles is guaranteed to be the same.

If $\angle A = \angle D$ and $\angle C = \angle F$, the remaining angles, $\angle B = \angle E$, are also equal. These relationships would indicate that $\triangle ABC$ is similar to $\triangle DEF$.

2. D

Similar triangles have the same shape, but not necessarily the same size and have the following properties:

1. Corresponding angles are equal.
   $\angle A = \angle A'$ and $\angle B = \angle B'$ and $\angle C = \angle C'$

2. Corresponding sides have proportional lengths.
   $\dfrac{a}{a'} = \dfrac{b}{b'} = \dfrac{c}{c'}$

Therefore, the ratio of corresponding sides are equal and the measure of corresponding angles are equal.

3. A

The two triangles are similar since the corresponding angles are equal.
$$\frac{3}{y} = \frac{19.5}{26}$$
$$3 \times 26 = 19.5 \times y$$
$$78 = 19.5y$$
$$78 \div 19.5 = y$$
$$4 = y$$
The length of side y is 4.0 units.

4. D

By definition, two triangles are congruent if all pairs of corresponding sides and angles are equal. In this case, all angles are the same, and two corresponding sides are marked as equal, so by SAS, the triangles are congruent.

5. B

The triangles are similar since they are formed using the shadows created by the same angle of the sun at the same point in time, and the remaining corresponding angles are equal. Therefore, corresponding sides will have equal ratios.
$$\frac{10.4}{11.2} = \frac{2.3}{x}$$
$$x = \frac{2.3 \times 11.2}{10.4}$$
$$x \approx 2.4769$$
The height of the statue, to the nearest tenth of a metre, is 2.5 m tall.

6. C

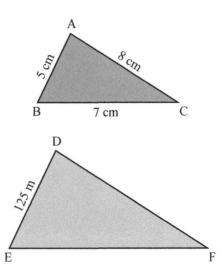

Let $\triangle ABC$ represent the triangular field drawn on the map and let $\triangle DEF$ represent the actual field. When the field is reproduced on the map using a scale factor, all its sides are scaled down in the same proportion.

Thus, the shortest side of the field drawn on the map represents the shortest side of the actual field.

Since all sides of ΔABC and ΔDEF are proportional, the two triangles are similar.

Since side AC (the longest side of ΔABC) corresponds to side DF of ΔDEF, it means that side DF is the longest side of the actual field.

$$\frac{AB}{DE} = \frac{AC}{DF}$$
$$\frac{5 \text{ cm}}{125 \text{ m}} = \frac{8 \text{ cm}}{DF}$$
$$DF = \frac{8 \times 125}{5} \text{ m}$$
$$DF = 200 \text{ m}$$

Thus, the longest side of the triangular field is 200 m.

7. 67.5

∠ABL = ∠CDL , ∠BAL = ∠DCL , and ∠ALB = ∠CLD.
Therefore, ΔLAB is similar to ΔLCD.
In similar triangles, the length of corresponding sides are proportional; thus, $\frac{LB}{LD} = \frac{AB}{CD}$

Step 1
Write the ratios of the corresponding sides.
$$\frac{LB}{LD} = \frac{AB}{CD}$$
$$\frac{12}{27} = \frac{30}{x}$$

Step 2
Solve for the unknown value.
$$\frac{12}{27} = \frac{30}{x}$$
$$12x = 810$$
$$\frac{12x}{12} = \frac{810}{12}$$
$$= 67.5$$

The length of bridge CD is 67.5 meters.

8. A

Recall the primary trigonometry ratio.

$$\cos \theta = \frac{\text{adjacent}}{\text{hypotenuse}} \qquad \cos \theta = \frac{12}{13}$$

$$\tan \theta = \frac{\text{opposite}}{\text{adjacent}} \qquad \tan \theta = \frac{5}{12}$$

From the given ratios the following triangle can be drawn

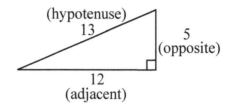

$$\sin \theta = \frac{\text{opposite}}{\text{hypotenuse}}$$
$$\sin \theta = \frac{5}{13}$$

9. B

$$\tan \theta = \frac{\text{opposite}}{\text{adjacent}}$$
$$\tan 72° = \frac{c}{a}$$

Since tan 72° = 3.1, it follows that $3.1 = \frac{c}{a}$.

10. C

The angle inside the triangle adjacent to 133° is 47° because they are supplementary angles (180° − 133° = 47°).
Therefore,
$$\sin 47° = \frac{\text{opposite}}{\text{hypotenuse}} = \frac{11.7}{x}$$
$$x = \frac{11.7}{\sin 47°}$$
$$x \approx 15.998 \text{ cm}$$
The length of side x, to the nearest tenth, is 16.0 cm.

11. A

Begin by sketching a diagram to represent the given problem.

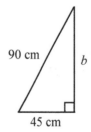

To solve, use the Pythagorean theorem
$c^2 = a^2 + b^2$.
Substitute 90 for c and 45 for a.
$(90)^2 = (45)^2 + b^2$

Now, solve for b.
$8100 = 225 + b^2$
$675 = b^2$
$b = \sqrt{675}$
$b = \approx 77.942$ cm

To the nearest centimetre, the length of the third side is 78 cm.

12. **B**

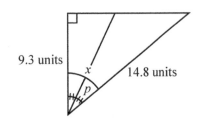

Using the cosine ratio, determine the angle that represents $2p$. The angle is labelled x in the diagram shown.

$\cos x = \dfrac{\text{adjacent}}{\text{hypotenuse}}$

$\cos x = \dfrac{9.3}{14.8}$

$\cos x = 0.628\,378$

$\cos^{-1}(0.628\,378) = x$
$x \approx 51.069°$

Since $x = 2p$, the measure of angle
$p = \dfrac{x}{2} \approx \dfrac{51.069°}{2} = 25.5°$.

13. **24.9**

Step 1
Apply the Pythagorean theorem in $\triangle BDC$ in order to determine by length of side BD.
$(BD)^2 + (CD)^2 = (BC)^2$
Substitute 63 for CD and 65 for BC
$(BD)^2 + (63)^2 = (65)^2$
$(BD)^2 + 3\,969 = 4\,225$
$(BD)^2 = 256$
$BD = \sqrt{256}$
$BD = 16$ m

Step 2
Apply the sine ratio in $\triangle ADB$ in order to determine the length of side AB.
$\sin 40° = \dfrac{BD}{AB}$
Substitute 16 for BD.
$\sin 40° = \dfrac{16}{AB}$
$AB\sin 40° = 16$
$AB = \dfrac{16}{\sin 40°}$
$AB \approx 24.89$ m
Correct to the nearest tenth of a metre, the length of side AB is 24.9 m.

14. **A**

Step 1
Label the diagram.

Let x represent the unknown angle between wire B and the ground. Since there are two right triangles in the diagram, use the smaller right triangle to solve for the height of the telephone pole. This is needed to solve for the unknown angle. Let y represent the height of the telephone pole.

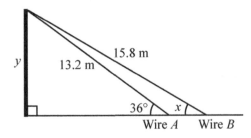

Step 2
Use the sine ratio to solve for y.
$\sin \theta = \dfrac{\text{opposite}}{\text{hypotenuse}}$
$\sin 36° = \dfrac{y}{13.2}$
$y = 13.2 \times \sin 36°$
$y \approx 7.759$ m

Step 3
Use the sine ratio to solve for x.
$\sin \theta = \dfrac{\text{opposite}}{\text{hypotenuse}}$
$\sin x \approx \dfrac{7.759}{15.8}$
$x \approx \sin^{-1}\left(\dfrac{7.759}{15.8}\right)$
$x \approx 29.411°$

To the nearest degree, the angle between wire B and the ground is 29°.

15. C

The tent is made up of two congruent right triangles. Use the cosine ratio to determine the value of $\frac{1}{2}x$, labelled y, as shown.

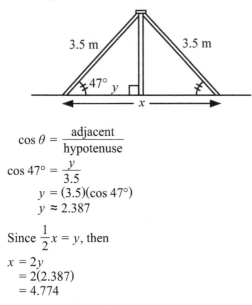

$$\cos \theta = \frac{\text{adjacent}}{\text{hypotenuse}}$$

$$\cos 47° = \frac{y}{3.5}$$

$$y = (3.5)(\cos 47°)$$

$$y \approx 2.387$$

Since $\frac{1}{2}x = y$, then

$$x = 2y$$
$$= 2(2.387)$$
$$= 4.774$$

The width of the tent at its base, rounded to the nearest tenth of a metre, is 4.8 m.

16. C

Let the distance from the top of the shorter building to the top of the taller building be w. Thus, $y = w + x$.

Step 1
Apply the tangent ratio to solve for x.

$$\tan \theta = \frac{\text{opposite}}{\text{adjacent}}$$

$$\tan 26° = \frac{x}{40}$$

$$x = 40(\tan 26°)$$

$$x \approx 19.509 \text{ m}$$

Step 2
Apply the tangent ratio to solve for w.

$$\tan \theta = \frac{\text{opposite}}{\text{adjacent}}$$

$$\tan 37° = \frac{w}{40}$$

$$w = 40(\tan 37°)$$

$$w \approx 30.142 \text{ m}$$

Step 3
Substitute the values for x and w into the equation $y = w + x$, and solve for y.

$$y \approx 19.509 + 30.142$$

$$y \approx 49.651 \text{ m}$$

Rounded to the nearest tenth of a metre, the height of the taller building is 49.7 m.

17. D

Step 1
Since there is a right angle from Lynn's house to the school to the café, determine the acute angle inside the right triangle formed from the café to the school.
$90° - 71° = 19°$

Step 2
To determine the total distance from the café to Marrah's house, determine the unknown side x by using the tangent ratio.

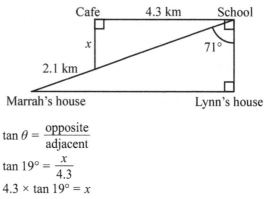

$$\tan \theta = \frac{\text{opposite}}{\text{adjacent}}$$

$$\tan 19° = \frac{x}{4.3}$$

$$4.3 \times \tan 19° = x$$

To the nearest tenth, $x = 1.5$ km.

Step 3
Calculate the total distance by adding the three distances that make up the route from the school to the café to Marrah's house.
$4.3 \text{ km} + 1.5 \text{ km} + 2.1 \text{ km} = 7.9 \text{ km}$

18. a) OR

The given diagram can be labelled as shown below.

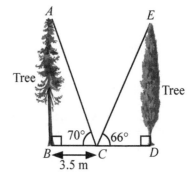

Diagram not to scale

In $\triangle ABC$, the length of the ladder, AC, can be determined as follows:

$$\cos 70° = \frac{BC}{AC}$$

Substitute 3.5 for BC.

$$\cos 70° = \frac{3.5}{AC}$$

$$AC \times \cos 70° = 3.5$$

$$AC = \frac{3.5}{\cos 70°}$$

$$AC \approx 10.23$$

The length of the ladder correct to the nearest tenth is 10.2 m.

b) OR

The distance between the bases of the two trees is equal to the distance from B to D. Since $BD = BC + CD$, it is necessary to determine the length of BC and CD.

Since $BC = 3.5$ m, solve for CD using the following procedure:

In $\triangle CDE$, $\cos 66° = \dfrac{CD}{CE}$

Substitute 10.23 for CE, since $CE = AC$.

$$\cos 66° = \frac{CD}{10.23}$$

$CD = 10.23 \times \cos 66°$

$CD = 4.2$ (to the nearest tenth)

Recall that $BD = BC + CD$.

Thus, $BD = 3.5 + 4.2 = 7.7$

To the nearest tenth, the distance between the bases of the two trees is 7.7 m.

19. D

$\sin A = \dfrac{h}{b}$ implies that $b \times \sin A = h$.

$\sin B = \dfrac{h}{a}$ implies that $a \times \sin B = h$.

Since the value of h is identical in each equation, it follows that $b \times \sin A = a \times \sin B$ or $b\sin A = a\sin B$.

20. B

In general, the law of sines states that $\dfrac{a}{\sin A} = \dfrac{b}{\sin B}$.

Thus, in the equation $\dfrac{80}{\sin 50°} = \dfrac{65}{\sin x°}$, the 50° angle must be opposite the side measuring 80 m and the $x°$ angle must be opposite the side measuring 65 m.

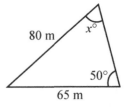

21. D

One form of the cosine law is

$$\cos A = \frac{b^2 + c^2 - a^2}{2bc}.$$

The equation $\cos x° = \dfrac{15^2 + 20^2 - 17^2}{2(15)(20)}$ implies that the side measuring 17 cm is opposite to the angle measuring $x°$ and the measures of the other sides of the triangle are 15 cm and 20 cm.

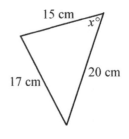

22. D

The law of cosines can be represented by the general equation $a^2 = b^2 + c^2 - 2bc\cos A$. This equation implies that angle A is opposite side a.

In the given triangle, angle R is opposite PQ, angle P is opposite QR, and angle Q is opposite PR.

Thus, the equation $(QR)^2 = (QP)^2 + (PR)^2 - 2(QP)(PR)\cos P$ correctly represents the law of cosines.

23. C

Begin by sketching triangle ABC and placing the given

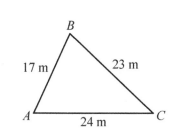

measurements in the appropriate location. One possible sketch is shown.

In the given sketch, $\angle A$ is opposite the side measuring 23 m. Since this is a side-side-side situation, determine the measure of $\angle A$ by applying the law of cosines as follows:

$$\cos A = \frac{(AB)^2 + (AC)^2 - (BC)^2}{2(AB)(AC)}$$

Substitute 17 for AB, 24 for AC, and 23 for BC.

$$\cos A = \frac{17^2 + 24^2 - 23^2}{2(17)(24)}$$

$$\cos A = \frac{336}{816}$$

$$\cos A \approx 0.4118$$

$$A \approx 65.68°$$

To the nearest degree, the measure of the angle opposite the side measuring 23 m is 66°.

24. C

The given triangle presents a side-angle-side situation, so use the law of cosines in order to solve for x.

The general form of the law of cosines is $a^2 = b^2 + c^2 - 2bc\cos A$. By making the appropriate substitutions, the equation becomes $x^2 = 37^2 + 37^2 - 2(37)(37)\cos(80°)$.

25. A

There is no side-side-side situation in $\triangle LMN$; therefore, use the sine law to determine the measure of $\angle M$ as follows:

To begin, determine the measure of $\angle L$, since $\angle L$ is opposite side MN.

$$\frac{MN}{\sin L} = \frac{LM}{\sin N}$$

Substitute 140 for MN, 120 for LM, and 43° for $\angle N$. Then, solve for $\angle L$.

$$\frac{140}{\sin L} = \frac{120}{\sin 43°}$$

$$120\sin L = 140\sin 43°$$

$$\sin L = \frac{140\sin 43°}{120}$$

$$\sin L = 0.795$$

$$\angle L = 52.7°$$

To the nearest degree, the measure of $\angle M$ is $180° - 43° - 53° = 84°$.

26. B

Because there is no side-angle-side situation in $\triangle ABC$, use the sine law to determine the measure of $\angle B$.

$$\frac{AC}{\sin B} = \frac{AB}{\sin C}$$

Substitute 6 for AC, 9 for AB, and 87° for $\angle C$. Then, solve for $\angle B$.

$$\frac{6}{\sin B} = \frac{9}{\sin 87°}$$

$$9\sin B = 6\sin 87°$$

$$\sin B = \frac{6\sin 87°}{9}$$

$$\sin B \approx 0.6658$$

$$\angle B \approx 41.7°$$

Rounded to the nearest degree, the measure of $\angle B$ is 42°.

27. 111

In order to determine the perimeter of $\triangle ABC$, find the length of each of the three sides of the triangle. The length of side BC is given, but the lengths of side AC and AB must be calculated.

Step 1

Calculate the measure of side AC in $\triangle DAC$. Use the cosine ratio to solve for side AC.

$$\cos \angle DAC = \frac{AC}{AD}$$

Substitute 20° for $\angle DAC$ and 38 for AD.

$$\cos 20° = \frac{AC}{38}$$

$$AC = 38\cos 20°$$

$$AC = 35.71 \text{ cm}$$

Step 2

Calculate the measure of side AB in $\triangle ABC$.

Use the law of cosines to determine AB as follows:

$(AB)^2 = (AC)^2 + (BC)^2 - 2(AC)(BC)\cos \angle ACB$

Substitute 35.71 for AC, 42 for BC, and 50° for $\angle ACB$. Then, solve for side AB.

$(AB)^2 = (35.71)^2 + (42)^2 - 2(35.71)(42)\cos 50°$

$(AB)^2 = 1\ 111.07$

$AB = 33.33$ cm

Step 3

Calculate the perimeter of $\triangle ABC$.

The perimeter of $\triangle ABC$ is

$42 + 35.71 + 33.33 = 111.04$ cm.

Rounded to the nearest centimetre, the perimeter of $\triangle ABC$ is 111 cm.

28. A

Step 1

Determine the distance from point S to point A in $\triangle SAB$ by applying the Sine Law.

$\dfrac{SA}{\sin \angle B} = \dfrac{SB}{\sin \angle BAS}$

The measure of $\angle BAS$ can be calculated as follows:

$\angle BAS = 180° - 49° - 42° = 89°$

Substitute 42° for $\angle B$, 50 for SB, and 89° for $\angle BAS$.

$\dfrac{SA}{\sin 42°} = \dfrac{50}{\sin 89°}$

$SA \times \sin 89° = 50 \times \sin 42°$

$SA = \dfrac{50 \times \sin 42°}{\sin 89°}$

$SA \approx 33.46$ m

Step 2

Solve for h in right triangle SAP.

$\tan \angle PSA = \dfrac{PA}{SA}$

Substitute 65° for $\angle PSA$, h for PA, and 33.46 for SA.

$\tan 65° = \dfrac{h}{33.46}$

$h = 33.46 \times \tan 65°$

$h \approx 71.76$ m

To the nearest metre, the height of the cliff is 72 m.

29. OR

Step 1

Determine the measure of angle AHT.

$\angle AHT = 180° - (\angle ATH + \angle TAH)$

$\angle AHT = 180° - (45° + 95°)$

$\angle AHT = 40°$

Step 2

Use the sine law to determine the distance from point T to point H.

$\dfrac{TH}{\sin TAH} = \dfrac{TA}{\sin AHT}$

$\dfrac{TH}{\sin 95°} = \dfrac{175}{\sin 40°}$

$TH = \dfrac{175\sin 95°}{\sin 40°}$

$TH = 271.215\ 6699\ldots$

Step 3

Round the answer to the neatest metre.

The distance from point T to point H is about 271 m.

30. B

In $\triangle NPR$, it is not a side-angle-side situation, so determine the distance between the Royal Caribbean and the Norwegian cruise ships by applying the law of sines as shown:

$\dfrac{RN}{\sin \angle RPN} = \dfrac{NP}{\sin \angle NRP}$

Substitute 85° for $\angle RPN$, 250 for NP, and 71° $(180° - 24° - 85°)$ for $\angle NRP$.

$\dfrac{RN}{\sin 85°} = \dfrac{250}{\sin 71°}$

$RN \times \sin 71° = 250 \times \sin 85°$

$RN = \dfrac{250 \times \sin 85°}{\sin 71°}$

$RN \approx 263.40$

To the nearest metre, the distance between the Royal Caribbean and the Norwegian cruise ships is 263 m.

31. C

Step 1

Label the diagram.

The given diagram can be labelled as follows:

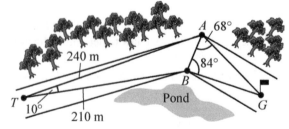

Step 2

Determine the distance from point A to point B.

In $\triangle ATB$, it is a side-angle-side situation; therefore, solve for AB by applying the cosine law.

$(AB)^2 = (TA)^2 + (TB)^2 - 2(TA)(TB)\cos \angle T$

Substitute 240 for TA, 210 for TB, and $10°$ for $\angle T$, and solve for AB.

$(AB)^2 = 240^2 + 210^2 - 2(240)(210)\cos 10°$

$(AB)^2 \approx 57\ 600 + 44\ 100 - 99\ 268.62$

$(AB)^2 \approx 2\ 431.38$

$\quad AB \approx \sqrt{2\ 431.38}$

$\quad AB \approx 49.31$

Step 3

Use $\triangle GAB$, and apply the sine law in order to determine the distance of BG.

$\dfrac{BG}{\sin \angle GAB} = \dfrac{AB}{\sin \angle G}$

Calculate the measure of $\angle G$ by subtracting the known angle measures of $\triangle ABG$ from $180°$.

$\angle G = 180° - 68° - 84° = 28°$

Substitute $68°$ for $\angle GAB$, 49.31 for AB, and $28°$ for $\angle G$, and solve for BG.

$\dfrac{BG}{\sin 68°} = \dfrac{49.31}{\sin 28°}$

$BG \times \sin 28° = 49.31 \times \sin 68°$

$\quad BG = \dfrac{49.31 \times \sin 68°}{\sin 28°}$

$\quad BG \approx 97.38$ m

To the nearest metre, the distance of BG is 97 m.

32. a) OR

$\triangle ABC$

$\tan B = \dfrac{AC}{BC}$

Substitute $20°$ for $\angle B$ and 90 for AC.

$\tan 20° = \dfrac{90}{BC}$

$BC \times \tan 20° = 90$

$BC = \dfrac{90}{\tan 20°}$

$BC \approx 247.27$

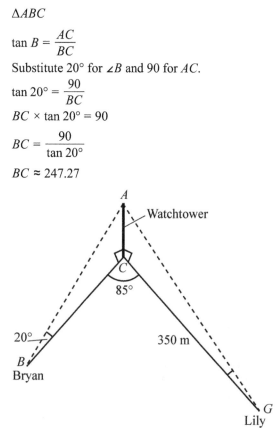

To the nearest metre, Bryan is 247 m from the base of the watchtower.

Solutions – Trigonometry

b) OR

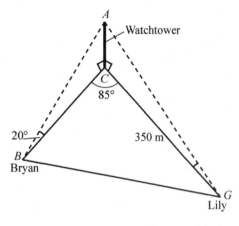

Connect B to G. In $\triangle BCG$, make use of the law of cosines as follows:

$(BG)^2 = (BC)^2 + (CG)^2 - 2(BC)(CG)\cos \angle BCG$

Substitute 247.27 for BC, 350 for CG, and 85° for $\angle BCG$.

$(BG)^2 = 247.27^2 + 350^2 - 2(247.27)(350)\cos 85°$

$(BG)^2 \approx 61\ 142.45 + 122\ 500 - 1585.70$

$(BG)^2 \approx 168\ 556.75$

$BG \approx \sqrt{168\ 556.75}$

$BG \approx 410.56$

To the nearest metre, Bryan and Lily are 411 m apart.

UNIT TEST — TRIGONOMETRY

1. Two different triangles are shown.

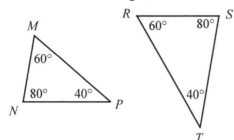

Which of the following equations is **incorrect** with respect to $\triangle MNP$ and $\triangle RST$?

A. $\dfrac{MN}{NP} = \dfrac{RS}{ST}$

B. $\dfrac{NP}{ST} = \dfrac{MP}{RT}$

C. $\dfrac{MN}{RS} = \dfrac{MP}{RT}$

D. $\dfrac{NP}{ST} = \dfrac{MN}{RT}$

2. Which of the following conditions does **not** guarantee that two triangles are congruent?

A. The measures of the three side lengths of the two triangles are the same.

B. The measures of the three interior angles of the two triangles are the same.

C. The measures of two of the interior angles and the side included by them are the same.

D. The measures of two of the side lengths and the interior angle included by them are the same.

Use the following information to answer the next question.

Mitchell made a drawing of a poster in the shape of a right triangle as shown.

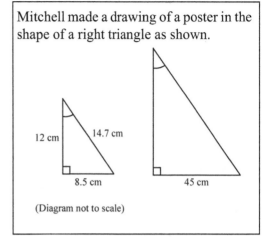

(Diagram not to scale)

3. If one of the sides of the actual poster is 45 cm, what are the actual lengths of the other two sides of the poster, correct to the nearest tenth of a centimetre?

A. 26.7 cm and 45 cm

B. 48.5 cm and 51.2 cm

C. 60.5 cm and 75.8 cm

D. 63.5 cm and 77.8 cm

Numerical Response

4. A 6 m high vertical pole casts a shadow 4 m long. The pole is right beside a building that casts a shadow with a length of 64 m. The approximate height in metres of the building is _____.

Use the following information to answer the next question.

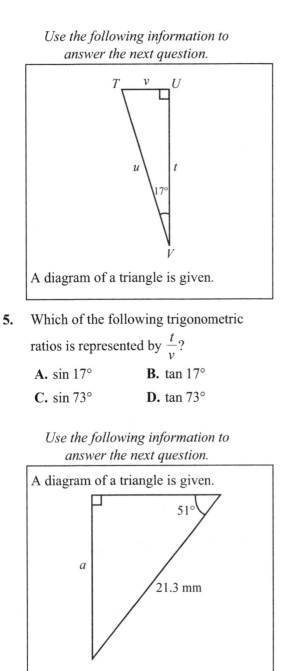

A diagram of a triangle is given.

5. Which of the following trigonometric ratios is represented by $\frac{t}{v}$?

A. $\sin 17°$ **B.** $\tan 17°$

C. $\sin 73°$ **D.** $\tan 73°$

Use the following information to answer the next question.

A diagram of a triangle is given.

6. To the nearest tenth of a millimetre, what is the length of side a?

  A. 13.4 mm   **B.** 16.6 mm

  C. 26.3 mm   **D.** 27.4 mm

7. The length of the hypotenuse of a right triangle is 30.5 cm. If the length of another side is 5.5 cm, what is the length of the third side of this triangle?

  A. 25 cm   **B.** 30 cm

  C. 31 cm   **D.** 36 cm

Use the following information to answer the next question.

A diagram of a triangle and a supplementary angle is given.

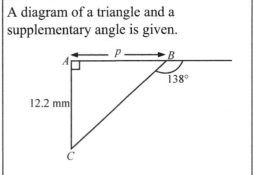

8. What is the length of side p?

  A. 8.2 mm   **B.** 9.1 mm

  C. 11.0 mm   **D.** 13.5 mm

Use the following information to answer the next question.

A design involving two right triangles is shown.

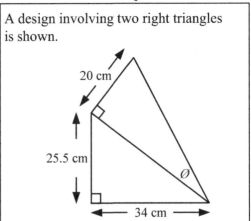

Numerical Response

9. To the nearest tenth, the measure of $\angle\theta$ in the design is _____ degrees.

To support a score clock in an arena, two cables are attached from the ceiling to the score clock, as shown.

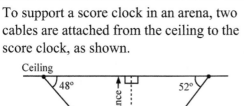

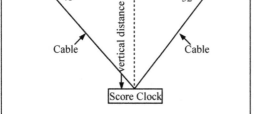

10. If the vertical distance between the top of the score clock and the ceiling is 16 m, then the distance, correct to the nearest tenth of a metre, between the two cables at the point where they are attached to the ceiling is

    A. 26.9 m   **B.** 29.4 m

    C. 30.2 m   **D.** 34.9 m

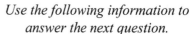

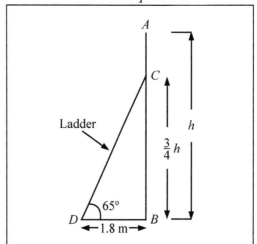

11. In order to paint a pole, George places a ladder against it. The foot of the ladder is 1.8 m away from the pole, and the top of the ladder rests against the pole at a position that is three-quarters up the pole. If the ladder is at an angle of 65° to the ground, what is the actual height of the pole, to the nearest thousandth?

    A. 5.193 m   **B.** 5.147 m

    C. 4.931 m   **D.** 4.903 m

     Trigonometry

When light is reflected off a smooth surface, such as polished glass, the path it follows can easily be determined. Almost 2 000 years ago, Hero of Alexandria concluded that the angle at which light strikes a mirror (the angle of incidence) is exactly equal to the angle at which it reflects (the angle of reflection).

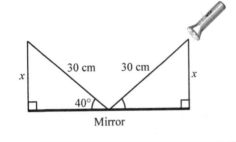

12. If the light from a flashlight reflects off a mirror at a 40° angle and the distance the light travels to the mirror is 30 cm, then, rounded to the nearest tenth of a centimetre, how far is the flashlight from the mirror?

   A. 19.3 cm   **B.** 23.0 cm

   C. 25.2 cm   **D.** 46.7 cm

A cellphone transmitter is placed at the top of a vertical tower. Cables are used to help support the tower. One end of a cable is anchored to the ground, and the other end is attached to an anchor at the top of the tower. As shown, two supporting cables are anchored to the ground at points A and B, which are 12 m apart. The angle between the ground and the cable anchored to points A and B is 62° and 72°, respectively.

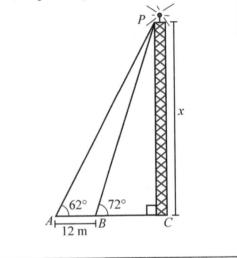

Numerical Response

13. To the nearest metre, the height of the tower is _____ m.

14. George built a shelf that was 50 cm in length. In order to keep it secure, he built two supports, *BE* and *CD*, as shown in the given diagram.

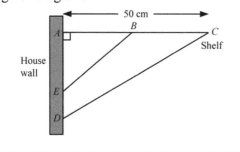

Open Response

a) If ∠*ADC* = 60°, what is the length of *CD* rounded to the nearest tenth of a centimetre?

b) If the distance between anchor points *A* and *E* is 20 cm, what is the distance between anchor points *D* and *E*, rounded to the nearest tenth of a centimetre?

15. The equation $\dfrac{60}{\sin 48°} = \dfrac{x}{\sin 62°}$ applies to which of the following acute triangles?

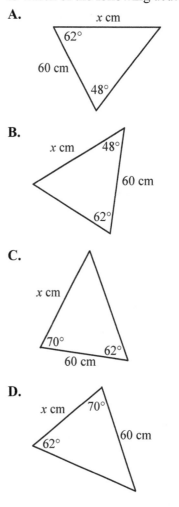

A.

x cm

62°

60 cm

48°

B.

x cm   48°

60 cm

62°

C.

x cm

70°   62°

60 cm

D.

x cm   70°

60 cm

62°

16. For which of the following triangles could the equation
$x^2 = 45^2 + 50^2 - 2(45)(50) \cos 78°$ be used to determine the length of side x?

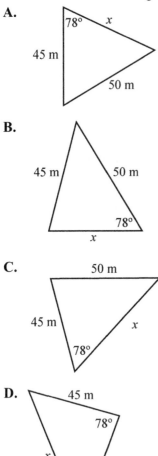

A.

78° x

45 m

50 m

B.

45 m   50 m

78°

x

C.

50 m

45 m x

78°

D.

45 m

78°

x

50 m

Use the following information to answer the next question.

In the given diagram, $\angle BAC = 84°$, $AD = 3.4$ m, $CD = 3.8$ m, and $AC = 3.5$ m.

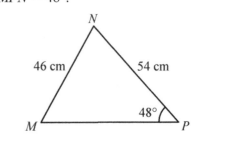

17. The measure of $\angle BAD$, correct to the nearest tenth, is

A. 26.1°   B. 24.7°

C. 19.4°   D. 17.2°

Use the following information to answer the next question.

The diagram illustrates triangle MNP, where $MN = 46$ cm, $NP = 54$ cm, and $\angle MPN = 48°$.

N

46 cm   54 cm

48°

M   P

18. Correct to the nearest tenth of a degree, what is the measure of $\angle NMP$?

A. 71.8°   B. 60.7°

C. 52.4°   D. 39.3°

Use the following information to answer the next question.

In triangle PQR, $PR = 12.2$ cm, $\angle R = 38°$, and $\angle P = 74°$.

19. Correct to the nearest tenth of a centimetre, the length of side PQ is

A. 7.8 cm   B. 8.1 cm

C. 14.3 cm   D. 18.4 cm

20.

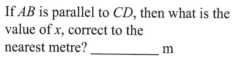

If *AB* is parallel to *CD*, then what is the value of *x*, correct to the nearest metre? _____ m

Use the following information to answer the next question.

An engineer needs to calculate the distance across a deep canyon. She takes a sighting from a point *A* and then from a point *C*, which are both on the same side of the canyon, to a point *B* on the opposite side of the canyon, as shown in the diagram.

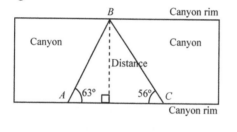

21. If points *A* and *C* are 70 m apart, then the distance across the canyon, correct to the nearest tenth of a metre, is

A. 51.9 m   B. 59.1 m

C. 60.3 m   D. 68.7 m

Use the following information to answer the next question.

The game of curling involves throwing rocks down a sheet of ice toward a bull's eye called the house which is painted under the ice surface. The diagram shows the path of a curling rock that is released from point *A*, strikes a stationary rock at point *B*, and comes to rest at point *C*.

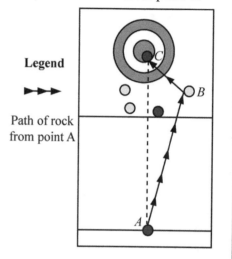

In the triangle formed by the rock's path, side *AB* is 24 m, side *BC* is 8.5 m, and angle *ABC* is 115°.

22. Rounded to the nearest tenth of a metre, what is the distance from point *A* to point *C*?

A. 31.2 m   B. 28.6 m

C. 25.4 m   D. 21.8 m

From a prison watchtower, there are two floodlights lighting the prison yard. The triangular shaded region in the given diagram represents the section of the prison yard lit by the two floodlights and has an area of 2 670 m².

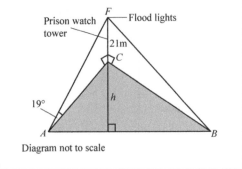

Diagram not to scale

23. If $\angle ACB = 98°$ and the length of side BC is 84.51m, then the height, h, of the shaded triangle that represents the section of the prison yard lit by the floodlights, to the nearest metre, is

A. 84 m   B. 80 m

C. 48 m   D. 44 m

24. An engineer is asked to calculate the width, w, of a river. He takes a sighting from point X and another sighting from point Y, both on the shore of the same side of the river to a point A on the opposite shore of the river. The engineer's measurements are shown in the diagram.

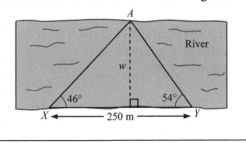

Open Response

a) What is the measure of $\angle XAY$? Justify your answer.

b) What is the width, w, of the river to the nearest tenth of a metre?

ANSWERS AND SOLUTIONS — UNIT TEST

1. D	7. B	13. 58	18. B	24. a) OR
2. B	8. D	14. a) OR	19. B	b) OR
3. D	9. 25.2	b) OR	20. 22	
4. 96	10. A	15. C	21. B	
5. D	11. B	16. D	22. B	
6. B	12. A	17. D	23. C	

1. D

In $\triangle MNP$ and $\triangle RST$, $\triangle MNP$ is similar to $\triangle RST$ since the angles in $\triangle MNP$ are equal to the angles in $\triangle RST$.

Thus, the ratios of corresponding sides are equal. The correct ratios are $\dfrac{MN}{NP} = \dfrac{RS}{ST}$, $\dfrac{NP}{ST} = \dfrac{MP}{RT}$, and $\dfrac{MN}{RS} = \dfrac{MP}{RT}$.

The incorrect ratio $\dfrac{NP}{ST} = \dfrac{MN}{RT}$ could be replaced with the correct ratios $\dfrac{NP}{ST} = \dfrac{MP}{RT}$ or $\dfrac{NP}{ST} = \dfrac{MN}{RS}$.

2. B

There are three approaches to verifying congruency:

1. **SSS:** The measures of the three side lengths of two triangles are the same.
2. **SAS:** The measures of two of the side lengths and the interior angle included by them are the same.
3. **ASA:** The measures of two of the interior angles and the side included by them are the same.

Therefore, if the measures of the three interior angles of the two triangles are the same, it does not guarantee congruency.

3. D

Since both triangles are right triangles and they have an equal angle at the top, the remaining angle will also be equal. The triangles are similar.

Therefore, the ratios of the corresponding sides are equal.

Label the larger triangle as follows:

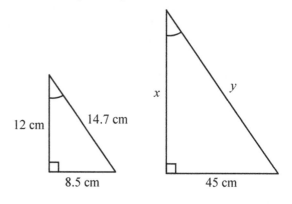

(Diagram not to scale)

$$\frac{x}{45 \text{ cm}} = \frac{12 \text{ cm}}{8.5 \text{ cm}}$$

$$x = \frac{12 \text{ cm} \times 45 \text{ cm}}{8.5 \text{ cm}} = 63.5 \text{ cm}$$

$$\frac{y}{45 \text{ cm}} = \frac{14.7 \text{ cm}}{8.5 \text{ cm}}$$

$$y = \frac{14.7 \text{ cm} \times 45 \text{ cm}}{8.5 \text{ cm}} = 77.8 \text{ cm}$$

The actual lengths of the other two sides of the poster are 63.5 cm and 77.8 cm.

4. 96

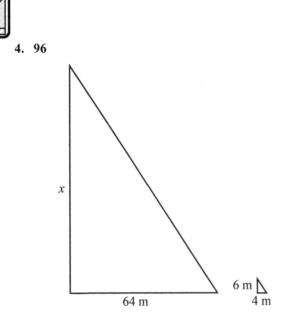

The triangles are similar since they are formed using the shadows created by the same angle of the sun at the same point in time, and the remaining corresponding angles are equal. Therefore, corresponding sides will have equal ratios.

$$\frac{x}{64} = \frac{6}{4}$$

$$x = \frac{6 \times 64}{4}$$

$$x = 96 \text{ m}$$

5. D

Step 1

Determine the primary trigonometric ratios for one of the acute angles.

Using 17° as the angle of reference, the sides are labelled t = adjacent, v = opposite, and u = hypotenuse.

The primary trigonometric ratios are as follows:

$$\sin \theta = \frac{\text{opposite}}{\text{hypotenuse}}$$

$$\sin 17° = \frac{v}{u}$$

$$\cos \theta = \frac{\text{adjacent}}{\text{hypotenuse}}$$

$$\cos 17° = \frac{t}{u}$$

$$\tan \theta = \frac{\text{opposite}}{\text{adjacent}}$$

$$\tan 17° = \frac{v}{t}$$

Step 2

Determine the primary trigonometric ratios for the other acute angle.

Since 180° − 90° − 17° = 73°, the third angle in the triangle is 73°.

Using 73° as the angle of reference, the sides are labelled t = opposite, v = adjacent, and u = hypotenuse.

$$\sin \theta = \frac{\text{opposite}}{\text{hypotenuse}}$$

$$\sin 73° = \frac{t}{u}$$

$$\cos \theta = \frac{\text{adjacent}}{\text{hypotenuse}}$$

$$\cos 73° = \frac{v}{u}$$

$$\tan \theta = \frac{\text{opposite}}{\text{adjacent}}$$

$$\tan 73° = \frac{t}{v}$$

Therefore, the trigonometric ratio represented by $\frac{t}{v}$ is tan 73°.

6. B

Use the sine ratio to determine the length of side a.

$$\sin \theta = \frac{\text{opposite}}{\text{hypotenuse}}$$

$$\sin 51° = \frac{a}{21.3}$$

$$a = (21.3)(\sin 51°)$$

$$a \approx 16.6 \text{ mm}$$

To the nearest tenth of a millimetre, the length of side a is 16.6 mm.

7. B

Begin with a sketch for clarity.

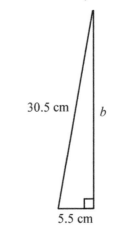

To solve, use the Pythagorean theorem $c^2 = a^2 + b^2$.

Substitute the value of the hypotenuse, ($c = 30.5$ cm), and the value of a, ($a = 5.5$ cm) into the equation.

$(30.5)^2 = (5.5)^2 + b^2$

Now, solve for b.

$930.25 = 30.25 + b^2$

$900 = b^2$

$b = \sqrt{900}$

$b = 30$ cm

The length of the third side is 30 cm.

8. **D**

Step 1

Calculate the angle inside the triangle at B.

The $138°$ angle is a supplementary angle to $\angle B$ inside the triangle.

$\angle B = 180° - 138°$
$\quad\quad = 42°$

Step 2

Calculate the length of p using the tangent ratio.

$\tan \angle B = \dfrac{\text{opposite}}{\text{adjacent}}$

$\tan 42° = \dfrac{12.2}{p}$

$p = \dfrac{12.2}{\tan 42°}$

$p = 13.5$ mm

The length of side p is 13.5 mm.

9. **25.2**

The given diagram can be labelled as shown below

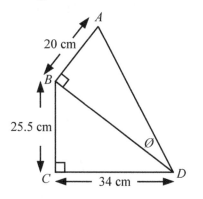

Apply the Pythagorean theorem to $\triangle BCD$ as follows:

$(BC)^2 + (CD)^2 = (BD)^2$

Substitute 25.5 for BC and 34 for CD.

$25.5^2 + 34^2 = (BD)^2$

$650.25 + 1156 = (BD)^2$

$1806.25 = (BD)^2$

$\sqrt{1806.25} = BD$

$42.5 = BD$

In $\triangle ABD$, $\tan \theta = \dfrac{AB}{BD}$

Substitute 20 for AB and 42.5 for BD.

$\tan \theta = \dfrac{20}{42.5}$

$\theta = \tan^{-1}\left(\dfrac{20}{42.5}\right)$

$\theta \approx 25.20$

To the nearest tenth, the measure of $\angle \theta$ is $25.2°$.

10. **A**

Label the diagram as follows:

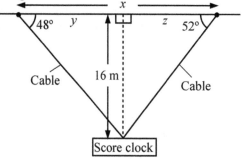

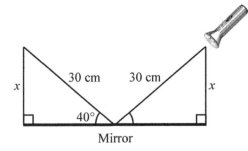

From the diagram, $x = y + z$. Therefore, determine the values of y and z to determine x. To determine y, use the tangent ratio.

$$\tan \theta = \frac{\text{opposite}}{\text{adjacent}}$$

$$\tan 48° = \frac{16}{y}$$

$$y = \frac{16}{\tan 48°}$$

$y = 14.4$ m

Similarly, determine z.

$$\tan \theta = \frac{\text{opposite}}{\text{adjacent}}$$

$$\tan 52° = \frac{16}{z}$$

$$z = \frac{16}{\tan 52°}$$

$z = 12.5$ m

Substitute these values into $x = y + z$.

$x = 14.4$ m $+ 12.5$ m

$x = 26.9$ m

The distance between the two cables is 26.9 m.

11. B

To determine the height of the pole (BA), first determine the distance BC. Use the tangent ratio.

$$\tan \theta = \frac{\text{opposite}}{\text{adjacent}}$$

$$\tan 65° = \frac{BC}{1.8}$$

$1.8 \times \tan 65° = BC$

$BC = 3.860$ m

Since $BC = \frac{3}{4} BA$,

$$BA = \frac{4}{3} BC$$

$$BA = \frac{4}{3}\left(3.860\right)$$

$BA = 5.147$ m

12. A

In the diagram, the distance between the flashlight and the mirror is the side of a right triangle opposite the 40° angle.

Since the hypotenuse of the triangle is 30 cm, use the sine ratio to determine the distance between the flashlight and the mirror. Let x equal the distance between the flashlight and the mirror.

$$\frac{x}{30} = \sin 40°$$

$x = \sin 40 \times 30$

$x = 19.3$ cm

Therefore, $\frac{x}{30} \doteq 0.643$

Multiply both sides of the equation by 30 cm.

$$\frac{x}{30} \times 30 \doteq 30 \times 0.643$$

$x \doteq 19.28$ cm $\doteq 19.3$ cm

13. 58

By looking at the larger triangle, you can determine that $\angle APC$ at the top is 28° and $\angle BPC$ is 18°. Let y represent the distance from the bottom of the transmitter to the anchor at point B.

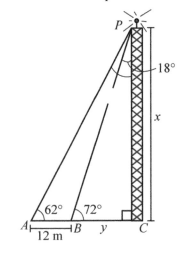

Step 1

Set up the tangent ratios.

$$\tan \theta = \frac{\text{opposite}}{\text{adjacent}}$$
$$\tan 28° = \frac{12 + y}{x}$$
$$\tan 18° = \frac{y}{x}$$

Rearrange the tangent ratios as follows by using the cross-product.

$x \tan 28° = 12 + y$
$x \tan 18° = y$

Step 2

From rearranging the tangent ratios in the previous step, we see that $y = x \tan 18°$, so we can substitute $x \tan 18°$ for y in the remaining tangent ratio, $x \tan 28° = 12 + y$, and then solve the resulting equation for x.

$$x \tan 28° = 12 + y$$
$$x \tan 28° = 12 + (x \tan 18°)$$
$$x \tan 28° - x \tan 18° = 12$$
$$x(\tan 28° - \tan 18°) = 12$$
$$x = \frac{12}{\tan 28° - \tan 18°}$$
$$x = \frac{12}{0.5317 - 0.3249}$$
$$x = \frac{12}{0.269}$$
$$x = 58 \text{ m}$$

Therefore, the height of the tower is 58 m.

14. a) OR

In $\triangle ACD$, the length of CD can be determined using the trigonometric ratio for angle $\angle ACD$ that involves sides AC and CD.

This is the sine ratio.

$$\sin \angle ACD = \frac{AC}{CD}$$
$$\sin 60° = \frac{AC}{CD}$$
$$\sin 60° = \frac{50}{CD}$$
$$CD \times \sin 60° = 50$$
$$CD = \frac{50}{\sin 60°}$$
$$CD \approx 57.7 \text{ cm}$$

To the nearest tenth of a centimetre, the length of CD is 57.7 cm.

b) OR

In order to determine the distance between anchor points D and E, it is necessary to find the distance between anchor points A and D because $AD = AE + DE$. Since $AE = 20$ cm, solve for AD as follows.

Step 1

Apply the Pythagorean theorem to $\triangle ACD$.
Substitute 57.74 for CD and 50 for AC.

$$(AD)^2 + (AC)^2 = (CD)^2$$
$$(AD)^2 + 50^2 = 57.74^2$$
$$(AD)^2 + 2\,500 \approx 3\,333.91$$
$$(AD)^2 \approx 833.91$$
$$AD \approx \sqrt{833.91}$$
$$AD = 28.9$$

Step 2

Recall that $AD = AE + DE$.
Substitute 20 for AE and 28.9 for AD.

$$AD = AE + DE$$
$$28.9 = 20 + DE$$
$$8.9 = DE$$

To the nearest tenth of a centimetre, the distance between anchor points D and E is 8.9 cm.

15. C

The equation $\frac{60}{\sin 48°} = \frac{x}{\sin 62°}$ implies that the side measuring 60 cm is opposite to the 48° angle and the unknown side length is opposite the 62° angle.

The triangle can look like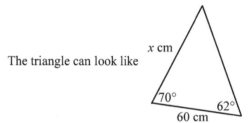

where the missing angle measurement is 48°.

16. D

The law of cosines states that $a^2 = b^2 + c^2 - 2bc \cos A$. Therefore, the equation $x^2 = 45^2 + 50^2 - 2(45)(50) \cos 78°$ applies to a triangle where the side-angle-side situation is given and the 78 ° angle is opposite the side measuring x.

17. D

The measure of $\angle BAD$ is equal to the measure of $\angle BAC$ minus the measure of $\angle CAD$. The measure of $\angle BAC$ is given, but it is necessary to determine the measure of $\angle CAD$.

Determine the measure of $\angle CAD$ by applying the law of cosines.

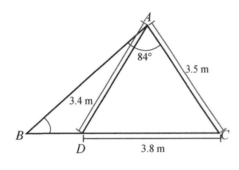

$$\cos \angle CAD = \frac{(AD)^2 + (AC)^2 - (CD)^2}{2(AD)(AC)}$$

Substitute 3.4 for AD, 3.5 for AC, and 3.8 for CD.

$$\cos \angle CAD = \frac{3.4^2 + 3.5^2 - 3.8^2}{2(3.4)(3.5)}$$
$$\cos \angle CAD = \frac{9.37}{23.8}$$
$$\cos \angle CAD = 0.3937$$
$$\cos \angle CAD = \cos^{-1}(0.3937)$$
$$\cos \angle CAD = 66.82$$

To the nearest tenth, the measure of $\angle CAD$ is 66.8°.

Thus,
$\angle BAD = 84° - 66.8°$
$\angle BAD = 17.2°$

18. B

Step 1

Since three measures in triangle MNP are given (a side, its corresponding opposite angle, and another side length), apply the sine law to determine the measure of angle NMP.

The sine law is stated as follows:

$$\text{Sine law} = \frac{a}{\sin A} = \frac{b}{\sin B} = \frac{c}{\sin C}$$

Therefore, $\dfrac{NP}{\sin \angle NMP} = \dfrac{MN}{\sin \angle MPN}$.

Step 2

Substitute 54 for NP, 46 for MN, and 48° for $\angle MPN$.

$$\frac{54}{\sin \angle NMP} = \frac{46}{\sin 48°}$$
$$46\sin \angle NMP = 54\sin 48°$$
$$\sin \angle NMP = \frac{54\sin 48°}{46}$$
$$\sin \angle NMP \approx 0.8724$$
$$\angle NMP \approx \sin^{-1}(0.8724)$$
$$\angle NMP \approx 60.74$$

To the nearest tenth, the measure of angle NMP is 60.7°.

19. B

Step 1

Begin by sketching ΔPQR and placing the given measurements in the appropriate locations.

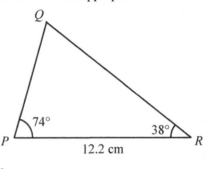

Step 2

Triangle PQR is not a side-angle-side situation; therefore, solve for PQ by using the sine law.

$$\frac{PQ}{\sin \angle PRQ} = \frac{PR}{\sin \angle PQR}$$

Side PR is opposite $\angle PQR$, and the measure of $\angle PQR = 180° - 74° - 38° = 68°$.

Substitute 38° for $\angle PRQ$, 12.2 for PR, and 68° for $\angle PQR$, and solve for side PQ.

$$\frac{PQ}{\sin 38°} = \frac{12.2}{\sin 68°}$$
$$PQ\sin 68° = 12.2\sin 38°$$
$$PQ = \frac{12.2\sin 38°}{\sin 68°}$$
$$PQ \approx 8.10 \text{ cm}$$

To the nearest tenth of a centimetre, the length of side PQ is 8.1 cm.

20. 22

Begin by determining the length of side BC.

In $\triangle ABC$, $\sin \angle ABC = \dfrac{AC}{BC}$

Substitute 65° for $\angle ABC$ and 19 for AC.

$\sin 65° = \dfrac{19}{BC}$

$BC \times \sin 65° = 19$

$BC = \dfrac{19}{\sin 65°}$

$BC \approx 20.96$

Since $\angle ABC$ and $\angle DCB$ are alternate angles, the measure of $\angle ABC$ is equal to the measure of $\angle DCB$. Thus, the measure of $\angle DCB$ is 65°.

In $\triangle BCD$, it is not a side-angle-side situation, so use the law of sines to determine the value of x as follows:

$\dfrac{x}{\sin \angle DCB} = \dfrac{BC}{\sin \angle CDB}$

Substitute 20.96 for BC, 65° for $\angle DCB$, and 61° (180° − 65° − 54°) for $\angle CDB$.

$\dfrac{x}{\sin 65°} = \dfrac{20.96}{\sin 61°}$

$x \times \sin 61° = 20.96 \times \sin 65°$

$x = \dfrac{20.96 \times \sin 65°}{\sin 61°}$

$x \approx 21.72$

The value of x, to the nearest metre, is 22 m.

21. B

Step 1

Label the diagram.

The given diagram can be labelled as shown.

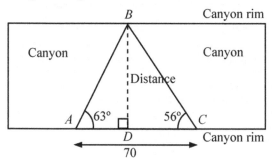

Step 2

Calculate the measure of $\angle B$.

$\angle B = 180° − 63° − 56° = 61°$

Step 3

Determine the length of either side AB or CB by applying the sine law with respect to $\triangle ABC$.

The length of AB can be determined as follows:

$\dfrac{AB}{\sin C} = \dfrac{AC}{\sin B}$

Substitute 56° for C, 70 for AC, and 61° for B. Solve for AB.

$\dfrac{AB}{\sin 56°} = \dfrac{70}{\sin 61°}$

$AB \times \sin 61° = 70 \times \sin 56°$

$AB = \dfrac{70 \times \sin 56°}{\sin 61°}$

$AB \approx 66.35$ m

Step 4

Solve for BD by examining $\triangle ADB$.

In $\triangle ADB$, $\sin A = \dfrac{BD}{AB}$

Substitute 63° for A and 66.35 for AB.

$\sin 63° = \dfrac{BD}{66.35}$

$BD = 66.35 \times \sin 63°$

$BD = 59.12$ m

To the nearest tenth, the distance across the canyon BD is 59.1 m.

A similar procedure can be used to determine the length of side BC, and then the sine ratio can be used with respect to $\triangle BCD$.

22. B

Step 1

Determine whether to apply the sine law or the cosine law in order to calculate the distance from point A to point C.

Since the given values for triangle ABC form a side-angle-side situation, apply the cosine law to determine the distance from point A to point C.

$(AC)^2 = (AB)^2 + (BC)^2 − 2(AB)(BC)\cos \angle B$

Step 2

Substitute the given values into the cosine equation, and solve for AC.

Substitute 24 for AB, 8.5 for BC, and 115° for $\angle B$.

$(AC)^2 = 24^2 + 8.5^2 − 2(24)(8.5)\cos (115°)$

$(AC)^2 \approx 576 + 72.25 + 172.43$

$(AC)^2 \approx 820.68$

$AC \approx \sqrt{820.68}$

$AC \approx 28.648$

The distance from point A to point C is 28.6 m.

23. C

Begin by determining the distance from point A to point C in the right triangle FAC as follows:

$$\tan \angle FAC = \frac{FC}{AC}$$

Substitute 19° for $\angle FAC$ and 21 for FC.
$$AC \times \tan 19° = 21$$

$$\tan 19° = \frac{21}{AC}$$

$$AC = \frac{21}{\tan 19°}$$

$$AC \approx 60.99$$

Next, determine the distance from point A to point B in $\triangle ACB$ by applying the law of cosines as shown:
$$(AB)^2 = (AC)^2 + (BC)^2 - 2(AC)(BC)\cos\angle ACB$$
Substitute 60.99 for AC, 84.51 forBC, and 98° for $\angle ACB$.
$$(AB)^2 = (60.99)^2 + (84.51)^2 - 2(60.99)(84.51)\cos98°$$
$$(AB)^2 \approx 319.78 + 7141.94 + 1434.67$$
$$(AB)^2 \approx 12\ 296.39$$
$$AB \approx 110.89$$

Recall that the area of a triangle is given by the formula $A = \frac{bh}{2}$.

Thus, for $\triangle ABC$,
$$\triangle ABC = \frac{AB \times h}{2}$$

Substitute 2 670 for the area of $\triangle ABC$ and 110.89 for AB.
$$2670 = \frac{110.89 \times h}{2}$$

$$110.89 \times h = 2670 \times 2$$

$$h = \frac{2670 \times 2}{110.89}$$

$$h \approx 48.16$$

The height, h, of the shaded triangle, to the nearest metre, is 48 m.

24. a) OR

The sum of the measures of the three interior angles of a triangle is equal to 180°.
Thus, $\angle X + \angle Y + \angle XAY = 180°$
Substitute 46° for $\angle X$ and 54° for $\angle Y$.
$$46° + 54° + \angle XAY = 180°$$
$$100° + \angle XAY = 180°$$
$$\angle XAY = 180° - 100°$$
The measure of $\angle XAY$ is 80°.

b) OR

The given diagram can be labelled as shown:

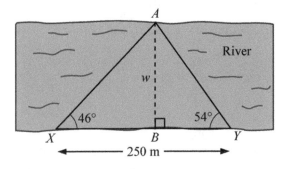

For $\triangle XAY$, apply the law of sines as follows:
$$\frac{XY}{\sin \angle XAY} = \frac{AX}{\sin \angle XAY}$$
Substitute 250 for XY, 80° for $\angle XAY$, and 54° for $\angle XYA$.
$$\frac{250}{\sin 80°} = \frac{AX}{\sin 54°}$$

$$AX \times \sin 80° = 250 \times \sin 54°$$
$$AX = \frac{250 \times \sin 54°}{\sin 80°}$$
$$AX \approx 205.37$$

$\triangle ABX$ is a right angle triangle; therefore,
$$\sin \angle X = \frac{AB}{AX}.$$
Substitute 46° for $\angle X$, w for AB, and 205.37 for AX.
$$\sin 46° = \frac{w}{205.37}$$
$$w = 205.37 \times \sin 46°$$
$$w \approx 147.73$$

The width of the river to the nearest tenth is 147.7 m.

Note: an alternate solution is shown:

In $\triangle XAY$, $\frac{XY}{\sin \angle XAY} = \frac{AY}{\angle AXY}$

$$\frac{250}{\sin 80°} = \frac{AY}{\sin 46°}$$
$$AY \times \sin 80° = 250 \times \sin 46°$$
$$AY = \frac{250 \times \sin 46°}{\sin 80°}$$
$$AY \approx 182.61$$

In $\triangle ABY$, $\sin \angle Y = \frac{AB}{AY}$

$$\sin 54° = \frac{w}{182.61}$$
$$w = 182.61 \times \sin 54°$$
$$w \approx 147.73$$
$$w = 147.7 \text{ m}$$

KEY Strategies for Success on Tests

KEY STRATEGIES FOR SUCCESS ON TESTS

THINGS TO CONSIDER WHEN TAKING A TEST

It is normal to feel anxious before you write a test. You can manage this anxiety by using the following strategies:

- Think positive thoughts. Imagine yourself doing well on the test.

- Make a conscious effort to relax by taking several slow, deep, controlled breaths. Concentrate on the air going in and out of your body.

- Before you begin the test, ask questions if you are unsure of anything.

- Jot down key words or phrases from any instructions your teacher gives you.

- Look over the entire test to find out the number and kinds of questions on the test.

- Read each question closely, and reread if necessary.

- Pay close attention to key vocabulary words. Sometimes, these words are **bolded** or *italicized*, and they are usually important words in the question.

- If you are putting your answers on an answer sheet, mark your answers carefully. Always print clearly. If you wish to change an answer, erase the mark completely, and ensure that your final answer is darker than the one you have erased.

- Use highlighting to note directions, key words, and vocabulary that you find confusing or that are important to answering the question.

- Double-check to make sure you have answered everything before handing in your test.

- When taking tests, students often overlook the easy words. Failure to pay close attention to these words can result in an incorrect answer. One way to avoid this is to be aware of these words and to underline, circle, or highlight them while you are taking the test.

- Even though some words are easy to understand, they can change the meaning of the entire question, so it is important that you pay attention to them. Here are some examples.

all	always	most likely	probably	best	not
difference	usually	except	most	unlikely	likely

Example

1. Which of the following expressions is **incorrect**?

    A. $3 + 2 \geq 5$

    B. $4 - 3 < 2$

    C. $5 \times 4 < 15$

    D. $6 \times 3 \geq 18$

TEST PREPARATION AND TEST-TAKING SKILLS

HELPFUL STRATEGIES FOR ANSWERING MULTIPLE-CHOICE QUESTIONS

A multiple-choice question gives you some information and then asks you to select an answer from four choices. Each question has one correct answer. The other choices are distractors, which are incorrect.

The following strategies can help you when answering multiple-choice questions:

- Quickly skim through the entire test. Find out how many questions there are, and plan your time accordingly.

- Read and reread questions carefully. Underline key words, and try to think of an answer before looking at the choices.

- If there is a graphic, look at the graphic, read the question, and go back to the graphic. Then, you may want to underline the important information from the question.

- Carefully read the choices. Read the question first and then each choice that goes with it.

- When choosing an answer, try to eliminate those choices that are clearly wrong or do not make sense.

- Some questions may ask you to select the best answer. These questions will always include words like *best*, *most appropriate*, or *most likely*. All of the choices will be correct to some degree, but one of the choices will be better than the others in some way. Carefully read all four choices before choosing the answer you think is the best.

- If you do not know the answer, or if the question does not make sense to you, it is better to guess than to leave it blank.

- Do not spend too much time on any one question. Make a mark (*) beside a difficult question, and come back to it later. If you are leaving a question to come back to later, make sure you also leave the space on the answer sheet, if you are using one.

- Remember to go back to the difficult questions at the end of the test; sometimes, clues are given throughout the test that will provide you with answers.

- Note any negative words like *no* or *not*, and be sure your answer fits the question.

- Before changing an answer, be sure you have a very good reason to do so.

- Do not look for patterns on your answer sheet, if you are using one.

HELPFUL STRATEGIES FOR ANSWERING WRITTEN-RESPONSE QUESTIONS

A written response requires you to respond to a question or directive indicated by words such as explain, predict, list, describe, show your work, solve, or calculate. The following strategies can help you when answering written-response questions:

- Read and reread the question carefully.

- Recognize and pay close attention to directing words such as *explain*, *show your work*, and *describe*.

- Underline key words and phrases that indicate what is required in your answer, such as *explain*, *estimate*, *answer*, *calculate*, or *show your work*.

- Write down rough, point-form notes regarding the information you want to include in your answer.

- Think about what you want to say, and organize information and ideas in a coherent and concise manner within the time limit you have for the question.

- Be sure to answer every part of the question that is asked.

- Include as much information as you can when you are asked to explain your thinking.

- Include a picture or diagram if it will help to explain your thinking.

- Try to put your final answer to a problem in a complete sentence to be sure it is reasonable.

- Reread your response to ensure you have answered the question.

- Ask yourself if your answer makes sense.

- Ask yourself if your answer sounds right.

- Use appropriate subject vocabulary and terms in your response.

ABOUT MATHEMATICS TESTS

WHAT YOU NEED TO KNOW ABOUT MATHEMATICS TESTS

To do well on a mathematics test, you need to understand and apply your knowledge of mathematical concepts. Reading skills can also make a difference in how well you perform. Reading skills can help you follow instructions and find key words, as well as read graphs, diagrams, and tables. They can also help you solve mathematics problems.

Mathematics tests usually have two types of questions: questions that ask for understanding of mathematics ideas and questions that test how well you can solve mathematics problems.

HOW YOU CAN PREPARE FOR MATHEMATICS TESTS

The following strategies are particular to preparing for and writing mathematics tests:

- Know how to use your calculator, and, if it is allowed, use your own for the test.

- Note taking is a good way to review and study important information from your class notes and textbook.

- Sketch a picture of the problem, procedure, or term. Drawing is helpful for learning and remembering concepts.

- Check your answer to practice questions by working backward to the beginning. You can find the beginning by going step by step in reverse order.

- Use the following steps when answering questions with graphics (pictures, diagrams, tables, or graphs):

  1. Read the title of the graphic and any key words.

  2. Read the test question carefully to figure out what information you need to find in the graphic.

  3. Go back to the graphic to find the information you need.

  4. Decide which operation is needed.

- Always pay close attention when pressing the keys on your calculator. Repeat the procedure a second time to be sure you pressed the correct keys.

TEST PREPARATION COUNTDOWN

If you develop a plan for studying and test preparation, you will perform well on tests.

Here is a general plan to follow seven days before you write a test.

COUNTDOWN: 7 DAYS BEFORE THE TEST

1. Use "Finding Out about the Test" to help you make your own personal test preparation plan.

2. Review the following information:

   – Areas to be included on the test

   – Types of test items

   – General and specific test tips

3. Start preparing for the test at least seven days before the test. Develop your test preparation plan, and set time aside to prepare and study.

COUNTDOWN: 6, 5, 4, 3, 2 DAYS BEFORE THE TEST

1. Review old homework assignments, quizzes, and tests.

2. Rework problems on quizzes and tests to make sure you still know how to solve them.

3. Correct any errors made on quizzes and tests.

4. Review key concepts, processes, formulas, and vocabulary.

5. Create practice test questions for yourself, and answer them. Work out many sample problems.

COUNTDOWN: THE NIGHT BEFORE THE TEST

1. Use the night before the test for final preparation, which includes reviewing and gathering materials needed for the test before going to bed.

2. Most importantly, get a good night's rest, and know you have done everything possible to do well on the test.

TEST DAY

1. Eat a healthy and nutritious breakfast.

2. Ensure you have all the necessary materials.

3. Think positive thoughts, such as "I can do this," "I am ready," and "I know I can do well."

4. Arrive at your school early, so you are not rushing, which can cause you anxiety and stress.

SUMMARY OF HOW TO BE SUCCESSFUL DURING A TEST

You may find some of the following strategies useful for writing a test:

- Take two or three deep breaths to help you relax.

- Read the directions carefully, and underline, circle, or highlight any important words.

- Look over the entire test to understand what you will need to do.

- Budget your time.

- Begin with an easy question or a question you know you can answer correctly rather than follow the numerical question order of the test.

- If you cannot remember how to answer a question, try repeating the deep breathing and physical relaxation activities. Then, move on to visualization and positive self-talk to get yourself going.

- When answering questions with graphics (pictures, diagrams, tables, or graphs), look at the question carefully, and use the following steps:

    1. Read the title of the graphic and any key words.

    2. Read the test question carefully to figure out what information you need to find in the graphic.

    3. Go back to the graphic to find the information you need.

- Write down anything you remember about the subject on the reverse side of your test paper. This activity sometimes helps to remind you that you do know something and are capable of writing the test.

- Look over your test when you have finished, and double-check your answers to be sure you did not forget anything.

NOTES

Practice Tests

PRACTICE TEST 1

Use the following information to answer the next question.

A model rocket was launched from a platform and its height, *h* metres, above the ground with respect to time, *t* seconds, was recorded. Some of the data obtained is shown in the table.

Time (s)	Height (m)
0	3
1	148
3	410
8	890
14	1 140
20	1 025
25	700

1. Which of the following graphs **best** represents the data shown in the table?

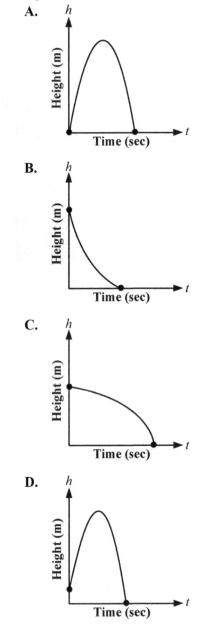

A.

B.

C.

D.

2. Which of the following quadratic relations has a corresponding graph that opens downward and has a second difference of -8.4?

A. $y = 8.4x^2 - 8.4$

B. $y = -8.4x^2 + 5$

C. $y = 4.2x^2 - 8.4$

D. $y = -4.2x^2 + 5$

Use the following information to answer the next question.

The partial graph of a parabola is shown.

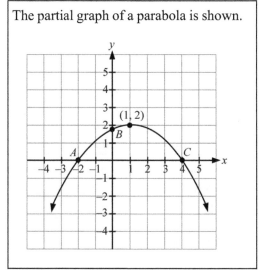

3. Which of the following statements about the graph of the parabola shown is correct?

A. The y-intercept is A, and the zeros occur at B and C.

B. The y-intercept is B, and the zeros occur at A and C.

C. The coordinates of the vertex are $(1, 2)$, and the zeros occur at A and B.

D. The coordinates of the vertex are $(-1, 2)$, and the zeros occur at A and B.

4. A partial table of values for the graph of $y = 2^x$ is shown.

x	-3	0	3
y	a	b	c

What are the respective values of a, b, and c?

A. -6, 0, and 6

B. -8, 0, and 6

C. $\dfrac{1}{6}$, 1, and 6

D. $\dfrac{1}{8}$, 1, and 8

5. The roots of the equation $ax^2 + bx - 16 = 0$ where a and b are real numbers, are 2 and 4. What is the maximum value of the quadratic function $y = ax^2 + bx - 16$?

A. 1

B. 2

C. 3

D. 4

6. A stone is thrown upward from the top of a building. The height of the stone, y in metres, above the ground is given by the function $y = -2x^2 + 8x + 27$, where x is the time in seconds. What is the maximum height attained by the stone?

A. 30 m

B. 35 m

C. 40 m

D. 45 m

Use the following information to answer the next multipart question.

7. A ball is thrown in the air from a balcony of an apartment building and falls to the ground. The height, y metres, of the ball with respect to the ground x seconds after being thrown is given by the equation $y = -4.9x^2 + 24.5x + 6$.

Open Response

a) On the grid below, draw a graph that represents the path of the ball. Make use of your graphing calculator.

b) What is the maximum height, to the nearest tenth, of the ball above the ground?

c) To the nearest tenth of a second, how long is the ball more than 25 m above the ground. Justify your answer.

d) To the nearest tenth, what are the domain and range for the path of the ball?

Use the following information to answer the next question.

The ordered pair $(K, -3)$ is the solution to the system of equations $8x + 3y = -41$ and $6x - 5y = -9$.

8. What is the value of K?

A. 1

B. $\dfrac{4}{25}$

C. -4

D. $\dfrac{-25}{4}$

Use the following information to answer the next question.

> Sally has this system of equations in her notebook.
> $2x - 3y = 3$
> $-x + 4y = 1$

9. In verifying that (3, 1) is a solution to this system of equations, Sally must replace x with 3

   A. and replace y with 1 in both equations

   B. and replace y with 1 in the first equation only

   C. and replace y with 1 in the second equation only

   D. in the first equation and replace y with 1 in the second equation

Use the following information to answer the next question.

> A rock concert drew 55 300 fans to a venue in London. The price of each ticket in sections A to M was $55, and the price of each ticket in sections N to Z was $85. The concert brought in a total of $3 740 500 in ticket sales.

10. How many tickets in sections N to Z were sold?

    A. 9 000

    B. 23 300

    C. 32 000

    D. 55 300

Use the following information to answer the next question.

> As part of an end of the year school function, a teacher and 23 students attend a special showing of a movie at a downtown theatre. All the students and the teacher each purchase a large bag of popcorn.

Open Response

11. If each large bag of popcorn sells for $4.75, what will be the total cost of the popcorn?

12. What is the midpoint of one of the diagonals of a parallelogram with vertices (−5, 5), (5, 10), (3, −1), and (−7, −6)?

    A. (−2, 4)

    B. (−6, −0.5)

    C. (4, 4.5)

    D. (−1, 2)

Use the following information to answer the next question.

Points $A(-2, 2)$, $B(1, -4)$, and $C(2, 6)$ are shown on the given coordinate plane.

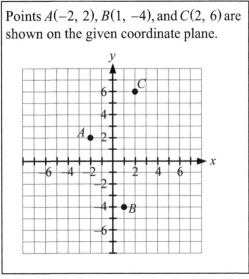

13. The perimeter of triangle ABC is equal to
   A. $\sqrt{178}$
   B. $\sqrt{784}$
   C. $\sqrt{5} + \sqrt{13} + 8$
   D. $3\sqrt{5} + 4\sqrt{2} + \sqrt{101}$

14. The equation of the circle with centre $(0, 0)$ that passes through the point $(5, -2)$ is
   A. $x^2 + y^2 = \sqrt{29}$
   B. $x^2 + y^2 = 29$
   C. $x^2 + y^2 = \sqrt{21}$
   D. $x^2 + y^2 = 21$

Use the following information to answer the next question.

Rami sketched the circle defined by the equation $x^2 + y^2 = 16$. Jacqueline decided to sketch a circle with a diameter that was twice as long as the diameter of Rami's circle.

15. Which of the following diagrams could represent a sketch of Jacqueline's circle?

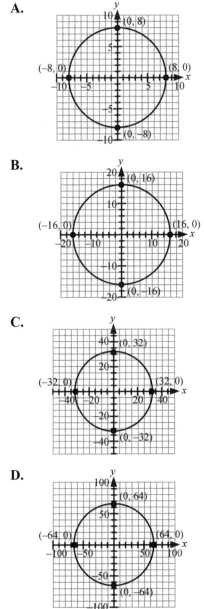

Use the following information to answer the next question.

The median of a triangle is a line segment from one vertex to the midpoint of the opposite side. The vertices of triangle *ABC* are *A*(−5, 0), *B*(−1, 4), and *C*(1, −1), as shown in the diagram.

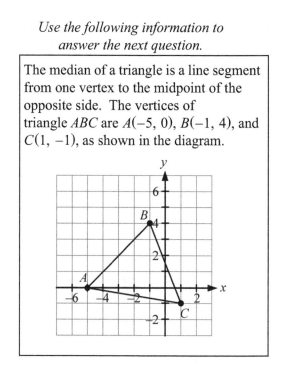

16. What is the length of the median from point *C* to line segment *AB*?

  A. 4 units

  B. 5 units

  C. 6 units

  D. 7 units

Numerical Response

17. The ordered pair $(1, K)$ is located on the right bisector of a line segment with endpoints $(2, -6)$ and $(-8, -4)$. The value of *K* is _____.

Use the following information to answer the next question.

The chart shows the slopes of six different pairs of lines.

	Slope of First Line	Slope of Second Line
Pair I	$\frac{3}{4}$	$\frac{3}{4}$
Pair II	-1	1
Pair III	$\frac{1}{2}$	-2
Pair IV	0	0
Pair V	$-\frac{8}{7}$	$\frac{7}{8}$
Pair VI	$\frac{5}{6}$	$\frac{6}{5}$

18. Perpendicular lines are given by pairs

  A. I and IV only

  B. III and V only

  C. II, III, and V only

  D. II, III, V, and VI only

Use the following information to answer the next question.

Cody is asked to use the diagram shown to verify that the perpendicular bisector of a chord of a circle passes through the centre of the circle.

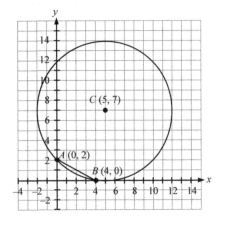

Cody's Plan

Determine the equation of the perpendicular bisector of chord AB, and then determine if the point $(5, 7)$ is on this perpendicular bisector.

Cody's Partial Solution

Step 1: Determine the slope, m, of chord AB.

$$m = \frac{2 - 0}{0 - 4} = -\frac{1}{2}$$

Step 2: Determine the midpoint, M, of chord AB.

$$M = \left(\frac{0 + 4}{2}, \frac{2 + 0}{2}\right) = (2, 1)$$

Step 3: Determine the equation of the perpendicular bisector of chord AB by applying the formula $y = m(x - x_1) + y_1$.

$$y = -\frac{1}{2}(x - 2) + 1$$
$$y = -\frac{1}{2}x + 1 + 1$$
$$y = -\frac{1}{2}x + 2$$

Step 4: Verify that the point $(5, 7)$ is on the line $y = -\frac{1}{2}x + 2$.

19. Which of the following statements with respect to Cody's plan and partial solution is **true**?
    A. Cody's plan is incorrect.
    B. Cody's plan and partial solution are both correct.
    C. Cody's partial solution is incorrect because he made his first error in step 1.
    D. Cody's partial solution is incorrect because he made his first error in step 3.

Use the following information to answer the next question.

Two different quadratic functions are defined by the equations $f(x) = 3(x - h)^2 - 7$ and $g(x) = -3(x - h)^2 + 7$.

20. If the value of h is the same for both equations, then the graphs will have the same
    A. range
    B. vertex
    C. y-intercepts
    D. axis of symmetry

21. The vertex of the parabola defined by the equation $y = -3(x - 2)^2 + 5$ is located at the coordinates
    A. $(-2, -5)$
    B. $(2, -5)$
    C. $(-2, 5)$
    D. $(2, 5)$

Use the following information to answer the next question.

> The following four transformations are applied, in the given order, to the graph of $y = x^2$:
>
> - a reflection about the x-axis
> - a vertical stretch about the x-axis by a factor of 3
> - a horizontal translation 2 units to the right
> - a vertical translation 4 units downward

22. Point $(3, 9)$ on the graph of $y = x^2$ becomes point (a, b) on the transformed graph. What are the values of a and b?

A. $a = 5$ and $b = -23$

B. $a = 5$ and $b = -31$

C. $a = 1$ and $b = -23$

D. $a = 1$ and $b = -31$

Use the following information to answer the next question.

> The graph of a parabola is shown.
>
>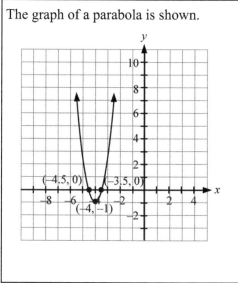

23. What is the equation of the given parabola?

A. $y = 4(x + 4)^2 + 1$

B. $y = 4(x + 4)^2 - 1$

C. $y = -4(x - 4)^2 + 1$

D. $y = -4(x + 4)^2 - 1$

24. The expanded form of the expression $\left(m - \dfrac{n}{5}\right)^2$ is

A. $m^2 + \dfrac{2}{5}mn - \dfrac{n^2}{5}$

B. $m^2 + \dfrac{2}{5}mn + \dfrac{n^2}{25}$

C. $m^2 - \dfrac{2}{5}mn + \dfrac{n^2}{25}$

D. $m^2 - \dfrac{2}{5}mn - \dfrac{n^2}{25}$

25. The expression $x + 3$ is **not** a factor of

A. $x^2 + 3x$

B. $x^2 - 9$

C. $x^2 + 6x + 9$

D. $x^2 + 13x - 30$

26. A factored form of a quadratic function that has zeros of $\dfrac{3}{5}$ and -6 is

A. $y = (5x - 3)(x + 6)$

B. $y = (5x + 3)(x + 6)$

C. $y = (3x - 5)(x - 6)$

D. $y = (3x + 5)(x - 6)$

Use the following information to answer the next question.

> Two equations are given.
>
> I. $x^2 + 4 = 0$
>
> II. $x^2 - 2x + 3 = 0$

27. Which of the following statements about these equations is **true**?

A. Both equations have real roots.

B. Both equations have non-real roots.

C. Equation I has real roots, and equation II has non-real roots.

D. Equation I has non-real roots, and equation II has real roots.

Use the following information to answer the next question.

To convert the quadratic function $y = 4x^2 - 4x - 3$ into the completed square form $y = a(x - h)^2 + k$, a student performed the following steps:

1. $y = 4(x^2 - x) - 3$

2. $y = 4\left(x^2 - x + \dfrac{1}{4}\right) - 3 - 1$

3. $y = 4\left(x - \dfrac{1}{2}\right)^2 - 4$

28. Which of the following statements about the student's solution is **true**?

    A. The student made an error in step 1.

    B. The student made an error in step 2.

    C. The student made an error in step 3.

    D. The student did not make an error.

29. Which of the following graphs could be a sketch of the quadratic function $y = -24x^2 + 1\ 000x - 3\ 250$?

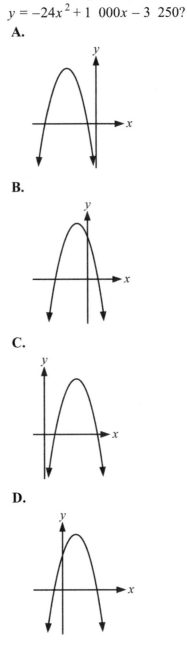

    A.

    B.

    C.

    D.

30. The solution to the quadratic equation $2x^2 + 5x + 1 = 0$ is

A. $x = \dfrac{-5 \pm \sqrt{13}}{4}$

B. $x = \dfrac{-5 \pm \sqrt{17}}{4}$

C. $x = \dfrac{-5 \pm \sqrt{15}}{2}$

D. $x = \dfrac{-5 \pm \sqrt{19}}{4}$

Use the following information to answer the next question.

The procedures used by four different students in order to solve the equation $3x^2 - 5x = 1$ by using a graphical approach are given:

Sergei

Graph $y_1 = 3x^2 - 5x$ and $y_2 = 1$. Determine the x-coordinate of each point of intersection of the two graphs.

Jeremy

Graph $y_1 = 3x^2$ and $y_2 = 1 + 5x$. Determine the x-coordinate of each point of intersection of the two graphs.

Alexi

Graph $y_1 = 3x^2 - 5x - 1$. Determine the zeros of the resulting graph.

Beyonce

Rewrite the equation as $x(3x - 5) - 1 = 0$. Graph $y_1 = x(3x - 5)$. Subtract 1 from each of the zeros of the graph of $y_1 = x(3x - 5)$.

31. The student who has an **incorrect** procedure is

A. Sergei

B. Jeremy

C. Alexi

D. Beyonce

Use the following information to answer the next question.

The graphs of $y = -2x - 2$ and $y = x^2 + x - 6$ are shown.

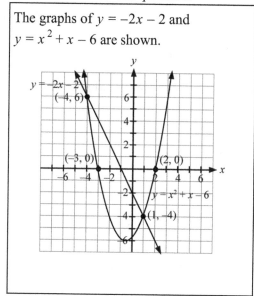

Numerical Response

32. The largest root of the quadratic equation $x^2 + x - 6 = -2(x + 1)$ is _____.

Use the following information to answer the next question.

The sails of two sailboards are similar triangles, as shown below.

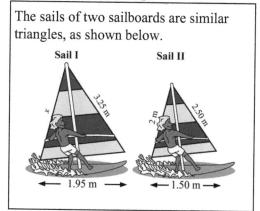

33. What is the length of side x of sail I?

A. 2.45 m

B. 2.6 m

C. 2.75 m

D. 3.8 m

Use the following information to answer the next question.

During an afternoon soccer game, Samira casts a 62 cm shadow, and Leah casts a 77 cm shadow.

34. If Leah is 158 cm tall, what is Samira's height, to the nearest cm?

   A. 124 cm

   B. 127 cm

   C. 143 cm

   D. 173 cm

35. The hypotenuse of a right triangle is $3x$, and the other two sides are 8 cm and 12 cm. What is the value of x, to the nearest hundredth?

   A. 4.81 cm

   B. 7.23 cm

   C. 11.16 cm

   D. 14.42 cm

Use the following information to answer the next question.

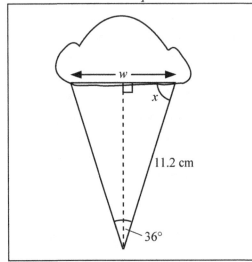

36. Rounded to the nearest tenth of a centimetre, the width, w, of the ice-cream cone's opening is

   A. 3.5 cm

   B. 5.4 cm

   C. 6.9 cm

   D. 10.7 cm

Use the following information to answer the next question.

A rectangular garden that has a length of 50 m will have a sidewalk built diagonally across it, as shown in the diagram. This sidewalk will be at a 32° angle to the longer side.

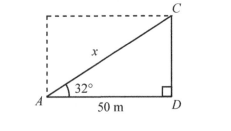

37. To the nearest metre, what is the length of the sidewalk?

   A. 42 m

   B. 57 m

   C. 59 m

   D. 94 m

Use the following information to answer the next question.

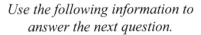

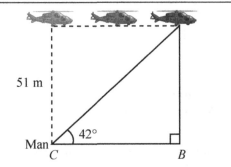

A rescue helicopter is at a height of 51 m above sea level. To save a drowning man at point C, the helicopter needs to lift him to point B on the shore with the help of a rope.

38. What is the distance that the man travels from point C to point B?

   A. 54.64 m

   B. 55.66 m

   C. 56.64 m

   D. 65.55 m

Use the following information to answer the next question.

> Standing beneath an apple tree, Ted spotted an apple at a height of 10 m. By throwing a rock at an angle of 45° from the ground, Ted managed to hit the apple and knock it from the tree. Standing in the same place, he saw another apple directly above where the first had been. This time, by throwing a rock at an angle of 50° from the ground, Ted knocked the second apple from the tree.

Numerical Response

39. Before Ted knocked them down, the distance between the two apples to the nearest tenth of a meter was _____ m.

40. The equation $\dfrac{50}{\sin 40°} = \dfrac{x}{\sin 58°}$ applies to which of the following acute triangles?

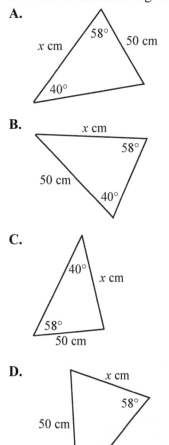

A.

B.

C.

D.

Use the following information to answer the next question.

A student drew the diagram shown in order to derive the law of cosines.

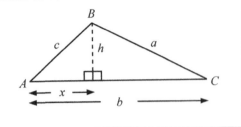

41. If the student correctly determined that $x^2 + h^2 = c^2$ and $(b-x)^2 + h^2 = a^2$, then which of the following equations is correct?

A. $x^2 + c^2 = (b-x)^2 + a^2$

B. $a^2 - (b-x)^2 = c^2 - x^2$

C. $h^2 = \dfrac{c^2 - x^2}{a^2 - (b-x)^2}$

D. $h^2 = \dfrac{a^2 + (b-x)^2}{x^2 + c^2}$

Use the following information to answer the next question.

The given diagram illustrates triangle RST, in which $RS = 37$ cm, $ST = 28$ cm, and $\angle R = 49°$.

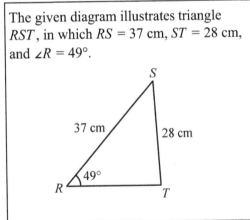

42. What is the measure of $\angle T$, rounded to the nearest tenth of a degree?

A. $85.8°$

B. $74.6°$

C. $60.2°$

D. $34.8°$

Use the following information to answer the next multipart question.

43. A weather balloon is flying in a field outside of London, Ontario. One end of a lightweight rope is attached to the base of the weather balloon, and the other end of the rope is anchored to the ground at point P. On a windy day, Rachel decides to determine the length of the rope, x, between P and the connection point located at the base of the weather balloon. She locates two points A and B that are 200 m apart and records the measurements shown in the diagram.

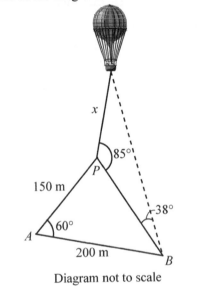

Diagram not to scale

Open Response

a) To the nearest metre, what is the distance from anchor point P to point B?.

b) What is the value of x to the nearest metre?

PRACTICE TEST 2

Use the following information to answer the next question.

A model rocket was launched from a platform. Its height (h) above the ground in metres with respect to the time (t) in seconds was recorded. The data obtained is shown in the table.

Time (s)	0	1	3	8	14	20	25
Height (m)	3	148	410	890	1 140	1 025	700

1. If a quadratic regression is done on the data, the **best** estimate of the height of the model rocket after 6 s is

   A. 680 m

   B. 725 m

   C. 780 m

   D. 820 m

2. Which of the following graphs could be the graph of the quadratic function $y = ax^2 - 12x + 7, a < 0$?

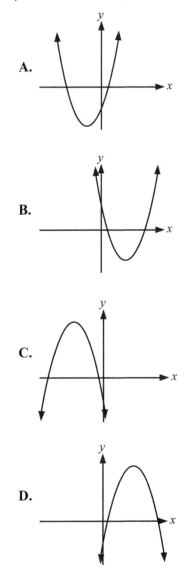

A.

B.

C.

D.

Use the following information to answer the next question.

The graphs of two different parabolas with the same vertex are shown in the diagram.

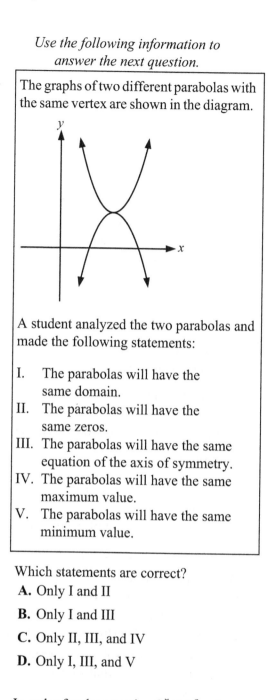

A student analyzed the two parabolas and made the following statements:

I.   The parabolas will have the same domain.
II. The parabolas will have the same zeros.
III. The parabolas will have the same equation of the axis of symmetry.
IV. The parabolas will have the same maximum value.
V.   The parabolas will have the same minimum value.

3. Which statements are correct?
    A. Only I and II

    B. Only I and III

    C. Only II, III, and IV

    D. Only I, III, and V

4. In order for the equation $2^x \times 2^a = 1$, $x \neq 0$, to be correct, the value of a must be
    A. 0

    B. 1

    C. x

    D. $-x$

5. What is the minimum value of the function $y = 4x^2 - 12x + 15$?
    A. -12

    B. -4

    C. 4

    D. 6

Use the following information to answer the next question.

A bullet is fired vertically at an initial speed of 100 m / s. The height, h metres, after t seconds is given by the equation $h = 100t - 5t^2$.

6. What is the maximum height attained by the bullet?
    A. 10 m

    B. 20 m

    C. 100 m

    D. 500 m

Use the following information to answer the next question.

Maj held a soccer ball in front of her. She kicked the ball, which followed a path that can be modelled by the equation $y = -4.9x^2 + 13.7x + 0.7$, where y is the height above the ground in metres and x is the time in seconds.

7. At what height above the ground was Maj holding the soccer ball when she kicked it?
    A. 0.0 m

    B. 0.7 m

    C. 1.4 m

    D. 2.8 m

Numerical Response

8. The path of a roller coaster car can be modelled by the function $h = -7t^2 + 61t + 98$ for the section of the ride where $1 \leq t \leq 10$. For this function, h is the height of the car above the ground in feet and t is the time in seconds elapsed since the beginning of the ride.

To the nearest tenth of a second, over what time period is the roller coaster car 200 feet or more above the ground?

_____

Use the following information to answer the next question.

Two students showed their partial solutions in solving this system of equations.

$4x + y = -14$
$3x + 2y = -8$

Minesh's Partial Solution

1. Multiply the first equation by 3.
2. Multiply the second equation by 4.
3. Subtract the second equation from the first equation.
   $12x + 3y = -42$
   $\underline{12x + 8y = -32}$
   ${-5y = -10}$
4. Solve for y.
5. Then, solve for x.

Cameron's Partial Solution

1. Rearrange the first equation in the form $y = -4x - 14$.
2. Rearrange the second equation in the form $y = -\dfrac{3}{2}x - 4$.
3. Graph both equations using technology.
4. Determine the point of intersection of the two lines.

9. Which of the following statements about these partial solutions is **true**?
   A. Minesh and Cameron each made an error that will lead to a wrong answer.
   B. Minesh's partial solution is wrong, and Cameron's partial solution is correct.
   C. Cameron's partial solution is wrong, and Minesh's partial solution is correct.
   D. Minesh's partial solution and Cameron's partial solution will both lead to the same correct answer.

Numerical Response

10. If $5x + y = 93$ and $2x + y = 48$, what is the value of y in the solution to this system of equations? _____

11. At a particular fast food restaurant, the cost of 2 hamburgers and 1 small french fries is $7.00. The cost of 1 hamburger and 2 small french fries is $5.75. What is the cost of 1 hamburgers?

A. $2.25

B. $2.50

C. $2.75

D. $2.80

Use the following information to answer the next question.

Harold invested his savings of $5 000, part at 4% per annum and the other part at 6% per annum. At the end of one year, the interest from the amount invested at 4% was $50 more than the interest from the amount invested at 6%.

12. If x represents the amount of money invested at 4% and y represents the amount of money invested at 6%, which of the following systems of equations could be solved to determine the amount of money invested at each rate?

A. $x + y = 5\ 000$ and $4x = 6y + 5\ 000$

B. $x + y = 5\ 000$ and $6y - 4x = 5\ 000$

C. $4x + 6y = 5\ 000$ and $x = y - 50$

D. $4x + 6y = 5\ 000$ and $x - 50 = y$

13. If point $(-3, 4)$ is the midpoint of point $A(2, 1)$ and point $B(x, 7)$, then the value of x is

A. -8

B. -6

C. 6

D. 8

Use the following information to answer the next question.

The given diagram represents a situation in which coast guard ship A is located 4 km west and 12 km north of a reference point denoted by $(0, 0)$, and coast guard ship B is located 1 km west and 8 km north of the reference point. A third coast guard ship, C, is located such that coast guard ship B is the midpoint of the line segment connecting coast guard ship A to coast guard ship C. Cruise ship D, which is sailing in the area, issues a distress signal. It is determined that the distance from coast guard ship A to cruise ship D is the same as the distance from coast guard ship A to coast guard ship C.

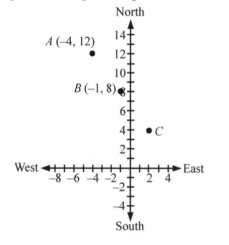

14. If the coordinates of cruise ship D are $(2, y)$, then the value of y is

A. 18

B. 20

C. 22

D. 24

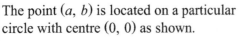

Use the following information to answer the next question.

The point (a, b) is located on a particular circle with centre $(0, 0)$ as shown.

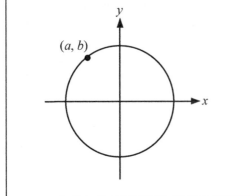

15. The radius of this circle is given by the expression

A. $a^2 + b^2$

B. $\sqrt{a^2 + b^2}$

C. $a^2 - b^2$

D. $\sqrt{a^2 - b^2}$

Use the following information to answer the next question.

A circle is defined by the equation $4x^2 + 4y^2 = 36$.

16. What is the length of the radius of this circle?

A. 2 units

B. 3 units

C. 6 units

D. 9 units

Use the following information to answer the next question.

A perpendicular bisector is a line that intersects the midpoint of another line at a right angle. Triangle PQR has vertices $Q(6, 2)$, $R(-2, 8)$ and $P(2, -4)$.

17. The equation of the perpendicular bisector of side QR is given by

A. $y = \dfrac{3}{4}x + 2$

B. $y = \dfrac{4}{3}x - \dfrac{1}{3}$

C. $y = \dfrac{4}{3}x + \dfrac{7}{3}$

D. $y = -\dfrac{3}{4}x + \dfrac{13}{2}$

18. To the nearest tenth, the shortest distance between the point $A(-1, 2)$ and the line $3x - 4y - 36 = 0$ is

A. 5.2 units

B. 8.4 units

C. 9.4 units

D. 11.0 units

19. The points $A(1, 5)$, $B(-3, 1)$, and $C(6, -4)$ are the vertices of triangle ABC. If the length of side AB is $\sqrt{32}$ units and the length of side AC is $\sqrt{106}$ units, then $\triangle ABC$ is

A. a scalene triangle

B. an isosceles triangle

C. a right angle triangle

D. an equilateral triangle

Use the following information to answer the next multipart question.

20. A soccer field is part of a sports complex. The given diagram shows the soccer field placed on a coordinate grid where the coordinates are expressed in yards.

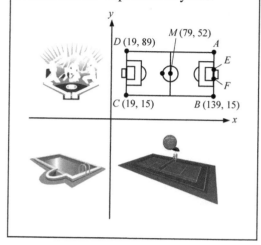

Open Response

a) Determine the coordinates of corner post *A*.

b) The soccer nets are centered on the back lines of the playing field and are 8 yards in width. Determine the coordinates of points *E* and *F* in the diagram. Justify your answer.

c) If player *P* located at coordinates $(54, 41)$ wants to pass the soccer ball to player *Q* located at coordinates $(83, 62)$, what is the minimum distance, to the nearest tenth, that the ball must travel? Show your work.

d) Verify that the diagonals of the playing field bisect each other at the centre mark *M*. Show your work.

21. The graph of $y = x^2$ is translated four units left and three units down. Which of the following graphs accurately depicts the new parabola?

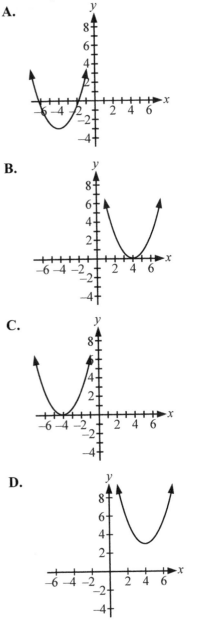

22. The graph of the function $y = x^2$ is transformed to become the function $y = -3(x - h)^2 + k$. Respectively, what are the equation of the axis of symmetry and the location of the vertex of the transformed function?

A. $x = k$ and (h, k)

B. $x = -h$ and $(-h, k)$

C. $x = h$ and (h, k)

D. $x = k$ and (k, h)

In the order shown, the following transformations were applied to the graph of $y = x^2$.

1. A vertical stretch by a factor of 2 about the x-axis.
2. A reflection in the x-axis.
3. A horizontal translation 2 units left.
4. A vertical translation 3 units up.

23. Which of the following graphs **best** represents the graph of the transformed function?

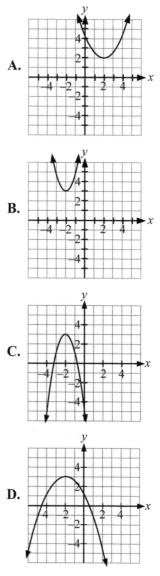

A.

B.

C.

D.

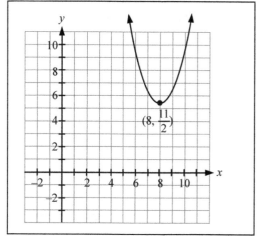

$(8, \frac{11}{2})$

24. If the ordered pair $\left(10, \frac{19}{2}\right)$ is on the given parabola, then the defining equation of the parabola is

   A. $y = (x - 8)^2 + \frac{11}{2}$

   B. $y = (x - 8)^2 - \frac{11}{2}$

   C. $y = 2(x - 8)^2 - \frac{11}{2}$

   D. $y = 2(x - 8)^2 + \frac{11}{2}$

25. If $-2(3x + 5)^2 = ax^2 + bx + c$, then the value of $a + c$ is
   A. -34
   B. -68
   C. -78
   D. -110

26. Which of the following expressions is **not** a factor of $9mn^2 - 12mn - 12m$?
   A. $3n + 2$
   B. $n - 4$
   C. $n - 2$
   D. $3m$

Use the following information to answer the next question.

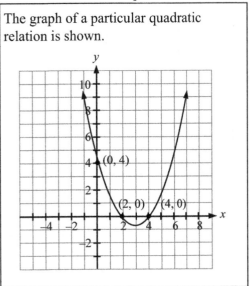

The graph of a particular quadratic relation is shown.

27. The equation of the quadratic relation is

A. $y = \dfrac{1}{2}(x + 2)(x + 4)$

B. $y = 2(x + 2)(x + 4)$

C. $y = \dfrac{1}{2}(x - 2)(x - 4)$

D. $y = 2(x - 2)(x - 4)$

28. Which of the following graphs represents a quadratic equation with no real roots?

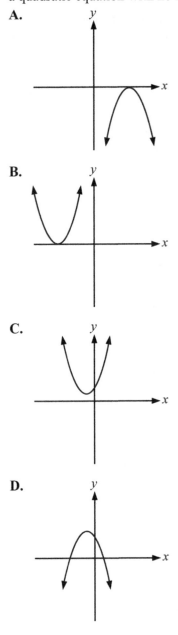

29. If the equation $y = 3x^2 + 42x + 142$ is expressed in completed square form $y = a(x - h)^2 + k$, the value of k is

A. -7

B. -5

C. 5

D. 7

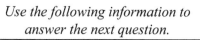

Use the following information to answer the next question.

Roman is attempting to sketch the graph of the quadratic function $y = -2(x^2 + 6x + 8)$. He makes the following four statements:

Statement I: The y-intercept of the graph is 8.

Statement II: The x-intercepts of the graph are -4 and -2.

Statement III: The vertex of the graph is $(3, -2)$.

Statement IV: The equation of the axis of symmetry of the graph is $x = -3$.

30. Which of Roman's statements are correct?

   A. Only II and IV

   B. Only II and III

   C. I, II, and III

   D. I, II, and IV

Use the following information to answer the next question.

A math teacher asks her class to solve the quadratic equation $6x^2 - 13x = 5$. The partial solutions of two students are given.

Rhett's solution:
$$6x^2 - 13x = 5$$
$$6x^2 - 13x - 5 = 0$$
$$6x^2 - 10x - 3x - 5 = 0$$
$$2x(3x - 5) - 1(3x - 5) = 0$$
$$(3x - 5)(2x - 1) = 0$$

Vlad's solution:
$$6x^2 - 13x = 5$$
$$6x^2 - 13x - 5 = 0$$
$$x = \frac{13 \pm \sqrt{(-13)^2 - 4(6)(-5)}}{2(6)}$$
$$x = \frac{13 \pm \sqrt{169 - 120}}{12}$$
$$x = \frac{13 \pm \sqrt{49}}{12}$$

31. Which of the following statements is **true**?

   A. Rhett's work and Vlad's work will each lead to a correct solution.

   B. Rhett's work and Vlad's work will each lead to an incorrect solution.

   C. Rhett's work will lead to a correct solution, and Vlad's work will lead to an incorrect solution.

   D. Rhett's work will lead to an incorrect solution, and Vlad's work will lead to a correct solution.

32. The cost, C, in dollars of manufacturing x Road Racer bicycles at Cycle World's production plant can be modelled by the function

$C = 2x^2 - 700x + 92\ 750.$

Open Response

a) What are two possible values for x if the cost, C, of manufacturing Road Racer bicycles is $62 750?

b) Algebraically, determine the number of Road Racer bicycles that must be manufactured to minimize the cost.

c) What is the minimum cost of manufacturing Road Racer bicycles?

d) To the nearest whole number, what is the fewest number of bicycles that can be manufactured for a cost of $50 000? Use a graphing calculator.

33. At 11:30 A.M on a sunny day, a 6 foot tall man casts an 8 foot long shadow. What is the approximate length of the shadow cast by a 45 foot high building at the same time?

A. 33.75 ft

B. 47.00 ft

C. 60.00 ft

D. 85.00 ft

Use the following information to answer the next question.

Jim wants to measure the width of a small river that is near his house. He draws the following diagram based on measurements that he knows, where A, B, and C represent points in a nearby park.

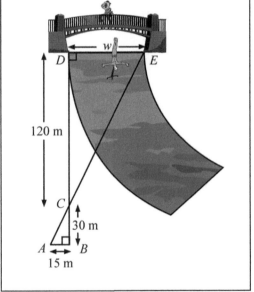

34. What is the width of the river?

A. 40 m

B. 60 m

C. 80 m

D. 240 m

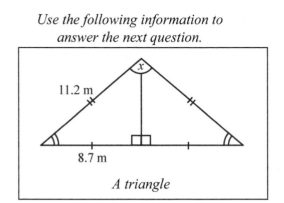

A triangle

35. What is the measure of angle *x* to the
nearest degree?

    A. 102°

    B. 78°

    C. 51°

    D. 39°

36. To estimate the amount of new water pipe
required for part of a golf course, the golf
course designer used the given diagram
with the indicated measurements.

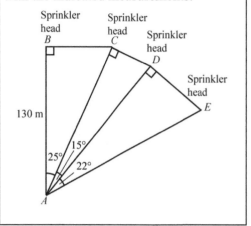

| **Open Response** |

a) What is the correct distance from the
sprinkler head at point *B* to the sprinkler
head at point *C*, to the nearest tenth of
a metre?

b) What is the correct distance from the
sprinkler head at point *D* to the sprinkler
head at point *E*, to the nearest metre?

Use the following information to answer the next question.

Acute △*MNP* is given.

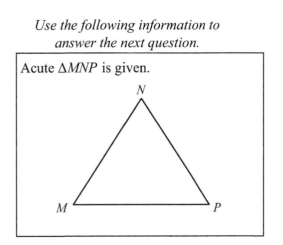

37. Which of the following equations correctly represents the law of sines with respect to △*MNP*?

A. $\dfrac{NP}{\sin M} = \dfrac{MP}{\sin P}$

B. $\dfrac{MN}{\sin P} = \dfrac{MP}{\sin N}$

C. $(MP)^2 = (MN)^2 + (NP)^2 - 2(MN)(NP)\sin M$

D. $(NP)^2 = (MN)^2 + (MP)^2 - 2(MN)(MP)\sin P$

38. Which of the following triangles represents the equation $x^2 = 80^2 + 95^2 - 2(80)(95)\cos 73°$?

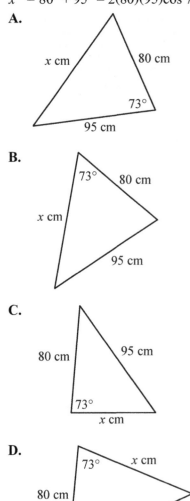

A.

B.

C.

D.

Use the following information to answer the next question.

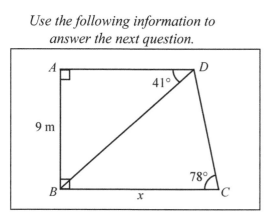

39. Correct to the nearest tenth, what is the length of side *x* in the given diagram?

    A. 9.2 m

    B. 11.2 m

    C. 12.3 m

    D. 13.7 m

Use the following information to answer the next question.

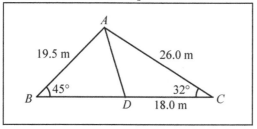

40. Correct to the nearest degree, what is the measure of ∠*ADB*?

    A. 58°

    B. 64°

    C. 68°

    D. 74°

Use the following information to answer the next question.

From a particular point, Jennifer determined that the angle of elevation to the top of her school was 18°. When she walked 12.5 m closer to the school, she determined that the angle of elevation to the top of the school was 29°, as illustrated in the diagram.

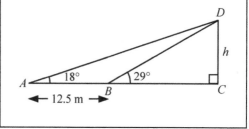

Numerical Response

41. Correct to the nearest metre, the height of the school, *h*, is _____ m.

Use the following information to answer the next question.

A boat is towing two wakeboarders. Wakeboarder 1 has a rope that is 65 feet long, and Wakeboarder 2 has a rope that is 70 feet long. At one point in time, the angle between the two ropes is 38°, as illustrated in the diagram.

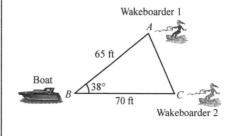

42. To the nearest tenth, how far apart are the wakeboarders at the given point in time?

    A. 4.4 ft

    B. 43.1 ft

    C. 44.2 ft

    D. 50.8 ft

Use the following information to answer the next question.

A construction site at the University of Toronto is in the shape of a kite. Because of the size of the area and the busy traffic around the university, a road was built through the site for construction vehicles only, as shown in the diagram.

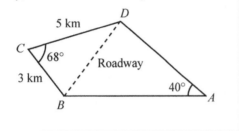

43. An equation that could be used to determine the length of the roadway, *BD*, in kilometres is

A. $BD = \dfrac{3\sin 68°}{\sin 40°}$

B. $BD = \dfrac{5\sin 68°}{\sin 40°}$

C. $BD = \sqrt{3^2 + 5^2 + 2(3)(5)\cos 68°}$

D. $BD = \sqrt{3^2 + 5^2 - 2(3)(5)\cos 68°}$

ANSWERS AND SOLUTIONS — PRACTICE TEST 1

1. D	8. C	18. C	28. D	38. C
2. D	9. A	19. D	29. C	39. 1.9
3. B	10. B	20. D	30. B	40. C
4. D	11. OR	21. D	31. D	41. B
5. B	12. D	22. B	32. 1	42. A
6. B	13. D	23. B	33. B	43. a) OR
7. a) OR	14. B	24. C	34. B	b) OR
b) OR	15. A	25. D	35. A	
c) OR	16. B	26. A	36. C	
d) OR	17. 15	27. B	37. C	

1. D

The shape of the graph can be determined either by using technology or by sketching the graph by hand. If a TI-83 graphing calculator is used the resulting graph will display as shown.:

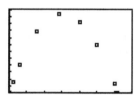

The shape of the graph models a parabola. Examine the first set of ordered pairs from the table to see that when time is 0, the height is 3. Therefore, the graph that best represents the data is graph D.

2. D

If the corresponding graph of the quadratic relation opens downward, $a < 0$ in the equation $y = ax^2 + bx + c$. Therefore, of the given quadratic equations, $y = -8.4x^2 + 5$ and $y = -4.2x^2 + 5$ are two possible equations. Using an appropriate table of values, calculate the second differences for each equation.

$y = -8.4x^2 + 5$

x	y	1st diff	2nd diff
1	−3.4		
		} 25.2	
2	−28.6		} −16.8
		} 42	
3	−70.6		} −16.8
		} 58.8	
4	−129.4		} −16.8
		} 75.6	
5	−205		} −16.8
		} 92.4	
6	−297.4		

$y = -4.2x^2 + 5$

x	y	1st diff	2nd diff
1	0.8		
		} 12.6	
2	−11.8		} −8.4
		} 21	
3	−32.8		} −8.4
		} 29.4	
4	−62.2		} −8.4
		} 37.8	
5	−100		} −8.4
		} 46.2	
6	−146.2		

The given quadratic relation that opens downward and has a second difference of −8.4 is $y = -4.2x^2 + 5$.

3. B

The graph of the function shown is a parabola that opens downward and has the following features:

- The vertex of the parabola is $(1, 2)$.
- The zeros are $x = -2$ and $x = 4$, which are points A and C, respectively.
- The parabola passes through the y-axis at point B.

Therefore, the y-intercept is B, and the zeros occur at A and C.

4. D

Substitute each x-value into the equation $y = 2^x$.

$y = 2^{(-3)} = \dfrac{1}{2^3} = \dfrac{1}{8}$

$y = 2^{(0)} = 1$ (Any number or variable with an exponent of zero is equal to 1; $x^0 = 1$.)

$y = 2^{(3)} = 8$

5. B

The roots of the equation $ax^2 + bx - 16 = 0$ are 2 and 4.

The x-coordinate of the vertex of the graph of $y = ax^2 + bx - 16$ is halfway between the two roots of the equation $ax^2 + bx - 16 = 0$.

Thus, the x-coordinate of the vertex of the graph of $y = ax^2 + bx - 16$ is $x = \dfrac{2+4}{2} = 3$.

Insert $x = 3$ into $y = ax^2 + bx - 16$.

$\Rightarrow$ the y (maximum) value $= 9a + 3b - 16$

However, $a(x - 2)(x - 4) = 0$

Expand this equation.

$\Rightarrow ax^2 - 6ax + 8a = 0$

$\Rightarrow 8a = -16$ (since $c = -16$ in the equation $ax^2 + bx - 16 = 0$

$\Rightarrow a = -2$

$\Rightarrow b = -6a = -6(-2) = 12$ (from the equation $ax^2 - 6ax + 8a = 0$)

Enter the values of a and b into the maximum value $9a + 3b - 16$.

Hence, the maximum value is $9 \times (-2) + 3 \times 12 - 16$

$= -18 + 36 - 16 = 2$

6. B

Determine the maximum height by completing the square.

$y = -2x^2 + 8x + 27$

$y = -2(x^2 - 4x) + 27$

$y = -2(x^2 - \underline{4x}) + 27$

$\left(\dfrac{-4}{2}\right)^2 = 4$

$y = -2(x^2 - 4x + \underline{4 - 4}) + 27$

$y = \underline{-2}(x^2 - 4x + 4 \underline{- 4}) + 27$

$y = -2(x^2 - 4x + 4)\underline{+8} + 27$

$= -2(x - 2)^2 + 35$

Here, the stone describes a parabolic path with vertex $(2, 35)$.

The stone reaches its maximum height in $x = 2s$.

The maximum height attained by the stone is 35 m.

7. a) OR

The window setting for the graph shown is x: [0, 7, 1] and y: [0, 50, 5].

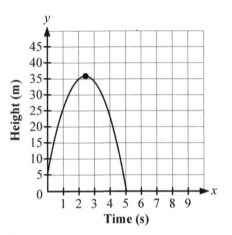

b) OR

The maximum height of the ball above the ground corresponds to the y-coordinate of the vertex (the highest point on the parabola). The vertex can either be determined graphically (using the maximum key on your calculator) or algebraically by completing the square as follows:

$y = -4.9x^2 + 24.5x + 6$

$y = -4.9(x^2 - 5x) + 6$

$y = -4.9(x^2 - 5x + 6.25 - 6.25) + 6$

$\rightarrow -\dfrac{5}{2} = -2.5, (-2.5)^2 = 6.25$

$y = -4.9(x^2 - 5x + 6.25) + 30.625 + 6$

$y = -4.9(x - 2.5)^2 + 36.625$

The coordinates of the vertex are (2.5, 36.625). To the nearest tenth, the maximum height of the ball above the ground is 36.6 m.

c) OR

In order to determine the number of seconds that the ball is more than 25 m above the ground, it is best to use a graphical approach. Choose an appropriate window setting, and then graph

$y_1 = -4.9x^2 + 24.5x + 6$ and $y_2 = 25$. Next, find the x-coordinate of each point of intersection of the two graphs. The difference of these two values will be the number of seconds the ball is more than 25 m above the ground. The x-coordinates of the two intersection points are about 4.04 and 0.96.

$4.04 - 0.96 = 3.08$

To the nearest tenth, the ball is more than 25 m above the ground for 3.1 s.

d) OR

The maximum height of the ball is 36.6 m, and the minimum height of the ball is 0 m (when the ball lands on the ground). Therefore, the range is $0 < y < 36.6$.

In order to determine the domain, first determine the number of seconds it takes the ball to land on the ground. This can be done by using the zero feature on your graphing calculator or by substituting 0 for y (since the height is 0 m when the ball lands on the ground) in the equation $y = -4.9x^2 + 24.5x + 6$ and then solving for x by using the quadratic formula as follows:

$-4.9x^2 + 24.5x + 6 = 0$
Substitute -4.9 for a, 24.5 for b, and 6 for c.

$$x = \frac{-24.5 \pm \sqrt{(24.5)^2 - 4(-4.9)(6)}}{2(-4.9)}$$

$$x = \frac{-24.5 \pm \sqrt{600.25 + 117.6}}{-9.8}$$

$$x = \frac{-24.5 \pm \sqrt{717.85}}{-9.8}$$

$x = \frac{-24.5 + \sqrt{717.85}}{-9.8}$ or $x = \frac{-24.5 - \sqrt{717.85}}{-9.8}$

$x \approx -0.234$ $x \approx 5.234$

The time cannot be negative, so to the nearest tenth, $x = 5.2$. Thus, the domain is $0 \le x \le 5.2$.

8. C

The point $(K, -3)$ must satisfy both equations.

Step 1
Substitute K for x and -3 for y into the equation $8x + 3y = -41$.
$$8x + 3y = -41$$
$$8(K) + 3(-3) = -41$$

Step 2
Solve for K.
$$8(K) + 3(-3) = -41$$
$$8K - 9 = -41$$
$$8K = -32$$
$$K = -4$$

Step 3
Check the solution of $K = -4$ by substituting -4 for x and -3 for y into the equation $6x - 5y = -9$.
$$6x - 5y = -9$$
$$6(-4) - 5(-3) = -9$$
$$-24 - (-15) = -9$$
$$-24 + 15 = -9$$
$$-9 = -9$$

The value of K works, so $K = -4$.

The equation $6x - 5y = -9$ could also have been used to determine the value for K.

9. A

To verify a solution to a system of equations, the solution must satisfy both equations. A particular point could satisfy one equation but not the other.

10. B

Step 1
Assign a different variable to each of the unknown quantities.
Let x represent the number of tickets sold in sections A to M.
Let y represent the number of tickets sold in sections N to Z.

Step 2
Set up a system of equations
The total number of tickets sold is represented by the equation $x + y = 55\ 300$.
Ticket sale revenue is represented by the equation $55x + 85y = 3\ 740\ 500$.
The following system of equations can be formed:
$(1) x + y \qquad = 55\ 300$
$(2) 55x + 85y = 3\ 740\ 500$

Step 3
Solve the system of equations using an algebraic approach.
Apply the method of elimination.
Multiply equation 1 by 55.
$55(x + y = 55\ 300) \rightarrow 55x + 55y = 3\ 041\ 500$
Substitute this equation back into the system of equations
$(1)\ 55x + 55y = 3\ 041\ 500$
$(2)\ 55x + 85y = 3\ 740\ 500$
Subtract equation 2 from equation 1.
$(1)\ \ 55x + 55y = 3\ 041\ 500$
$(2)\ -\underline{(55x + 85y = 3\ 740\ 500)}$
$\qquad -30y = -699\ 000$
Solve for y.
$-30y = -699\ 000$
$\quad y = 23\ 300$
Thus, 23 300 tickets were sold in sections N to Z.

11. OR

The total cost of the popcorn is $114 ($4.75 \times 24)$.

12. D

Begin by sketching the parallelogram

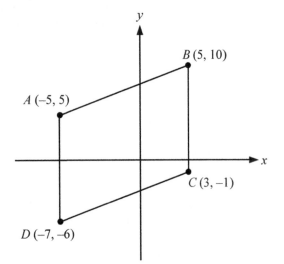

Here, you want the midpoint of diagonals AC and BD.

Using the midpoint formula:

$$M_{AC} = \left(\frac{-5+3}{2}, \frac{5+(-1)}{2} \right)$$

$$M_{AC} = (-1, 2)$$

$$M_{AC} = \left(\frac{-7+5}{2}, \frac{-6+10}{2} \right)$$

$$M_{AC} = (-1, 2)$$

In both cases, the midpoint is $(-1, 2)$.

13. D

Step 1

Using the distance formula
$d = \sqrt{(x_2 - x_1)^2 + (y_2 - y_1)^2}$, find the distances d_{AC}, d_{AB}, and d_{BC}.

$$\begin{aligned} d_{AC} &= \sqrt{(-2-2)^2 + (2-6)^2} \\ &= \sqrt{(-4)^2 + (-4)^2} \\ &= \sqrt{16+16} \\ &= \sqrt{32} \\ &= \sqrt{16(2)} \\ d_{AC} &= 4\sqrt{2} \end{aligned}$$

$$\begin{aligned} d_{AB} &= \sqrt{(-2-1)^2 + [2-(-4)]^2} \\ &= \sqrt{(-3)^2 + 6^2} \\ &= \sqrt{9+36} \\ &= \sqrt{45} \\ &= \sqrt{9(5)} \\ d_{AB} &= 3\sqrt{5} \end{aligned}$$

$$\begin{aligned} d_{BC} &= \sqrt{(1-2)^2 + (-4-6)^2} \\ &= \sqrt{(-1)^2 + (-10)^2} \\ &= \sqrt{1+100} \\ d_{BC} &= \sqrt{101} \end{aligned}$$

Step 2

Find the perimeter by adding the distances d_{AC}, d_{AB}, and d_{BC}.

$$d_{AC} + d_{AB} + d_{BC} = 4\sqrt{2} + 3\sqrt{5} + \sqrt{101}$$

The perimeter is equal to $3\sqrt{5} + 4\sqrt{2} + \sqrt{101}$.

14. B

Begin by calculating the length of the radius using the distance formula.

$$\begin{aligned} d &= \sqrt{(x_2 - x_1)^2 + (y_2 - y_1)^2} \\ &= \sqrt{(5-0)^2 + (-2-0)^2} \\ &= \sqrt{25+4} \\ &= \sqrt{29} \end{aligned}$$

The length of the radius is $\sqrt{29}$.

Substitute the calculated value of r into the general equation of a circle and simplify.

$$x^2 + y^2 = r^2$$
$$x^2 + y^2 = (\sqrt{29})^2$$
$$x^2 + y^2 = 29$$

Therefore, the equation $x^2 + y^2 = 29$ describes a circle with centre $(0, 0)$ that passes through the point $(5, -2)$.

15. A

Since the equation $x^2 + y^2 = r^2$ represents a circle with centre $(0, 0)$ and radius r, then the radius of the circle defined by $x^2 + y^2 = 16$ is:

$r^2 = 16$
$r = \sqrt{16}$
$r = 4$

The radius of the circle $x^2 + y^2 = 16$ is 4 units.

Since the diameter represents twice the radius, the diameter of the circle $x^2 + y^2 = 16$ is 8 units.

Jacqueline sketches a circle with a diameter that is twice as long as the diameter of $x^2 + y^2 = 16$, so the diameter of Jacqueline's circle is 16 units.

Since diameter represents twice the radius, the radius of Jacqueline's circle is 8 units. The sketch that could represent her circle is one with a radius of 8 units and a centre at $(0, 0)$.

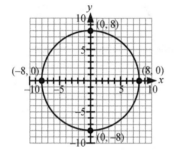

16. B

Step 1
Apply the midpoint formula
$M = \left(\dfrac{x_1 + x_2}{2}, \dfrac{y_1 + y_2}{2} \right)$ to determine the midpoint of AB. Substitute -5 for x_1, -1 for x_2, 0 for y_1, and 4 for y_2.

$M_{AB} = \left(\dfrac{-5 - 1}{2}, \dfrac{0 + 4}{2} \right)$
$M_{AB} = (-3, 2)$

The midpoint of AB is $(-3, 2)$.

Step 2
Appply the distance formula
$d = \sqrt{(x_2 - x_1)^2 + (y_2 - y_1)^2}$ to calculate the distance from $C(1, -1)$ to the midpoint of $AB(-3, 2)$.

$d = \sqrt{(-3 - 1)^2 + (2 - (-1))^2}$
$ = \sqrt{(-4)^2 + 3^2}$
$ = \sqrt{16 + 9}$
$ = \sqrt{25}$
$ = 5$

The length of the median from point C to line segment AB is 5 units.

17. 15

Step 1
To determine the value of K, first determine the equation of the right bisector of the line segment with the given endpoints.

Using the slope formula, calculate the slope of the line segment with endpoints $(2, -6)$ and $(-8, -4)$.

$m = \dfrac{y_2 - y_1}{x_2 - x_1}$
$ = \dfrac{-4 - (-6)}{-8 - 2}$
$ = \dfrac{2}{-10}$
$ = -\dfrac{1}{5}$

The right bisector of the line segment with the given endpoints is perpendicular to the given line segment. Perpendicular lines have slopes that are negative reciprocals of one another. The negative reciprocal of $-\dfrac{1}{5}$ is $\dfrac{5}{1}$. Therefore, the slope of the right bisector is 5.

Now, determine the midpoint of the line segment with endpoints $(2, -6)$ and $(-8, -4)$.

$M = \left(\dfrac{x_1 + x_2}{2}, \dfrac{y_1 + y_2}{2} \right)$
$ = \left(\dfrac{2 + (-8)}{2}, \dfrac{-6 + (-4)}{2} \right)$
$ = \left(\dfrac{-6}{2}, \dfrac{-10}{2} \right)$
$ = (-3, -5)$

Finally, use the point-slope form of the equation of a line to determine the equation of the right bisector.

$y = m(x - x_1) + y_1$
$y = 5(x - (-3)) + (-5)$
$y = 5(x + 3) - 5$
$y = 5x + 15 - 5$
$y = 5x + 10$

Step 2

Solve for K.

Since the ordered pair $(1, K)$ is located on the right bisector defined by the equation $y = 5x + 10$, substitute 1 for x and K for y into the equation and solve for K.

$K = 5(1) + 10$

$K = 15$

Note: This can also be verified graphically.

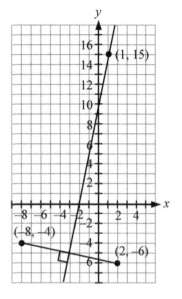

18. **C**

Two lines are perpendicular if their slopes are negative reciprocals of each other.

$(M_1 \times M_2 = 1)$

Therefore, the perpendicular lines are given by pairs II, III, and V only.

19. **D**

Step 1

The circle with chord AB and the perpendicular bisector of AB is shown.

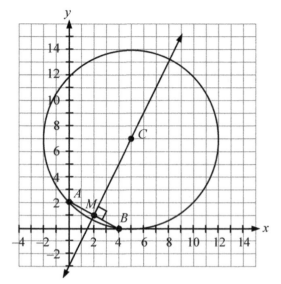

To verify that the perpendicular bisector of a chord of a circle passes through the centre of the circle, determine the equation of the perpendicular bisector of chord AB, and then determine if the point $(5, 7)$ is on this perpendicular bisector.

Determine the slope, m, of chord AB.

$$m = \frac{2 - 0}{0 - 4} = -\frac{1}{2}$$

Step 2

Determine the midpoint, m, of chord AB.

$$m = \left(\frac{0 + 4}{2}, \frac{2 + 0}{2}\right) = (2, 1)$$

Step 3

Determine the equation of the perpendicular bisector of chord AB by applying the formula $y = m(x - x_1) + y_1$.

Recall that the slope of chord AB is $-\frac{1}{2}$; therefore, the slope of the perpendicular bisector must be 2 (since perpendicular slopes are negative reciprocals of each other).

Now, substitute 2 for m and 2 for x_1 and 1 for y_1 into the equation $y = m(x - x_1) + y_1$.

$y = 2(x - 2) + 1$

$y = 2x - 4 + 1$

$y = 2x - 3$

Step 4

Verify that the point $(5, 7)$ is on the line $y = 2x - 3$.

Therefore, Cody's partial solution is incorrect because he made his first error in step 3.

20. D

The h-value causes a horizontal translation (shifting the parabola left or right) and affects the axis of symmetry. If the h-value is the same for both equations, the axis of symmetry will be the same for the graphs of both functions.

For a quadratic function of the form $y = a(x - h)^2 + k$, the range, vertex, and y-intercepts are affected by the parameter k.

21. D

The graph of a quadratic function of the form $y = a(x - h)^2 + k$ has its vertex at the coordinates (h, k).

The coordinates of the vertex of the function $y = -3(x - 2)^2 + 5$ are $(2, 5)$.

22. B

All points on the transformed graph must satisfy the given transformations.
A reflection about the x-axis will change $(3, 9)$ to $(3, -9)$.
A vertical stretch about the x-axis by a factor of 3 will change $(3, -9)$ to $(3, -27)$.
A horizontal translation 2 units to the right changes $(3, -27)$ to $(5, -27)$.
A vertical translation 4 units downward changes $(5, -27)$ to $(5, -31)$.
The respective values of a and b are 5 and -31.

23. B

The parabola shown can have an equation of the form $y = a(x - h)^2 + k$, where (h, k) is the vertex.
Since the vertex is at $(-4, -1)$, $h = -4$ and $k = -1$.

Step 1
Substitute -4 for h and -1 for k into $y = a(x - h)^2 + k$.
$y = a(x + 4)^2 - 1$

Step 2
Since the graph passes through the point $(-3.5, 0)$, substitute -3.5 for x and 0 for y into $y = a(x + 4)^2 - 1$. Solve for a.
$0 = a((-3.5) + 4)^2 - 1$
$0 = a\left(\frac{1}{2}\right)^2 - 1$
$0 = \frac{a}{4} - 1$
$\frac{a}{4} = 1$
$a = 4$

Step 3
Substitute 4 for a in the equation $y = a(x + 4)^2 - 1$.
$y = 4(x + 4)^2 - 1$
The graph illustrates the equation $y = 4(x + 4)^2 - 1$.

24. C

In general, $(a - b)^2 = a^2 - 2ab + b^2$.

Step 1
Substitute m for a and $\frac{n}{5}$ for b into $a^2 - 2ab + b^2$.
$\left(m - \frac{n}{5}\right)^2 = m^2 - 2(m)\left(\frac{n}{5}\right) + \left(\frac{n}{5}\right)^2$

Step 2
Simplify.
$m^2 - \frac{2}{5}mn + \frac{n^2}{25}$

25. D

$x^2 + 3x$ factors to $x(x + 3)$.
$x^2 - 9$ factors to $(x + 3)(x - 3)$.
$x^2 + 6x + 9$ factors to $(x + 3)(x + 3) = (x + 3)^2$.
$x^2 + 13x - 30$ factors to $(x + 15)(x - 2)$.

Therefore, $x + 3$ is not a factor of $x^2 + 13x - 30$.

26. A

A factored form of a quadratic function is $f(x) = a(x - r)(x - s)$. The given quadratic function has zeros of $\frac{3}{5}$ and -6. It follows that $r = \frac{3}{5}$ and $s = -6$.

Substitute $\frac{3}{5}$ for r and -6 for s into the equation $y = a(x - r)(x - s)$.
$y = a\left(x - \frac{3}{5}\right)(x + 6)$

An equivalent equation where $a = 5$ is as follows:
$y = 5\left(x - \frac{3}{5}\right)(x + 6)$
$y = (5x - 3)(x + 6)$

A factored form of the given quadratic function is $y = (5x - 3)(x + 6)$.

27. B

To determine the nature of the roots of each quadratic equation, graph each equation, and determine if there are any x-intercepts.

- $y = x^2 + 4$

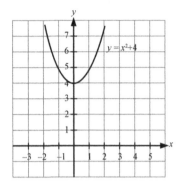

- $y = x^2 - 2x + 3$

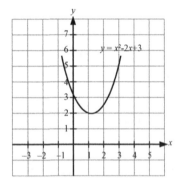

Since neither graph intersects the x-axis, the roots of both equations are non-real.

28. D

Step 1

Identify and remove the common factor from the x^2- and x-term of the expression. In this case, the common factor is 4.

$$y = 4(x^2 - x) - 3$$

Step 2

Identify the resulting coefficient for the x-term.

$$y = 4(x^2 - \underline{x}) - 3$$

Divide this value by 2, and then square it.

$$\left(\frac{-1}{2}\right)^2 = \frac{1}{4}$$

Step 3

Both add and subtract this value inside the brackets.

$$y = 4\left(x^2 - x + \frac{1}{4} - \frac{1}{4}\right) - 3$$

Step 4

Move the value that will not contribute to a perfect square outside the brackets. Multiply this value by the common factor that was removed previously.

$$y = 4\left(x^2 - x + \frac{1}{4} - \frac{1}{4}\right) - 3$$

To move $-\frac{1}{4}$ outside the brackets, multiply it by 4, and it becomes -1.

$$y = 4\left(x^2 - x + \frac{1}{4}\right) - 1 - 3$$

Step 5

Factor the trinomial inside the brackets to form a perfect square, and collect like terms outside the bracket.

$$y = 4\left(x - \frac{1}{2}\right)^2 - 4$$

The student's solution matches the given solution; therefore, there is no error.

29. C

Use a graphing calculator to get the following graph of the function $y = -24x^2 + 1\ 000x - 3\ 250$.

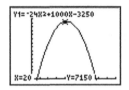

The graph is displayed using these window settings: $x:[-10, 50, 5]\ y:[-200, 8\ 500, 500]$

Therefore, this graph could be a sketch of the quadratic function $y = -24x^2 + 1\ 000x - 3\ 250$.

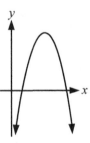

30. B

Solve $2x^2 + 5x + 1 = 0$ using the quadratic formula.

$$x = \frac{-b \pm \sqrt{b^2 - 4ac}}{2a}$$

Substitute 2 for a, 5 for b, and 1 for c into the quadratic formula.

$$x = \frac{-(5) \pm \sqrt{(5)^2 - 4(2)(1)}}{2(2)}$$

$$x = \frac{-5 \pm \sqrt{25 - 8}}{4}$$

$$x = \frac{-5 \pm \sqrt{17}}{4}$$

31. D

Sergei's procedure will yield the following graphs

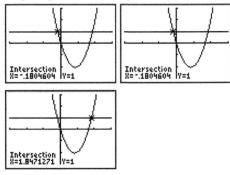

and the solution the equation $3x^2 - 5x = 1$ to the nearest hundredth is $x = -0.18$ or $x = 1.85$.

Jeremy's procedure will yield the following graphs:

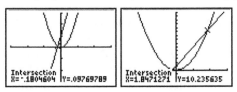

The solution to the equation $3x^2 - 5x = 1$ to the nearest hundredth is $x = -0.18$ or $x = 1.85$.

Alexi's procedure will yield the following graphs:

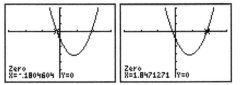

The solution to the equation $3x^2 - 5x = 1$ to the nearest hundredth is $x = -0.18$ or $x = 1.85$.

Beyonce's procedure will yield the following graphs:

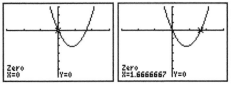

Subtract 1 from each of the zeros. The solution to the equation $3x^2 - 5x = 1$ to the nearest hundredth is $x = -1$ or $x = 0.67$.

Therefore, the student with the incorrect procedure is Beyonce.

32. 1

The roots of the quadratic equation $x^2 + x - 6 = -2(x + 1)$ are found by determining the x-coordinate of each point of intersection of the two graphs. The points of intersection are $(-4, \ 6)$ and $(1, \ -4)$. The roots are -4 and 1; therefore, the largest root is 1.

33. B

Since the triangles are similar, the ratio of corresponding sides are equal; therefore,

$$\frac{x}{1.95 \text{ m}} = \frac{2.00 \text{ m}}{1.50 \text{ m}}$$

$$x = \frac{2.00 \text{ m} \times 1.95 \text{ m}}{1.50 \text{ m}}$$

$$x = 2.6 \text{ m}$$

34. B

Begin with a diagram for clarity.

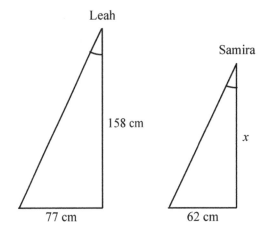

The triangles are similar since they are created using the shadows created by the same angle of the sun at the same point in time, and the remaining corresponding angles are equal. Therefore, corresponding sides will have equal ratios.

$$\frac{77}{158} = \frac{62}{x}$$

$$x = \frac{62 \times 158}{77}$$

$$x \approx 127 \text{cm}$$

35. A

To solve, use the Pythagorean theorem $c^2 = a^2 + b^2$.

Substitute the values of the hypotenuse, $c = 3x$, and sides, $a = 8$ cm, $b = 12$ cm into the equation.

$$(3x)^2 = (8)^2 + (12)^2$$

Simplify and solve for x.

$$9x^2 = 64 + 144$$

$$9x^2 = 208$$

$$x^2 = 23.\overline{1}$$

$$x = \sqrt{23.\overline{1}}$$

$$x \approx 4.81 \text{ cm}$$

36. C

Step 1

Determine the angle that will be used to solve for w. Since the cone is made up of two right triangles, the line passing through 36° will bisect that angle as well as the width of the ice-cream cone's opening. Thus, the angle in the triangle is 18°.

Step 2

Label the opposite side with the letter y.

Note: $w = 2y$

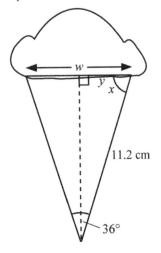

Step 3

Identify the ratio to use to solve for y.

The required angle is 18°.

Identify the sides you have to work with.

The side measuring 11.2 cm is the hypotenuse.

The side labelled y is the opposite side.

The trigonometric ratio that uses the opposite side and the hypotenuse is sine.

$$\sin \theta = \frac{\text{opposite}}{\text{hypotenuse}}$$

Step 4

Substitute the known values from the triangle into the sine ratio.

$$\sin 18° = \frac{y}{11.2}$$

Step 5

Use cross products to solve for y.

$$\frac{\sin 18°}{1} = \frac{y}{11.2}$$

$$\sin 18°(11.2) = y(1)$$

$$3.46 = y$$

Step 6

Solve for w.

Since $w = 2y$,

$$w = 2(3.46) = 6.92$$

Step 7

Round answer to the nearest tenth of a centimetre.

$6.92 \to 6.9$

The opening of the ice-cream cone is 6.9 cm wide.

37. C

As shown in the diagram, triangle ACD is a right triangle, where AC (the sidewalk) is the hypotenuse, AD is the length of the garden (50 m), CD is the width, and angle A is 32°. Given this information, use the cosine ratio to determine the length, x, of the sidewalk.

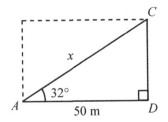

$$\cos A = \frac{\text{adjacent}}{\text{hypotenuse}}$$

$$\cos 32° = \frac{50}{x}$$

$$x(\cos 32°) = 50$$

$$x = \frac{50}{\cos 32°}$$

$$x \approx 58.96 \text{ m}$$

To the nearest metre, the length of the sidewalk is 59 m.

38. C

Since the helicopter is at a height of 51 m from sea level, label the diagram.

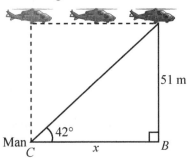

Label line CB as x.

To determine the length of x, use the tangent ratio.

$$\tan 42° = \frac{\text{opposite}}{\text{adjacent}}$$

$$\tan 42° = \frac{51}{x}$$

$$x = \frac{51}{\tan 42°}$$

$$x \approx 56.64 \text{ m}$$

From point C to point B, the man travels 56.64 m.

39. 1.9

Step 1

Sketch the problem.

Let x represent the distance between the two apples, y represent the distance from Ted to the base of the tree, and w represent the distance from the ground to the second apple.

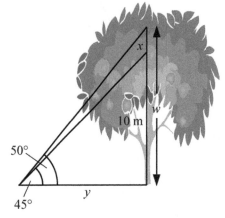

Step 2

Solve for y in the first triangle by using the tangent ratio.

$$\tan \theta = \frac{\text{opposite}}{\text{adjacent}}$$

$$\tan 45° = \frac{10}{y}$$

$$y = \frac{10}{\tan 45°}$$

$$= 10 \text{ m}$$

Step 3

Solve for w in the second triangle by using the tangent ratio again.

$$\tan \theta = \frac{\text{opposite}}{\text{adjacent}}$$

$$\tan 50° = \frac{w}{10}$$

$$w = 10 \times \tan 50°$$

$$\approx 11.9 \text{ m}$$

The diagram shows that $w = 10 + x$, and it follows that $x = w - 10$.

$x = 11.9 \text{ m} - 10 \text{ m} = 1.9 \text{ m}$

The distance between the two apples was 1.9 m.

40. C

The equation $\dfrac{50}{\sin 40°} = \dfrac{x}{\sin 58°}$ implies that the side measuring 50 cm is opposite to the 40° angle and the side measuring x cm is opposite to the 58° angle.

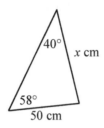

41. B

Since $x^2 + h^2 = c^2$, $h^2 = c^2 - x^2$.
Since $(b - x)^2 + h^2 = a^2$, $h^2 = a^2 - (b - x)^2$.
Since the value of h is identical in each equation, it follows that $a^2 - (b - x)^2 = c^2 - x^2$.

42. A

Since three measures are given, namely a side with its corresponding opposite angle and another side length, apply the sine law in order to determine the measure of $\angle T$.

$$\frac{RS}{\sin T} = \frac{ST}{\sin R}$$

Substitute 37 for RS, 28 for ST, and 49° for $\angle R$.

$$\frac{37}{\sin T} = \frac{28}{\sin 49°}$$

Solve for $\sin T$.
$28(\sin T) = 37(\sin 49°)$

$$\sin T = \frac{37(\sin 49°)}{28}$$

$$\sin T \cong 0.997\ 295$$

Solve for the value of $\angle T$.
$\angle T = \sin^{-1}(0.997\ 295)$
$ \cong 85.8°$

The measure of $\angle T$, to the nearest tenth of a degree, is 85.8°.

43. a) OR

The given diagram can be labelled as shown below.

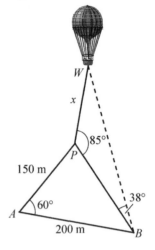

In $\triangle ABP$, make use of the law of cosines as follows:
$(PB)^2 = (AP)^2 + (AB)^2 - 2(AP)(AB)\cos A$
Substitute 150 for AP, 200 for AB, and 60° for A.
$(PB)^2 = 150^2 + 200^2 - 2(150)(200)\cos 60°$

$(PB)^2 = 22\ 500 + 400 - 300$

$(PB)^2 = 32\ 500$

$PB = \sqrt{32\ 500}$

$PB \approx 180.28$

To the nearest metre, the distance from anchor point P to point B is 180 m.

b) OR

The given diagram can be labelled as shown below.

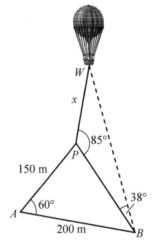

In $\triangle BPW$, make use of the law of sines as follows:

$\angle BWP = 180° - 85° - 38° = 57°$

Therefore, $\dfrac{PB}{\sin \angle BWP} = \dfrac{PW}{\sin \angle PBW}$

$\dfrac{180.28}{\sin 57°} = \dfrac{x}{\sin 38°}$

$x \times \sin 57° = 180.28 \times \sin 38°$

$x = \dfrac{180.28 \times \sin 38°}{\sin 57°}$

$x \approx 132.34$

To the nearest metre, the value of x is 132 m.

ANSWERS AND SOLUTIONS — PRACTICE TEST 2

1. B	11. C	b) OR	28. C	35. A
2. C	12. A	c) OR	29. B	36. a) OR
3. B	13. A	d) OR	30. A	b) OR
4. D	14. B	21. A	31. B	37. B
5. D	15. B	22. C	32. a) OR	38. A
6. D	16. B	23. C	b) OR	39. C
7. B	17. C	24. A	c) OR	40. D
8. 4.2	18. C	25. B	d) OR	41. 10
9. D	19. B	26. B	33. C	42. C
10. 18	20. a) OR	27. C	34. B	43. D

1. B

Step 1

Determine the quadratic equation that best models the data.

The regression equation representing the data (to one decimal) is $h = -4.8t^2 + 148.5t + 5.9$.

Step 2

Determine the height of the model rocket after 6 s by substituting 6 for t in the regression equation.

$h = -4.8(6)^2 + 148.5(6) + 5.9$
$= 724.1$ m

Therefore, the best estimate of the height of the rocket after 6 s is 725 m.

2. C

Since $a < 0$, the graph of $y = ax^2 - 12x + 7$ must open downward.
Graph two test equations, such as

$y = -2x^2 - 12x + 7$ and $y = -\frac{1}{2}x^2 - 12x + 7$.

Therefore, graph C could be the graph of the quadratic function $y = ax^2 - 12x + 7$, $a < 0$.

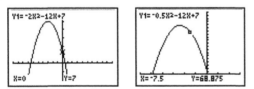

3. B

The domain of the quadratic relation
$y = ax^2 + bx + c, (a \neq 0)$ will always be $x \in \mathbf{R}$. This is true regardless of the direction of opening.

The zeros are the x-coordinate of each ordered pair where the parabola touches or intersects the x-axis.

The parabola that opens upward has no zeros, whereas the parabola that opens downward will have two zeros.

The axis of symmetry is a vertical line that passes through the vertex of the parabola. Since the two parabolas share the same vertex, they will have the same equation of the axis of symmetry.

A maximum value occurs when the parabola opens down, and a minimum value occurs when the parabola opens up. Since the parabolas each have different directions of opening, one will have a minimum value, and one will have a maximum value.

Therefore, the only correct statements are I and III.

4. D

Any number or variable with an exponent of zero is equal to 1; $x^0 = 1$.
Therefore, $2^0 = 1$. Applying the product rule,
$2^x \times 2^{-x} = 2^{x+(-x)} = 2^0 = 1$
Therefore, the value of a must be $-x$.

5. D

Step 1

Change the form of the function by completing the square.
$y = 4x^2 - 12x + 15$
$y = 4(x^2 - 3x) + 15$
$y = 4\left(x^2 - 3x + \frac{9}{4} - \frac{9}{4}\right) + 15$
$y = 4\left(x^2 - 3x + \frac{9}{4}\right) - 9 + 15$
$y = 4\left(x - \frac{3}{2}\right)^2 + 6$

This equation is of the form $y = a(x - h)^2 + k$,
where $a = 4$, $h = \frac{3}{2}$, and $k = 6$.

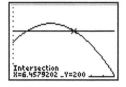

Step 2

Determine the minimum value of the function.

The vertex, (h, k), of the given parabola is $\left(\frac{3}{2}, 6\right)$,

and the parabola opens upward since $a > 0$.
The minimum value of the given quadratic function
is equal to the value of k.

Therefore, the minimum value of the function is 6.

6. **D**

Use a TI-83 Plus graphing calculator to graph the
equation $y = 100t - 5t^2$.

Then use the MAXIMUM feature and a window
setting such as $x: [1, 20, 2]$ $y: [0, 600, 50]$.

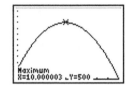

The function's maximum value occurs when
$x = 10$; therefore, the maximum height attained by
the bullet can be determined as follows:

$h = 100t - 5t^2$
$h = 100(10) - 5(10)^2$
$h = 500$ m

7. **B**

When Maj initially kicks the ball, no time has passed,
so $x = 0$.

Substitute 0 for x into the equation.

$y = -4.9x^2 + 13.7x + 0.7$
$y = -4.9(0)^2 + 13.7(0) + 0.7$
$y = 0.7$

Therefore, Maj was holding the soccer ball 0.7 m
above the ground when she kicked it.

8. **4.2**

Use a TI-83 Plus graphing calculator to plot the line
$y = 200$ and the parabola $y = -7x^2 + 61x + 98$.

Then use the INTERSECTION feature to find the
intersection points of the two graphs.

The first intersection point is (2.256, 200).

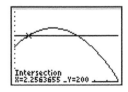

The second intersection point is (6.458, 200).

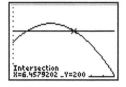

Therefore, the roller coaster car is 200 feet or more
above the ground for 6.458 – 2.256 = 4.2 s to the
nearest tenth.

9. **D**

In solving the system of equations, Minesh chose the
method of elimination, while Cameron chose the
method of graphing with technology. No mistake
was made in either partial solution, so both will yield
the same correct answer.

10. **18**

Step 1
Label the equations.
① $5x + y = 93$
② $2x + y = 48$

Step 2
Solve the system by elimination. Subtract equation
② from equation ① .
① $5x + y = 93$
② $\underline{2x + y = 48}$
$\quad\; 3x + 0 = 45$
$\quad\quad\; x = \dfrac{45}{3}$
$\quad\quad\; x = 15$

Step 3
To find y, substitute 15 for x in one of the equations.
In this case, use equation ② .
$\quad\; 2x + y = 48$
$2(15) + y = 48$
$\quad 30 + y = 48$
$\quad\quad\;\; y = 48 - 30$
$\quad\quad\;\; y = 18$
The value of y is 18.

11. C

Let H be the cost of 1 hamburger.
Let F be the cost of 1 small french fries.

Create a system representing the two cases.

(1) $2H + F = 7.00$
(2) $H + 2F = 5.75$

Subtract the equations, and solve for H.

$$
\begin{array}{ll}
(1) \times 2 & 4H + 2F = 14.00 \\
(2) & \underline{-(H + 2F = 5.75)} \\
& 3H = 8.25 \\
& H = 2.75
\end{array}
$$

Thus, one hamburger costs \$2.75.

12. A

Step 1
Determine the first equation.
If x represents one portion of the total amount of invested money and y represents the other portion, the equation can be written as \$5 000 being equal to the sum of x and y.
① $x + y = 50$

Step 2
Determine the second equation.
$0.04x$ = interest earned on the amount invested at 4%
$0.06y$ = interest earned on the amount invested at 6%
Since the interest earned on the x-amount of invested money is \$50 more than the interest earned on the y-amount of invested money, the equation can be written as the x-amount multiplied by its interest rate being equal to the y-amount multiplied by its interest rate plus 50.
② $0.04x = 0.06y + 50$

Step 3
Multiply the second equation by 100.
$$
\begin{array}{ll}
② & 0.04x = 0.06y + 50 \\
100 \times ② & 4x = 6y + 5\ 000
\end{array}
$$
The system of equations is $x + y = 50$ and $4x = 6y + 50$.

13. A

Using the midpoint formula,
$$m = \left(\frac{x_1 + x_2}{2}, \frac{y_1 + y_2}{2} \right).$$ Thus,

$$m_{AB} = \left(\frac{2 + x}{2}, \frac{1 + 7}{2} \right)$$

$$m_{AB} = \left(\frac{2 + x}{2}, 4 \right)$$

$$\frac{2 + x}{2} = -3$$
$$2 + x = -6$$
$$x = -8$$

14. B

First, determine the coordinate of point C by using the midpoint formula $m = \left(\frac{x_1 + x_2}{2}, \frac{y_1 + y_2}{2} \right).$

$$m_{AC} = \left(\frac{-4 + x}{2}, \frac{12 + y}{2} \right)$$

Thus,
$$
\begin{array}{c}
\frac{-4 + x}{2} = -1 \\
x \\
-4 + x = -2 \\
x = 2
\end{array}
$$

and
$$
\begin{array}{c}
\frac{12 + y}{2} = 8 \\
12 + y = 16 \\
y = 4
\end{array}
$$

Since point C is at $(2, 4)$, use the distance formula $d = \sqrt{(x_2 - x_1)^2 + (y_2 - y_1)^2}$ to find the distance from point C to point A.
$$d_{AC} = \sqrt{(-4 - 2)^2 + (12 - 4)^2}$$
$$d_{AC} = \sqrt{(-6)^2 + (8)^2}$$
$$d_{AC} = \sqrt{36 + 64}$$
$$d_{AC} = \sqrt{100}$$
$$d_{AC} = 10$$

Thus, the distance from point A to point D must also be 10.

$d_{AD} = \sqrt{(-4-2)^2 + (12-y)^2}$ (Note: D is the point $(2, y)$).

$10 = \sqrt{(-6)^2 + (12-y)^2}$

$10 = \sqrt{36 + (12-y)^2}$

Square both sides.

$100 = 36 + (12-y)^2$

Subtract 36 from both sides.

$64 = (12-y)^2$

Take the square root of both sides.

$\pm 8 = 12 - y$

Thus, $8 = 12 - y$ or $-8 = 12 - y$.

$-4 = -y$ or $-20 = -y$

Solve for y in both cases.

$4 = y$ or $20 = y$

The value for y is 20, since a y-coordinate of 4 would be the same location as cruise ship C.

15. B

Find the length of the radius using the distance formula.

$d = \sqrt{(x_2 - x_1)^2 + (y_2 - y_1)^2}$

$= \sqrt{(a - 0)^2 + (b - 0)^2}$

$= \sqrt{a^2 + b^2}$

The radius of this circle is given by the expression $\sqrt{a^2 + b^2}$.

16. B

Simplify the given equation by dividing each term of the equation by the GCF of 4.

$\dfrac{4x^2}{4} + \dfrac{4y^2}{4} = \dfrac{36}{4}$

$x^2 + y^2 = 9$

Since the equation $x^2 + y^2 = r^2$ represents a circle with centre $(0, 0)$ and radius r, it follows that:

$r^2 = 9$

$r = \sqrt{9}$

$r = 3$

Thus, the radius of the circle defined by the equation $4x^2 + 4y^2 = 36$ is 3 units.

17. C

Using the slope formula $m = \dfrac{y_2 - y_1}{x_2 - x_1}$, find the slope of QR.

$m = \dfrac{8 - 2}{-2 - 6}$

$m = \dfrac{6}{-8}$

$m = -\dfrac{3}{4}$

The slope of the perpendicular bisector will be $\dfrac{4}{3}$, which is the negative reciprocal of $\dfrac{-3}{4}$.

The midpoint of QR can be found by using the midpoint formula

$M = \left(\dfrac{x_1 + x_2}{2}, \dfrac{y_1 + y_2}{2} \right)$

$M_{QR} = \left(\dfrac{6 + (-2)}{2}, \dfrac{2 + 8}{2} \right)$

$M_{QR} = (2, 5)$

The perpendicular bisector of QR has a slope of $\dfrac{4}{3}$ and passes through the point $(2, 5)$.

Using the point-slope form, the equation of this line can be determined as follows:

$y = m(x - x_1) + y_1$

$y = \dfrac{4}{3}(x - 2) + 5$

$y = \dfrac{4}{3}x - \dfrac{8}{3} + 5$

Use a common denominator.

$y = \dfrac{4}{3}x - \dfrac{8}{3} + \dfrac{15}{3}$

$y = \dfrac{4}{3}x + \dfrac{7}{3}$

18. C

Step 1

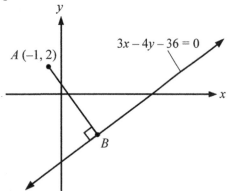

Sketch a graph that shows the line, the external point, and a perpendicular line segment from the external point to the given line.

Step 2

Determine the equation of the perpendicular line through point $A(-1, 2)$.

Write $3x - 4y - 36 = 0$ in the slope-intercept form $y = mx + b$.

$$3x - 36 = 4y$$
$$\frac{3x}{4} - \frac{36}{4} = \frac{4y}{4}$$
$$\frac{3}{4}x - 9 = y$$

The slope of the line is $m = \frac{3}{4}$ (the coefficient of x).

The slope of the perpendicular line is $-\frac{4}{3}$ (the

negative reciprocal of $\frac{3}{4}$).

The equation of the perpendicular line with slope $-\frac{4}{3}$ that passes through point $A(-1, 2)$ can be determined as follows:

$$y = m(x - x_1) + y_1$$
$$y = -\frac{4}{3}(x - (-1)) + 2$$
$$y = -\frac{4}{3}(x + 1) + 2$$
$$y = -\frac{4}{3}x - \frac{4}{3} + 2$$

Use a common denominator.

$$y = -\frac{4}{3}x - \frac{4}{3} + \frac{6}{3}$$
$$y = -\frac{4}{3}x + \frac{2}{3}$$

The equation of the perpendicular line is

$$y = -\frac{4}{3}x + \frac{2}{3}.$$

Step 3

Determine the point of intersection, B.

Substitute $y = \frac{3}{4}x - 9$ into $y = -\frac{4}{3}x + \frac{2}{3}$, and solve the system of equations.

$$\frac{3}{4}x - 9 = -\frac{4}{3}x + \frac{2}{3}$$
$$\frac{3}{4}x + \frac{4}{3}x = 9 + \frac{2}{3}$$
$$\frac{9}{12}x + \frac{16}{12}x = \frac{27}{3} + \frac{2}{3}$$
$$\frac{25}{12}x = \frac{29}{3}$$
$$x = \frac{29}{3} \times \frac{12}{25}$$
$$x = \frac{348}{75}$$
$$x = 4.64$$

Find the y-coordinate. Substitute $x = 4.64$ into the equation $y = \frac{3}{4}x - 9$.

$$y = \frac{3}{4}(4.64) - 9$$
$$y = 3.48 - 9$$
$$y = -5.52$$

The point of intersection is $B(4.64, -5.52)$.

Step 4

Determine the distance from the point to the line. Use the distance formula,

$d = \sqrt{(x_2 - x_1)^2 + (y_2 - y_1)^2}$, and points $A(-1, 2)$ and $B(4.64, -5.52)$.

$$d_{AB} = \sqrt{(4.64 - (-1))^2 + (-5.52 - 2)^2}$$
$$d_{AB} = \sqrt{(5.64)^2 + (-7.52)^2}$$
$$d_{AB} = \sqrt{88.36}$$
$$d_{AB} = 9.4$$

The distance between the point and the line is 9.4 units.

19. B

First, use the distance formula

$d = \sqrt{(x_2 - x_1)^2 + (y_2 - y_1)^2}$ to determine the length of side BC.

$$d_{BC} = \sqrt{(-3 - 6)^2 + (1 - (-4))^2}$$
$$d_{BC} = \sqrt{(-9)^2 + 5^2}$$
$$d_{BC} = \sqrt{106}$$

$\triangle ABC$ is an isosceles triangle (two equal sides). Note: this is not a right triangle because the three sides will not satisfy the Pythagorean theorem.

20. a) OR

Corner post A has the same x-coordinate as corner post B and the same y-coordinate as corner post D. Therefore, the coordinates of A are $(139, 89)$.

b) OR

Since soccer net EF is centered on the back line AB, begin by determining the midpoint of AB by using the midpoint formula $M = \left(\dfrac{x_1 + x_2}{2}, \dfrac{y_1 + y_2}{2}\right)$.

$$M_{AB} = \left(\frac{139 + 139}{2}, \frac{15 + 89}{2}\right)$$

$$M_{AB} = \left(\frac{278}{2}, \frac{104}{2}\right)$$

$$M_{AB} = (139, 52)$$

Recall that the width of soccer net EF is 8 yards. Therefore, the y-coordinate of point E must be 4 more than the y-coordinate of the midpoint of AB. The coordinates of point E are $(139, 56)$.
The y-coordinates of point F must be 4 less than the y-coordinate of the midpoint of AB. The coordinates of point F are $(139, 48)$.

c) OR

In order to determine the minimum distance the soccer ball must travel from player P to player Q, determine the length of the line segment PQ by applying the distance formula.

$$d = \sqrt{(x_2 - x_1)^2 + (y_2 - y_1)^2}$$

$$d_{PQ} = \sqrt{(83 - 54)^2 + (62 - 41)^2}$$

$$d_{PQ} = \sqrt{(29)^2 + (21)^2}$$

$$d_{PQ} = \sqrt{841 + 441}$$

$$d_{PQ} = \sqrt{1\,282}$$

$$d_{PQ} \approx 35.81$$

The minimum distance, to the nearest tenth, that the soccer ball must travel from player P to player Q is 35.8 yards.

d) OR

In order to verify that the diagonals of the playing field bisect each other at the centre mark, M, show that the midpoint of diagonal BD is the same as the midpoint of diagonal AC by making use of the midpoint formula $M = \left(\dfrac{x_1 + x_2}{2}, \dfrac{y_1 + y_2}{2}\right)$.

$$M_{BD} = \left(\frac{139 + 19}{2}, \frac{15 + 89}{2}\right)$$

$$M_{AC} = \left(\frac{139 + 19}{2}, \frac{89 + 15}{2}\right)$$

$$M_{BD} = \left(\frac{158}{2}, \frac{104}{2}\right) \qquad M_{AC} = \left(\frac{158}{2}, \frac{104}{2}\right)$$

$$M_{BD} = (79, 52) \qquad\qquad M_{AC} = (79, 52)$$

Thus, the diagonals of the playing field bisect each other at $(79, 52)$. This corresponds to the coordinates of the centre mark M.

21. A

The graph of the new parabola can be obtained by translating the graph of $y = x^2$ four units left and three units down, as shown in the following diagram.

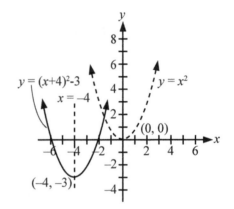

22. C

Since the equation $y = -3(x - h)^2 + k$ is in the form $y = a(x - h)^2 + k$, it follows that:

- The equation of the axis of symmetry is $x = h$.
- The vertex is (h, k).

23. C

Apply the given transformations to the graph of $y = x^2$ to get the following result:

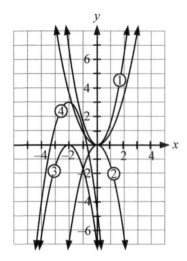

Therefore, graph C best represents the graph of the transformed function.

24. A

The parabola shown has an equation of the form $y = a(x - h)^2 + k$, where (h, k) is the vertex.

Since the vertex is at $\left(8, \dfrac{11}{2}\right)$, $h = 8$ and $k = \dfrac{11}{2}$.

Substitute 8 for h and $\dfrac{11}{2}$ for k into

$y = a(x - h)^2 + k$ to get $y = a(x - 8)^2 + \dfrac{11}{2}$.

Since the parabola passes through the point $\left(10, \dfrac{19}{2}\right)$ substitute 10 for x and $\dfrac{19}{2}$ for y in the

equation $y = a(x - 8)^2 + \dfrac{11}{2}$.

$$\frac{19}{2} = a(10 - 8)^2 + \frac{11}{2}$$
$$\frac{19}{2} = a(2)^2 + \frac{11}{2}$$
$$\frac{19}{2} = 4a + \frac{11}{2}$$
$$\frac{19}{2} - \frac{11}{2} = 4a$$
$$\frac{8}{2} = 4a$$
$$4 = 4a$$
$$1 = a$$

Substitute 1 for a in the equation $y = (x - 8)^2 + \dfrac{11}{2}$

to get $y = 1(x - 8)^2 = \dfrac{11}{2}$ or $y = (x - 8)^2 + \dfrac{11}{2}$.

25. B

Step 1

Rewrite the squared binomial as a product, and then use the FOIL method to expand it.

$-2(3x + 5)^2$
$= -2(3x + 5)(3x + 5)$
$= -2\left(\begin{array}{l}(3x)(3x) + (3x)(5) \\ + (3x)(5) + (5)(5)\end{array}\right)$
$= -2(9x^2 + 15x + 15x + 25)$
$= -2(9x^2 + 30x + 25)$

Step 2

Apply the distributive property to distribute -2 to all terms in the brackets.

$-2(9x^2 + 30x + 25)$
$= -2(9x^2) - 2(30x) - 2(25)$
$= -18x^2 - 60x - 50$

According to the expression given in the form of $ax^2 + bx + c$, $a = -18$ and $c = -50$.

Therefore, the value of $a + c = -18 + -50 = -68$.

26. B

Step 1

To factor $9mn^2 - 12mn - 12m$, begin by factoring out the greatest common factor (GCF) of $3m$ from each term of the expression.

$9mn^2 - 12mn - 12m = 3m(3n^2 - 4n - 4)$

Step 2

Factor the trinomial in the expression

$3m\left(3n^2 - 4n - 4\right)$.

To factor $\left(3n^2 - 4n - 4\right)$, find two numbers that have a product of -12 (from $a \times c$) and a sum of -4 (the b-value). In this case, the numbers are 2 and -6.

Rewrite the expression by replacing the term $-4n$ with $2n$ and $-6n$.

$= 3m\left[3n^2 - 4n - 4\right]$
$= 3m\left[3n^2 + 2n - 6n - 4\right]$

Group the terms inside the brackets.

$= 3m\left[3n^2 + 2n - 6n - 4\right]$
$= 3m\left[\left(3n^2 + 2n\right) + \left(-6n - 4\right)\right]$

Step 3

Remove the GCF from each group.

$= 3m\left[\left(3n^2 + 2n\right) + \left(-6n - 4\right)\right]$
$= 3m\left[n(3n + 2) - 2(3n + 2)\right]$

Factor out the common binomial.

$= 3m\left[n(3n + 2) - 2(3n + 2)\right]$
$= 3m(n - 2)(3n + 2)$

The expression that is not a factor of

$9mn^2 - 12mn - 12m$ is $n - 4$.

27. C

The x-intercepts of the graph shown are at $x = 2$ and $x = 4$. Therefore, substitute 2 for r and 4 for s in the equation $y = a(x - r)(x - s)$.
$y = a(x - 2)(x - 4)$
The ordered pair $(0, 4)$ is a point on the graph.
Solve for a in the equation $y = a(x - 2)(x - 4)$ by substituting 0 for x and 4 for y.
$4 = a((0) - 2)((0) - 4)$
$4 = a(-2)(-4)$
$4 = 8a$
$a = \dfrac{4}{8} = \dfrac{1}{2}$

Therefore, the equation of the quadratic relation in the form $y = a(x - r)(x - s)$ is

$y = \dfrac{1}{2}(x - 2)(x - 4)$.

28. C

The graph of a quadratic equation with no real roots has no x-intercepts.

This graph does not intersect the x-axis, has no x-intercepts, and therefore, has no real roots.

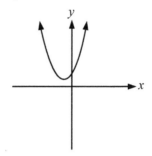

29. B

Step 1

Identify and remove the common factor from the x^2- and x-terms of the expression.

In this case, the common factor is 3.

$y = 3\left(x^2 + 14x\right) + 142$

Step 2

Divide the resulting coefficient for the x-term by 2, and then square it.

$y = 3\left(x^2 + \underline{14x}\right) + 142$

$\left(\dfrac{14}{2}\right)^2 = 49$

Both add and subtract this value inside the brackets.

$y = 3\left(x^2 + 14x + \underline{49 - 49}\right) + 142$

Step 3

Move the value that will not contribute to a perfect square outside the brackets.

When -49 is moved outside the brackets, it becomes $3(-49) = -147$ because of the distributive property.

$y = \underline{3}\left(x^2 + 14x + 49 \underline{-49}\right) + 142$
$y = 3\left(x^2 + 14x + 49\right) \underline{-147} + 142$

Step 4

Factor the trinomial inside the brackets to form a perfect square, and collect like terms outside the brackets.

$y = 3(x + 7)^2 - 5$

When the equation $y = 3x^2 + 42x + 142$ is written in the completed square form $y = a(x - h)^2 + k$, it becomes $y = 3(x + 7)^2 - 5$.

The k-value is -5.

30. A

Step 1

Determine the x-intercepts by letting $y = 0$.

$0 = -2(x^2 + 6x + 8)$
$0 = -2(x + 2)(x + 4)$
$x = -2$ or $x = -4$

Step 2

Find the y-intercept by substituting 0 for x.

$y = -2((0)^2 + 0 + 8)$
$y = -16$

Step 3

Find the midpoint of the x-intercepts in order to find the equation of the axis of symmetry.

$M = \left(\dfrac{x_1 + x_2}{2}\right), \left(\dfrac{y_1 + y_2}{2}\right)$

$= \left(\dfrac{-2 + (-4)}{2}\right), \left(\dfrac{0 + 0}{2}\right)$

$= (-3, 0)$

The equation of the axis of symmetry is $x = -3$.

Step 4

Find the vertex. Substitute -3 for x in the equation $y = -2(x^2 + 6x + 8)$.

$y = -2((-3)^2 + 6(-3) + 8)$

$y = -2(9 - 18 + 8)$

$y = 2$

The vertex is $(-3, 2)$.

Therefore, the only correct statements are II and IV.

31. B

Step 1

Solve the equation using Rhett's method.

To follow Rhett's method, solve by factoring.

Begin by rearranging the equation $6x^2 - 13x = 5$ to $6x^2 - 13x - 5 = 0$.

Factor by decomposition, find two numbers that have a product of -30 and a sum of -13. In this case, those numbers are 2 and -15.

$6x^2 - 13x - 5 = 0$
$6x^2 + 2x - 15x - 5 = 0$
$2x(3x + 1) - 5(3x + 1) = 0$
$(2x - 5)(3x + 1) = 0$

This solution does not match Rhett's partial solution.

Step 2

Solve the equation using Vlad's method.

To follow Vlad's method, solve using the quadratic formula.

Begin by rearranging the equation $6x^2 - 13x = 5$ to $6x^2 - 13x - 5 = 0$.

Apply the quadratic formula $x = \dfrac{-b \pm \sqrt{b^2 - 4ac}}{2a}$.

Substitute 6 for a, -13 for b, and -5 for c into the quadratic formula.

$x = \dfrac{-(-13) \pm \sqrt{(-13)^2 - 4(6)(-5)}}{2(6)}$

$x = \dfrac{13 \pm \sqrt{169 + 120}}{12}$

$x = \dfrac{13 \pm \sqrt{289}}{12}$

$x = \dfrac{13 \pm 17}{12}$

This solution does not match Vlad's partial solution. Therefore, Rhett and Vlad both had incorrect solutions.

32. a) OR

Solve for x by substituting \$62 750 for C in the equation $C = 2x^2 - 700x + 92\ 750$ as follows:

$62\ 750 = 2x^2 - 700x + 92\ 750$

$0 = 2x^2 - 700x + 300$

$0 = 2(x^2 - 350x + 150)$

The two numbers that have a sum of -350 and a product of 15 000 are -50 and -300.

$0 = 2(x - 50)(x - 300)$

Therefore, $x - 50 = 0$ or $x - 300 = 0$
$x = 50$ or $x = 300$

The equation $2x^2 - 700x + 300 = 0$ can also be solved by using the quadratic formula

$x = \dfrac{-b \pm \sqrt{b^2 - 4ac}}{2a}$ as shown:

Substitute 2 for a, -700 for b, and 30 000 for c.

$$x = \frac{-(-700) \pm \sqrt{(-700)^2 - 4(2)(300)}}{2(2)}$$

$$x = \frac{700 \pm \sqrt{4900 - 2400}}{4}$$

$$x = \frac{700 \pm \sqrt{2500}}{4}$$

$$x = \frac{700 \pm 500}{4}$$

$$x = \frac{700 + 500}{4} = \frac{1200}{4} = 300$$

or $x = \dfrac{700 - 500}{4} = \dfrac{200}{4} = 50$

b) OR

In order to determine the number of Road Racer bicycles that must be manufactured to minimize the cost, complete the square of the equation $C = 2x^2 - 700x + 92\ 750$, as follows:

$$C = 2x^2 - 700x + 92\ 750$$

$$C = 2(x^2 - 350x) + 92\ 750$$

$$\frac{-350}{2} = -175, (-175)^2 = 30\ 625$$

$$C = 2(x^2 - 350x + 30\ 625 - 30\ 625) + 92\ 750$$

$$C = 2(x^2 - 350x + 30\ 625) - 61\ 250 + 92\ 750$$

$$C = 2(x - 175)^2 + 31\ 500$$

The minimum value of C is 31 500, when $x = 175$. Thus, 175 Road Racer bicycles have to be manufactured to minimize the cost.

c) OR

The minimum cost of manufacturing the Road Racer bicycles is $31 500.

d) OR

First, choose an appropriate window setting on your graphing calculator. Next, graph $y_1 = 2x^2 - 700x + 92\ 750$ and $y_2 = 500$. Finally, determine the x-coordinate of the first point of intersection of the two graphs. This x-coordinate is about 78.823. Thus, the fewest number of bicycles that can be manufactured for a cost of $50 000 is 78.

33. C

Begin with a diagram for clarity.

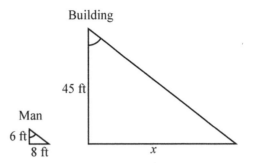

The triangles are similar since they are formed using the shadow created by the same angle of the sun at the same point in time. The remaining corresponding angles are equal. Therefore, corresponding sides will have equal ratios.

$$\frac{8}{6} = \frac{x}{45}$$

$$x = \frac{8 \times 45}{6}$$

$$x = 60 \text{ ft}$$

34. B

In the diagram, $\angle B = \angle D = 90°$.
Thus, $AB \parallel DE$, and segments AE and DB are transversals. Therefore, $\angle A = \angle E$. It follows that $\angle DCE = \angle BCA$.
Thus $\triangle ABC$ is similar to $\triangle EDC$.
Draw the two triangles with the same orientation.

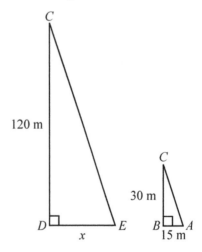

Since $\triangle ABC$ is similar to $\triangle EDC$, $\dfrac{BC}{DC} = \dfrac{AB}{DE}$.

Substitute the given values into this equation.

$$\dfrac{30}{120} = \dfrac{15}{W}$$

$$W = \dfrac{15 \times 120}{30} = 60$$

Therefore, the width of the river is 60 m.

35. A

The given triangle is made up of two congruent right triangles. Label the top angle of each right triangle as angle y, as shown below.

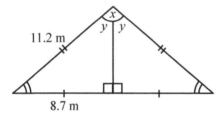

A triangle

Determine the measure of angle y.

$$\sin \theta = \dfrac{\text{opposite}}{\text{hypotenuse}}$$

$$\sin y = \dfrac{8.7}{11.2}$$

$$y = \sin^{-}1 = \left(\dfrac{8.7}{11.2}\right)$$

$$y \approx 50.97°$$

Since $x = 2y$, angle $x \approx 2(51°) \approx 102°$.

36. a) OR

In $\triangle ABC$, the distance BC can be determined as follows:

$$\tan 25° = \dfrac{BC}{AB}$$

Substitute 130 for AB.

$$\tan 25° = \dfrac{BC}{130}$$

$$BC = 130 \times \tan 25°$$

$$BC \approx 60.62$$

The distance from the sprinkler head at point B to the sprinkler head at point C, to the nearest tenth of a metre, is 60.6 m.

b) OR

In order to determine the distance from the sprinkler head at point D to the sprinkler head at point E, first find the length of AD. This can be done as follows:

In $\triangle ABC$, $\cos 25° = \dfrac{AB}{AC}$.

Substitute 130 for AB.

$$\cos 25° = \dfrac{130}{AC}$$

$$AC \times \cos 25° = 130$$

$$AC = \dfrac{130}{\cos 25°}$$

$$AC \approx 143.44$$

In $\triangle ACD$, $\cos 15° = \dfrac{AC}{AD}$

Substitute 143.44 for AC.

$$\cos 15° = \dfrac{143.44}{AD}$$

$$AD \times \cos 15° = 143.44$$

$$AD = \dfrac{143.44}{\cos 15°}$$

$$AD \approx 148.50$$

Now use the tangent ratio.

$$\tan (A) = \dfrac{DE}{AD}$$

$$\tan (22°) = \dfrac{DE}{148.50}$$

$$DE = 60$$

The distance from the sprinkler head at point D to the sprinkler head at point E, to the nearest metre, is 60 m.

37. B

The general form of the law of sines is

$\dfrac{a}{\sin A} = \dfrac{b}{\sin B} = \dfrac{c}{\sin C}$. This equation implies that side a is opposite angle A, side b is opposite angle B, and side c is opposite angle C.

In the given triangle, NP is opposite $\angle M$, MN is opposite $\angle P$, and MP is opposite $\angle N$.

Therefore, the equation $\dfrac{MN}{\sin P} = \dfrac{MP}{\sin N}$ correctly represents the law of sines.

38. A

The equation $x^2 = 80^2 + 95^2 - 2(80)(95)\cos 73°$ is a form of the law of cosines.

The equation implies that side x is opposite to the $73°$ angle and the measures of the other sides of the triangle are 80 cm and 95 cm.

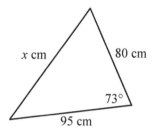

39. C

Step 1

Determine the length of side BD.

Use the sine ratio to determine the length of side BD in $\triangle BAD$.

$$\sin \angle ADB = \frac{AB}{BD}$$

Substitute $41°$ for $\angle ADB$ and 9 for AB. Solve for BD.

$$\sin 41° = \frac{9}{BD}$$
$$BD\sin 41° = 9$$
$$BD = \frac{9}{\sin 41°}$$
$$BD = 13.72 \text{ m}$$

Step 2

Determine the measure of $\angle D$ in $\triangle CBD$.

In $\triangle BAD$, $\angle ABD = 180° - 90° - 41° = 49°$.

In $\triangle CBD$, $\angle CBD = 90° - 49° = 41°$.

In $\triangle CBD$, $\angle BDC = 180° - 41° - 78° = 61°$.

Step 3

Solve for x.

In $\triangle CBD$, since it is not a side-angle-side situation, use the sine law.

$$\frac{BC}{\sin \angle BDC} = \frac{BD}{\sin \angle BCD}$$

Substitute x for BC, 13.72 for BD, $61°$ for $\angle BDC$, and $78°$ for $\angle BCD$.

$$\frac{x}{\sin 61°} = \frac{13.72}{\sin 78°}$$
$$x\sin 78° = 13.72\sin 61°$$
$$x = \frac{13.72\sin 61°}{\sin 78°}$$
$$x = 12.27 \text{ m}$$

Correct to the nearest tenth, the length of side x is 12.3 m.

40. D

Step 1

Determine the length of side AD.

In $\triangle ACD$, the measures of two sides of the triangle and the measure of the angle contained between those sides are given, so solve for AD by applying the cosine law.

$$(AD)^2 = (AC)^2 + (DC)^2 - 2(AC)(DC)\cos C$$

Substitute 26.0 for AC, 18.0 for DC, and 32 for C.

$$(AD)^2 = 26.0^2 + 18.0^2 - 2(26.0)(18.0)\cos 32°$$
$$(AD)^2 = 206.227$$
$$AD = \sqrt{206.227}$$
$$AD = 14.36$$

Step 1

Determine the measure of $\angle ADB$.

In $\triangle ABD$, the measure of a side with its corresponding opposite angle and another side length are known, so apply the sine law to determine the measure of $\angle ADB$.

$$\frac{AB}{\sin \angle ADB} = \frac{AD}{\sin \angle ABD}$$

Substitute 19.5 for AB, 14.36 for AD, and $45°$ for $\angle ABD$.

$$\frac{19.5}{\sin \angle ADB} = \frac{14.36}{\sin \angle 45°}$$
$$14.36 \times \sin \angle ADB = 19.5 \times \sin \angle 45°$$
$$\sin \angle ADB = \frac{19.5 \times \sin 45°}{14.36}$$
$$\sin \angle ADB \approx 0.9602$$
$$\angle ADB \approx 73.8°$$

Correct to the nearest degree, the measure of $\angle ADB$ is $74°$.

41. 10

Step 1

Determine the length of side BD by applying the sine law.

In $\triangle ABD$, observe that $\angle ABD = 180° - 29° = 151°$. Thus, the measure of $\angle ADB$ is $180° - 151° - 18° = 11°$.

$$\frac{BD}{\sin \angle A} = \frac{AB}{\sin \angle ADB}$$

Substitute $18°$ for $\angle A$, 12.5 for AB, and $11°$ for $\angle ADB$.

$$\frac{BD}{\sin 18°} = \frac{12.5}{\sin 11°}$$
$$BD \times \sin 11° = 12.5 \times \sin 18°$$
$$BD = \frac{12.5 \times \sin 18°}{\sin 11°}$$
$$BD \approx 20.24 \text{ m}$$

Step 2

Solve for h in right triangle BCD.

Substitute 29° for $\angle DBC$, h for DC, and 20.24 for BD.

$$\sin \angle DBC = \frac{DC}{BD}$$
$$\sin 29° = \frac{h}{20.24}$$
$$h = 20.24 \times \sin 29°$$
$$h \approx 9.81 \text{ m}$$

The height of the school, to the nearest metre, is 10 m.

42. C

In $\triangle ABC$, it is a side-angle-side situation; therefore, solve for the distance from A to C as follows:

$$(AC)^2 = (BA)^2 + (BC)^2 - 2(BA)(BC)\cos \angle ABC$$

Substitute 65 for BA, 70 for BC, and 38 degrees for $\angle ABC$.

$$(AC)^2 = 65^2 + 70^2 - 2(65)(70)\cos 38°$$

$$(AC)^2 \approx 4225 + 4900 - 7171.90$$

$$(AC)^2 \approx 1954.10$$

$$AC \approx \sqrt{1954.10}$$

$$AC \approx 44.21$$

To the nearest tenth, the wakeboarders are 44.2 feet apart.

43. D

In $\triangle BCD$, it is a side-angle-side situation; therefore, solve for BD by applying the law of cosines as shown:

$$(BD)^2 = (CB)^2 + (CD)^2 - 2(CB)(CD)\cos \angle BCD$$

Substitute 3 for CB, 5 for CD, and 68° for $\angle BCD$.

$$(BD)^2 = 3^2 + 5^2 - 2(3)(5)\cos 68°$$

$$BD = \sqrt{3^2 + 5^2 - 2(3)(5)\cos 68°}$$

Thus, the equation $BD = \sqrt{3^2 + 5^2 - 2(3)(5)\cos 68°}$ could be used to determine the length of the roadway, BD.

Appendices

Formula Sheet

Quadratic Relations

Standard form:	$y = a(x-h)^2 + k$
Factored form:	$y = a(x-r)(x-s)$
General form:	$y = ax^2 + bx + c, \quad a \neq 0$
Quadratic formula:	$x = \dfrac{-b \pm \sqrt{b^2 - 4ac}}{2a}$

Factoring Polynomials

Perfect squares:	$(a+b)^2 = a^2 + 2ab + b^2$ $(a-b)^2 = a^2 - 2ab + b^2$
Difference of squares:	$a^2 - b^2 = (a-b)(a+b)$

Expanding polynomials

Distributive property:	$a(x+y) = ax + ay$

Analytic Geometry

Midpoint formula:	$M_{AB} = \left(\dfrac{x_1 + x_2}{2}, \dfrac{y_1 + y_2}{2} \right)$
Distance formula:	$d = \sqrt{(x_2 - x_1)^2 + (y_2 - y_1)^2}$
Slope:	$m = \dfrac{y_2 - y_1}{x_2 - x_1}$
Equation of a circle:	$x^2 + y^2 = r^2$
Equation of a line:	$y = mx + b$

Trigonometry

Right Triangles

Primary trigonometric ratios:	Sine ratio: $\sin A = \dfrac{\text{opposite}}{\text{hypotenuse}}$
	Cosine ratio: $\cos A = \dfrac{\text{adjacent}}{\text{hypotenuse}}$
	Tangent ratio: $\tan A = \dfrac{\text{opposite}}{\text{adjacent}}$

Acute Triangles

Law of sines:	$\dfrac{a}{\sin A} = \dfrac{b}{\sin B} = \dfrac{c}{\sin C}$
Law of cosines:	$a^2 = b^2 + c^2 - 2bc \cos A$

NOTES

NOTES

NOTES

NOTES